LEVEL UP

GAMIFICATION IN PHARMA MARKETING

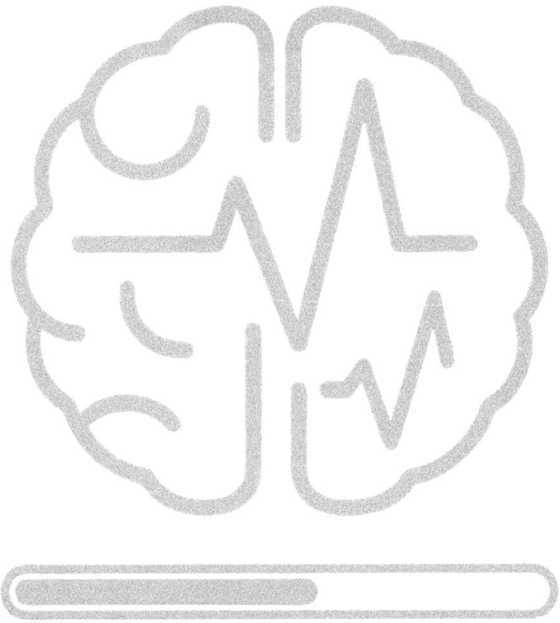

How Playful Innovation is Reshaping Engagement in Healthcare

LEVEL UP

GAMIFICATION IN PHARMA MARKETING

Subba Rao Chaganti

™ **PharmaMed Press**

An imprint of BSP Books Pvt. Ltd.
4-4-309/316, Giriraj Lane,
Sultan Bazar, Hyderabad - 500 001,
Telangana, India.

Level Up: Gamification in Pharma Marketing
by Subba Rao Chaganti

Disclaimer: The authors and the publishers have taken due care to provide the authentic, reliable and up to date information related to the subject. However, neither the authors nor the publisher shall be responsible for any liability for any damage caused as a result of use of this book. The respective user must check the accuracy from other sources too.

Published by

Pharma Med PRESS
An Imprint of BSP Books Pvt. Ltd.

™ **PharmaMed Press**

An imprint of BSP Books Pvt. Ltd.
4-4-309/316, Giriraj Lane, Sultan Bazar, Hyderabad - 500 001,
Telangana, India.
Phone: 040-23445688
E-mail: info@pharmamedpress.net
www.bspbooks.net/www.pharmamedpress.net

ISBN: 978-93-47311-07-9 (Paperback)

Disclaimer

This book, *Level Up: Gamification in Pharma Marketing*, is an original work of authorship created for educational and informational purposes. The frameworks, strategic analyses, narrative case studies, and practical tools presented herein reflect the independent intellectual contribution of the author.

To support content development, the author utilized select AI tools for language refinement, drafting assistance, and research synthesis. All AI-generated inputs were critically reviewed, edited, and contextualized by the author, who assumes full responsibility for the accuracy, originality, and interpretation of the final content.

Mentions of real companies, programs, and technologies (e.g., Mango Health, mySugr, AstraZeneca, Pfizer, Roche, Novartis, GSK, and others) are based on public sources, cited references, and verifiable reports. Some case narratives may be adapted or fictionalized for illustrative purposes. No proprietary or confidential internal data has been used.

All brand names, trademarks, and service marks cited are the property of their respective owners and are used solely for educational commentary under fair use principles. Their inclusion does not imply endorsement or affiliation.

This book does not constitute medical, legal, or regulatory advice. Readers are advised to consult qualified professionals and relevant regulatory agencies (such as the FDA, EMA, GDPR, HIPAA) before applying any strategies, especially in clinical, compliance-sensitive, or patient-facing contexts.

The author and publisher disclaim any liability for consequences arising from the application or interpretation of the contents herein.

If any content is believed to infringe upon copyright or other rights unintentionally, please notify the author or publisher. Appropriate corrective steps will be taken.

Acknowledgements

Writing Level Up: Gamification in Pharma Marketing has been an adventure as dynamic as the subject itself—full of insights, iteration, and the joy of rediscovery. At its heart, this book is about designing better engagement for a more human, more effective pharmaceutical industry. I owe its realization to many.

To the passionate professionals in pharma marketing, medical affairs, sales force training, and patient advocacy—your openness to rethink traditional paradigms and experiment with new frontiers like gamification is what inspired this project. Your curiosity, creativity, and courage are what will truly transform healthcare engagement.

I am deeply grateful to the global community of behavioral scientists, game designers, technologists, and healthcare innovators whose research, products, and case studies informed the pages of this book. In particular, the pioneering work of Jane McGonigal, BJ Fogg, Richard Ryan and Edward Deci, Yu-kai Chou, and so many others laid the theoretical groundwork that now enables meaningful play in medicine.

A heartfelt thanks to my publishers, Naresh Daver, Nikunjesh Shah, and the entire team at PharmaMed Press. Your enduring commitment to building a meaningful library of pharmaceutical knowledge has made it possible to bring these ideas to life with both professionalism and passion.

To my family—my wife Mahalakshmi, whose encouragement keeps my intellectual engine running; my children Srinivasa Phanindra, Geetha, Lavanya, Satya Shankara Aditya, Sowmya, and Chaitanya—each of whom inspires me with their dedication and creativity; and my beloved grandchildren Aditi, Eesha, Surya, and Shriya, who remind me daily that learning is most powerful when it's playful. Thank you for your love, patience, and belief in my work.

And finally, to every pharma brand manager, digital strategist, trainer, or medical rep who dares to ask, "What if healthcare could be more engaging?"—this book is for you.

Keep playing forward.

Subba Rao Chaganti

Preface

It began, as many meaningful explorations do, with a question.

How do we make people care?

In over five decades of working in pharmaceutical marketing, I've seen science deliver astonishing breakthroughs—life-saving therapies, revolutionary diagnostics, and precision interventions that were the stuff of science fiction when I started out. But alongside this scientific progress, I've also seen something far more human—and far more fragile—play out: the gap between knowing and doing.

Doctors know the guidelines. Patients know the importance of adherence. Reps know the message. And yet, something is often missing.

Engagement.

Connection.

Motivation.

That is where my curiosity about gamification began. Not as a buzzword or a marketing tactic, but as a serious, structured approach to solving one of pharma's most persistent problems: how do we move people—from awareness to action, from passive receipt to active participation?

Gamification, I quickly realized, is more than badges, leaderboards, or shiny apps. At its best, it is the thoughtful application of behavioral science, psychology, design thinking, and digital technologies to humanize the healthcare experience. It recognizes that we are not rational robots. We are emotional, story-driven, feedback-seeking beings. And yes—sometimes, we are more likely to take our medication if doing so unlocks a reward or completes a level.

This book is the result of years of research, interviews, case studies, and conversations with marketers, MSLs, developers, designers, and patients. I wanted to write a book that not only explains the what and how of gamification—but one that tells the stories of those who have used it meaningfully, ethically, and effectively in pharmaceutical marketing.

You will read about:

A mobile app that turned daily medication into a point-scoring mission.

A pharma sales team that absorbed complex oncology content through immersive simulations.

A patient with cancer who found solace and strength in a galaxy of gamified stories.

A training program that reduced knowledge gaps by 70% in five days—because it felt like play, not work.

Each chapter explores a different dimension—anchored in science, enlivened by narrative, and supported by real-world metrics. I've tried to strike a balance between accessibility and intelligence, a free-flowing yet grounded tone, and technical expertise where necessary, while always maintaining a human touch.

This is not a book only for game designers or digital marketers. It is for:

Pharma brand managers wondering how to improve engagement.

CX strategists designing interventions that stick.

Medical affairs leaders training field forces more effectively.

Data scientists building smarter nudges.

And anyone who believes that behavior change is at the heart of better healthcare.

We are entering an era where healthcare will be increasingly participatory. Where patients will not just consume information but interact with it. Where the difference between a life extended and a life cut short may hinge on something as simple—and profound—as a reminder delivered with joy.

If gamification can help us save lives, inform minds, and move hearts—then surely, it deserves serious consideration and strategic application.

This book is my contribution to that conversation.

Let's level up together.

Subba Rao Chaganti
Farmington, Connecticut
October 2025

Contents

Disclaimer ...(v)

Acknowledgements ...(vii)

Preface ...(ix)

PART I: UNDERSTANDING GAMIFICATION

Chapter 1: What is Gamification—and Why should Pharma Care? 5

- Defining Gamification: Mechanics, Dynamics, Aesthetics 8
- Differentiating Gamification from Serious Games and Edutainment 11
- The Psychological Underpinnings 14

Chapter 2: A Brief History of Gamification 17

- Game Theory Roots in Behavioral Economics 21
- The Rise of Digital Gaming and Behavioral Tech 24
- Timeline: From Pong to *Pokémon Go* to Pharma Apps 28

Chapter 3: Pioneers who Played to Win 32

- Jane McGonigal: Games for Good 36
- BJ Fogg: Behavior Design and Persuasive Technology 39
- Richard Ryan & Edward Deci: Self-Determination Theory 43
- Yu-Kai Chou: The Octalysis Framework 47
- The Implications of their Models in Healthcare Engagement 51

PART II: GAMIFICATION COMES TO PHARMA

Chapter 4: The why of Gamification in Pharma Marketing 59

- Engagement Deficits in Traditional Pharma Models 63
- "Fractures in the Flow: HCP Learning Fatigue, Patient Non-Adherence, and MSL Training Overload" 68
- "The Motivational Bridge: Why Gamification might be What Healthcare Needs" 72

Chapter 5: The Anatomy of a Gamified Experience 76

- Game Mechanics: Points, Badges, Leaderboards, Avatars, and Challenges 80
- Designing for Behavior Change: Nudges, Feedback Loops, and Progress Tracking 84
- Designing for Different Audiences: HCPs, Patients, and Reps 89

Chapter 6: The Digital Enablers 93

- Mobile-first Healthcare Evolution 98
- AI for Personalization and Adaptive Challenge 102
- IoT and Wearables: Real-time Triggers and Adherence Feedback 106
- Case Highlight: Mango Health App – Gamified Medication Adherence and behavior Tracking 110

PART III: PHARMA CASE STUDIES IN ACTION

Chapter 7: From Scripts to Scores – Gamifying Adherence 118

- Case Study: Mango Health — Gamifying the Pill Routine 122
- Case Study: MySugr — Diabetes Management Made Playful 125
- Case Study: Smart Inhalers & Connected Pillboxes – When IoT Meets Gamification 129
- Story: A Type 2 Diabetic's Journey: From Neglect to Habit Formation 132

Chapter 8: The Training Game – Educating Sales Reps & MSLs 136

- When Learning is Passive, Retention is Fragile 137
- Case Study: Abbott Brazil & Atrivity – When Trivia Meets Transformation 140
- From 27.5% to 7.5% in 5 Days: Closing the Gap with a Game 143
- Case Study: AstraZeneca's "Go to Jupiter" Onboarding that didn't Feel like Orbiting Bureaucracy 146
- Beyond Office Hours: When Reps Played On 149
- Case Study: Oncology Product Simulation (Biopharma) 152
- Immersive 3D Learning: When New Worlds Speed Real Readiness 155

Chapter 9: Doctors Who Game – Gamifying HCP Education and Engagement 161

- Why Doctors Play: The Quiet Power of Points, Peers, and Practice 165
- Case Study: The Game of Guidelines — When Protocols became Play 168
- When 40% Meant more than a Number 172
- Retention by Design: When Learning Turned into Play 175

Chapter 10: Patients as Players – Emotional and Social Gamification 178

- Case Study: Novartis – Galaxies of Hope 182
- Empathy-Based Storytelling for Neuroendocrine Cancer Support 185
- Headspace & Fitbit: Rewiring Wellness through Sleep, Steps and Stillness 188
- The Patient as Hero in their Own Narrative 191

Chapter 11: VR, Pain & Play 194

- Case Study: Johns Hopkins – Bandit's Shark Showdown (Stroke Rehab) 198

- Case Study: SnowWorld VR – Easing Burn Pain with a Snowball Fight 202
- Rewiring Pain and Possibility: How Immersive Games Engage the Brain 206

PART IV: DESIGNING FOR IMPACT

Chapter 12: The Science of Engagement – Metrics that Matter 216

- Measuring Engagement: DAUs, MAUs, Stickiness, Compliance 220
- KPIs in Gamification: What we Measure is What we Become 224
- The Infinit Study: When Research became a Game–and a Habit 228
- The Telltale Numbers: When 60% More Entries Meant 30% Fewer Goodbyes 231

Chapter 13: Ethics in the Game 234

- Motivation vs. Manipulation 237
- When Games Go Too Far: The Perils of Dark Patterns and Over-Gamification 241
- The Fine Point of Trust: Data Privacy, Consent, and Fairness in the Age of Health Gamification 245
- The Hidden Rulebook: Playing by Regulations in the Game of Health 249

Chapter 14: Where Gamification Fails – Lessons from Misfires 253

- Tokenization without Motivation: When the Game Loses its Soul 258
- Bad Game Design: When the Game Itself is the Problem 261
- When we Forget why the Game Works 264

PART V: FUTURE HORIZONS

Chapter 15: Playing it Right — A Strategic Playbook for Pharma Brand Managers 274

- Defining the Strategic Objective: Start with Why 279
- Mapping the Player Types and Motivation Models 282
- Designing Mechanics Aligned with Behavior Science 285
- Prototyping, Testing, and Regulatory Alignment 289
- Execution Blueprint: From Concept to Launch 293
- Measuring what Matters — KPIs, ROI, and Continuous Optimization 297
- Agile Rollouts and Metric Dashboards – Learning while Doing 301
- "Leveling Up Adhera™: A Gamified Cardiovascular Drug Launch" 304

Chapter 16: The Next Level 308

- Hyper-Personalized Gamified Care Pathways 312
- AI Co-Pilots and Adaptive Challenges 316
- Blockchain and Reward Tokenization in Healthcare 320
- Predictive Analytics and Real-time Gamification 323

Epilogue: The Joy of Play in a Serious World 327

- Gamification is not a Gimmick 331
- Ten Real-World Case Studies of Gamification in Pharma 334

APPENDICES

- Appendix A: Glossary of Gamification Terms 351
- Appendix B: Scientific References and Citations 356
- Appendix C: Gamification Templates and Checklists 360

About the Author 363

PART I: UNDERSTANDING GAMIFICATION

Chapter 1: What is Gamification—and Why Should Pharma Care?

Chapter 2: A Brief History of Gamification

Chapter 3: Pioneers who Played to Win

Part I

Understanding Gamification

Introduction: The Game behind the Pill

In 2016, I met a cardiologist in Hyderabad who told me a story I've never forgotten.

He had a middle-aged patient recovering from a bypass surgery—motivated, educated, and terrified of relapse. The prescription was standard: beta blockers, statins, a strict diet, and daily walks. The problem wasn't medical. It was motivational. On follow-up, the patient confessed: "Doctor saab, I feel like I'm fighting a battle without a scoreboard."

The phrase struck me.

A scoreboard.

We all need one. Something to show progress. To reward effort. To tell us we're not just complying—we're advancing. For this man, recovery felt invisible. Every walk was a chore. Every pill, a lonely ritual. He wasn't lazy. He was unengaged.

Now imagine if that same man received a chirp on his phone each time he took his medication. A gentle "well done" when he completed a walk. A daily progress bar, a friendly avatar, maybe even a virtual badge when he hit seven days straight.

That's not fantasy. That's gamification.

We think of games as distractions. Entertainment. Pastimes. But games are ancient, powerful, and deeply human. Soldiers in trenches played chess. Patients in chemotherapy wards play Candy Crush. Children recovering from burns are immersed in virtual snowball fights. In our hardest moments, we reach for play—not as escape, but as meaning-making.

Gamification takes the essence of games—progression, feedback, goals, reward—and brings it into real life. Into healthcare. Into pharma.

And in doing so, it addresses a silent epidemic in medicine: not lack of drugs, but lack of engagement.

In this section, we'll unpack the foundational questions:

- What exactly is gamification—and what is it not?
- Where did it come from? Who shaped it?
- Why are tech giants, behavioral economists, and now pharma companies investing in it?

We'll journey through early experiments in behavior change, meet thinkers like Jane McGonigal and BJ Fogg, and trace the arc from psychology labs to mobile apps that nudge patients to take control of their lives.

This is not just a theoretical chapter. It is a story of how play—that most underestimated force—may become one of pharma's most powerful tools.

Because in the end, patients aren't just looking for information. They're looking for a reason to keep going. And sometimes, that reason is as simple as a ding, a badge, a score, or a story.

The game behind the pill is just beginning.

Let's understand how it works.

Chapter 1

What is Gamification – and Why should Pharma Care?

A few years ago, I was speaking at a pharmaceutical marketing workshop in Mumbai when a young brand manager raised her hand and asked, half-jokingly, "Sir, do we really expect patients to play games with their medicines?"

The room chuckled. But she wasn't wrong to ask. For years, healthcare has carried a kind of sacred seriousness—illness as gravity, compliance as duty. And play? That belonged in amusement parks and weekend apps, not in oncology wards or chronic care plans.

But I asked her to consider this: What if playing a game made someone more likely to take their medicine? What if it helped them manage a disease better than any brochure ever could?

That's not just theory. It's already happening.

Games, Stripped Down

Let's start at the beginning. Gamification is not about turning everything into a video game. It's not adding cartoon mascots to serious things. At its core, gamification is about borrowing the elements that make games engaging—like goals, points, feedback, progress bars, challenges—and applying them to real-world activities.

Not to entertain.

To motivate.

Think about a typical health task: taking pills every day, going for a walk, logging glucose levels. These are simple, but not easy. They're repetitive, often thankless, and come without visible reward.

Games change that dynamic. They create structure, feedback, and stakes.

Suddenly, a daily walk becomes a mission. A completed medication schedule earns a badge. Logging meals unlocks progress on a virtual journey.

And that shift—from passive obligation to active participation—can be powerful.

From Silicon Valley to the Pharmacy Shelf

Gamification, as a term, entered the mainstream around 2010, but its roots run deeper—into behavioral psychology, educational theory, and even war-time propaganda posters that rewarded "fuel-saving citizens." But it was the tech industry that scaled it—Uber, Duolingo, Fitbit, Apple Watch—each using subtle nudges, progress metrics, and reward systems to encourage consistency.

And pharma noticed.

Because the industry has a stubborn, unyielding problem: people don't always do what's best for them.

- Up to 50% of patients don't take chronic disease medications as prescribed.
- Physicians, overwhelmed with information, forget to apply new clinical guidelines.
- Sales reps forget 80% of product knowledge within weeks of training.

Pamphlets don't fix this. Neither do emails. But a carefully designed gamified system might.

Not by tricking.

But by tapping into human nature—our need to progress, achieve, and feel seen.

Real People, Real Games

Take Mango Health, for instance. A medication adherence app that rewards users with points for taking pills on time. Or MySugr, which turns diabetes self-management into a game with challenges and rewards. Or AstraZeneca's Go to Jupiter—a gamified training platform for MSLs that saw reps voluntarily completing modules outside of work hours.

These aren't flukes. They're engineered. Purposeful. Evidence-backed.

And more importantly—they work.

Gamification does not trivialize health. It re-humanizes it.

So, Why Should Pharma Care?

Because we're in an era where science alone is not enough.

We have the molecules. We have the algorithms. But without behavior change—without attention, motivation, and participation—we have only potential, not impact.

Gamification isn't a panacea. But it is a tool. A surprisingly potent one. Especially in a world where screens dominate attention and patients are as overwhelmed as their doctors.

Pharma should care because, increasingly, the choice isn't between gamification and tradition.

It's between relevance and irrelevance.

As I told that young brand manager that day in Mumbai:

We're not asking patients to play games.

We're inviting them to become players in their own health stories.

And that's not gimmickry. That's empowerment.

Let's explore how it works.

Defining Gamification: Mechanics, Dynamics, Aesthetics

A few winters ago, I visited a close friend recovering from a knee replacement. The surgery had gone well. The physiotherapy? Less so. Every session was a struggle. The movements were small, painful, repetitive. She hated it.

Then her teenage grandson brought over an old Nintendo Wii.

Within days, she was bowling virtually. Swinging her arm with gusto. Smiling. Competing with her family. She was, essentially, doing the same motions her physical therapist had prescribed—only now with points, applause, and the occasional celebratory music.

"Strange, isn't it?" she said, laughing. "When the game says 'good job, 'I believe it more than when the nurse says it."

That, in essence, is the power—and precision—of gamification.

But what exactly is it? To define it, we must unpack its three fundamental layers: mechanics, dynamics, and aesthetics. Each plays a different role. Together, they create a system that doesn't just instruct behavior—but draws people into it.

1. **Mechanics: The Building Blocks**

   If gamification were a body, the mechanics would be the skeleton. These are the tangible, programmable rules and components—what the system does.

   - Points: for every pill logged, module completed, or step taken.
   - Badges: to mark milestones—7 days of adherence, 100% product mastery.
   - Levels: that signal progress, from novice to expert.
   - Leaderboards: that add a touch of competition—between reps, HCPs, or even clinics.
   - Challenges or Quests: time-bound missions with defined goals.

   Mechanics give structure. They tell the user: There is a goal. And there is a way to win.

   But structure alone doesn't motivate.

2. **Dynamics: The Unfolding Behavior**

   Mechanics are programmed. Dynamics are what emerge when humans interact with those mechanics. They are unpredictable, emotional, social. They are how the game actually feels.

   - A patient begins checking in daily—not just to earn points, but because missing a day feels like a loss.
   - A field rep returns to a training app late at night—not for a badge, but to stay ahead of her peers on the leaderboard.
   - A doctor re-engages with a guideline module—not because it's required, but because it's become a habit.

   Dynamics are about behavior in motion. They transform task into tension, compliance into curiosity.

   They're what made my friend bowl through her pain—because now, she wanted to win.

3. **Aesthetics: The Emotional Experience**

   The third layer—often ignored in technical conversations—is aesthetics. Not in the sense of pretty visuals, but in the sense of how the experience makes us feel.

   - Is it playful?
   - Is it serious and meaningful?
   - Is it empowering?
   - Is it soothing?

   For a child with asthma using a gamified inhaler, the aesthetic may be whimsical. For an oncologist training on immunotherapy, it may be sleek and professional. The look, feel, sound—even the rhythm of the interaction—matters deeply.

   Because the right aesthetic evokes the emotional buy-in needed for behavior to stick.

   And in healthcare, emotion is not fluff. It's fuel.

The Interplay: A Delicate Ecosystem

When done right, these three elements create more than just a game-like experience. They create a motivational ecosystem.

The mechanics give shape.

The dynamics give life.

The aesthetics give meaning.

This is why slapping a leaderboard onto a pill reminder app doesn't work. Or why "points for everything" can backfire. It's not about layering rewards on top of routines. It's about aligning design with psychology, and action with purpose.

My friend eventually finished her therapy. The *Wii* (the Nintendo game) sat idle again. But she said something that stayed with me:

"I stopped being a patient for a while. I was just someone playing. And I got better along the way."

That's gamification at its best. Not a distraction. Not manipulation.

Just intelligent design that respects human nature.

As we continue, we'll explore how these elements have been used in the real world—by pharma companies, healthcare startups, and digital health pioneers—to drive behavior not by force, but by invitation.

Let's keep playing.

Differentiating Gamification from Serious Games and Edutainment

A few years ago, I was invited to review a new "serious game" built by a healthcare startup for patients with chronic heart failure. It opened with a digital avatar of a smiling cardiologist who explained salt restrictions and diuretic schedules. Then came a mini-game where you guided a character through a supermarket, picking low-sodium foods. Every right choice earned stars. Every wrong one prompted a short video.

It was well-meaning. It was educational. But after a few minutes, I found myself drifting. So did the patients.

Compare that to something like Mango Health—an app that doesn't look like a game at all. There are no cartoon characters. No animated doctors. Just subtle gamified elements: medication reminders, streak counters, progress dashboards, rewards for consistency. Patients weren't "playing a game." They were living their lives—just with a nudge of motivation and a visible sense of progress.

And that's the difference.

Gamification is not about making a game.

It's about making life feel more game-like—in ways that support behavior change.

The Confusion of Labels

In the world of health tech and pharma marketing, terms like gamification, serious games, and edutainment are often used interchangeably. But they are not the same thing—and confusing them leads to poor design and poor outcomes.

So let's clarify.

1. **Gamification: Invisible Mechanics, Visible Motivation**

   Gamification is the use of game elements in non-game contexts to drive engagement, motivation, or behavior.

   - It doesn't require a storyline or a playable world.

- There's no "level" in the traditional sense—only progress toward a real-world goal.
- It often lives within an app, a dashboard, a training module—but doesn't look like a game.

The goal is not entertainment. It is sustained participation.

When a pharma rep gets a badge for completing an oncology module, or a patient sees a streak of 10 green dots for 10 days of medication adherence, that's gamification.

And it works because it's light-touch, ambient, and behaviorally aligned.

2. **Serious Games: Games with Purpose, Not Just Play**

   Serious games, by contrast, are fully developed game environments with a clear educational or training goal.

   - Think simulations where reps interact with virtual doctors.
   - Or VR rehab programs where patients use gamified arms to rebuild muscle control.
   - These are complete games, built with narratives, challenge structures, and win conditions.

   The user plays consciously. They enter the experience knowing it's a simulation. The immersion is part of the learning.

   Serious games are powerful—but resource-intensive, and not always practical for daily touchpoints.

   Gamification, on the other hand, can be threaded into daily routines without requiring deep immersion.

3. **Edutainment: Entertainment First, Education Second**

   Then there's edutainment—the hybrid genre that tries to teach by entertaining.

   It often lives in the world of children's media, health cartoons, explainer videos, or animated characters that explain blood pressure through stories. When done well, it creates curiosity. When done poorly, it condescends.

   Edutainment tells you something useful while trying to keep your attention.

But it doesn't always drive sustained behavior change—because knowing something is not the same as doing something. That gap—the knowing-doing gap—is precisely what gamification aims to bridge.

A Useful Metaphor

Think of it this way:

- Edutainment is like a teacher in costume—trying to make learning fun.
- Serious games are like medical flight simulators—complex, realistic, high-stakes practice.
- Gamification is the subtle background rhythm—the Fitbit buzz, the Duolingo streak, the nudge that says: "Just one more step. You're doing great."

It doesn't replace content. It wraps around it, guiding behavior gently, persistently, and often invisibly.

In medicine—and especially in pharma—we don't always need to entertain.

But we do need to engage.

We need people to stay curious, stay active, stay compliant—not for a week, but for a lifetime.

Gamification does that not by changing what we do, but by changing how it feels.

And that difference—small, silent, structural—is sometimes all it takes.

The Psychological Underpinnings

Why Gamification Works? (When it Does)

A few years ago, I was visiting a rehabilitation center in Boston when I met an elderly woman named Ruth, recovering from a minor stroke. Her speech had returned, her memory was sharp, but the physical therapy—particularly her hand exercises—were stagnating. She knew what to do. She wasn't doing it. Her therapist, a thoughtful young woman named Claire, tried everything—reminders, encouragement, even lectures. Nothing stuck.

Then Claire added a small twist: she gave Ruth a paper calendar, and every day she completed her therapy, she got to place a gold star on that day.

The stars were meaningless, of course. No prizes. No points. But after a week, Ruth's compliance jumped from sporadic to daily. "It just feels good," she said, tapping her calendar proudly. "I like seeing the chain grow."

That moment—that quiet, shimmering motivation—is the beating heart of gamification.

Not gimmicks.

Not noise.

But psychology, structured with empathy.

1. **Intrinsic vs. Extrinsic Motivation: The Quiet Tug-of-War**

   We like to think of motivation as a single force. But psychologists have long known it has two distinct sources:

   - Extrinsic motivation comes from outside—rewards, punishments, social approval, deadlines. It's the bonus for hitting a sales target, the badge for finishing a course.
   - Intrinsic motivation comes from within—curiosity, purpose, joy in the task itself. It's the satisfaction of mastering something hard, the delight in progress, the pride in self-discipline.

   Gamification works when it respects the balance between the two.

   Used poorly, it leans too heavily on the extrinsic—do X to get Y—and ends up training people like lab rats. The engagement disappears the moment the reward does.

But used wisely, it awakens intrinsic motivation. It shines a light on progress. It recognizes effort. It celebrates mastery. It helps people see themselves changing—and that is far more powerful than any leaderboard.

Ruth didn't do her exercises for the gold stars. She did them for what the stars represented: agency, momentum, dignity.

2. **Flow: The Sweet Spot of Challenge and Skill**

In the 1970s, psychologist Mihaly Csikszentmihalyi introduced a concept now central to gamified design: flow.

Flow is the mental state where we are fully absorbed in what we're doing—focused, challenged, and alive. Not bored. Not anxious. Just engaged. Time blurs. Self-consciousness fades.

We've all experienced it—writing something that flows, solving a puzzle, getting lost in a task. Games are masters of flow. They calibrate challenge precisely to our skill level—too easy and we disengage; too hard and we give up. The sweet spot pulls us in.

Gamified systems aim to engineer flow:

- A patient's app increases difficulty gradually—first a one-day streak, then three, then seven.
- A rep training module adapts content to the learner's pace—enough to stretch, never to overwhelm.
- An HCP platform offers immediate feedback, small wins, and visible mastery.

It's not magic. Its design is aligned with psychology.

And flow, when reached, feels less like work and more like play—the kind of play that teaches, heals, and transforms.

3. **Engagement Loops: The Invisible Habits of Action**

Gamification, at its core, is a system of loops—feedback loops and engagement loops—designed to reinforce behavior.

A typical loop looks like this:

Trigger → Action → Feedback → Motivation → Repeat

- You get a nudge (a reminder or visual cue)
- You act (take the pill, complete the lesson, enter your blood pressure)

- You receive immediate feedback (progress bar updates, a congratulatory message)
- You feel a sense of accomplishment or anticipation
- The behavior becomes more likely to repeat

Over time, the loop becomes a habit. Not through coercion, but through design that aligns with how our brains work.

Think of the rings on an Apple Watch. They're just circles. But they close only if you move. And once you've seen them close, you want to see it again. You crave the loop.

In pharma, a well-designed engagement loop might mean the difference between:

- A patient taking their full course—or stopping halfway.
- A rep mastering product knowledge—or just skimming.
- A doctor updating their practice—or reverting to old norms.

The Science of Behavior Meets the Art of Design

These concepts— intrinsic drive, flow, and engagement loops—aren't new. But in the hands of thoughtful designers and healthcare professionals, they become something more:

A system that nudges.

A rhythm that sustains.

A story that makes someone want to act, not just know they should.

That's what gamification really is.

Not points.

Not prizes.

Patterns—built on psychology, reinforced by emotion, guided by insight.

And like all good medicine, it begins not with a technology, but with a question:

"What will make this person want to keep going—tomorrow, and the day after that?"

The answer, more often than we think, lies in the mind—not the molecule.

Chapter 2

A Brief History of Gamification

In 1943, during the height of World War II, the U.S. government launched a public campaign called "Victory Gardens." Citizens were encouraged to grow vegetables in their backyards. Every seed packet distributed came with a star chart. Every harvest weighed was recorded. Neighbors compared numbers. The more you contributed, the more visible your effort became.

It was wartime logistics, yes. But it was also an early form of something else—something we now call gamification.

Because the truth is, long before we had the word, we had the instinct. To motivate, we didn't just instruct—we challenged. We tracked. We rewarded. We made it feel like progress.

This instinct—to transform the mundane into the meaningful through structure and feedback—has quietly run through history. It just didn't have a name until the 21st century.

The Roots: Psychology Before Play

In the 1950s and 60s, psychologists like B.F. Skinner were busy studying operant conditioning—the idea that behavior could be shaped by reinforcement. Press a lever, get a pellet. Over time, this principle evolved into behavioral design, laying the groundwork for much of what gamification became.

Meanwhile, educators were exploring learning through play, especially for children. Games weren't just distractions—they were delivery systems for knowledge and motivation. From Sesame Street to math flashcard games, we were beginning to realize: the brain learns better when it wants to.

But these insights mostly stayed in the realm of classrooms and laboratories—until technology caught up.

The Rise of Digital Play

The 1980s and 90s brought the golden age of video games—Tetris, Super Mario, SimCity. What fascinated psychologists and designers alike wasn't just the games themselves—it was how they made people persist.

- Players failed repeatedly—but kept trying.
- They faced challenges—but found them enjoyable.
- They learned systems, strategies, even math—without realizing it.

These games weren't lectures. They were experiences.

Game designers had stumbled onto something behaviorists had long suspected: engagement is not about simplicity. It's about structure, feedback, and perceived control.

By the early 2000s, the tech world began asking a new question:

"What if we used these same principles… for things that weren't games?"

Gamification Gets a Name

The term "gamification" began appearing around 2002. It was clumsy, almost apologetic—coined by British game designer Nick Pelling, who described it as "applying game-like elements to non-game tasks."

But the real explosion came between 2010 and 2012, when apps like Foursquare and Nike+ turned routine behaviors—checking in at a location, going for a run—into competitive, shareable, trackable actions. You didn't just exercise. You leveled up. You earned badges. You challenged friends.

Suddenly, everyone—from Silicon Valley startups to government departments—wanted in.

- Duolingo taught languages with streaks and hearts.
- LinkedIn showed your profile strength as a progress bar.
- Starbucks turned coffee purchases into a loyalty quest.
- Fitbit tracked your steps and celebrated your streaks.
- Even airline miles and credit card points—quietly gamified systems all along—took on more visibility and design.

The term went mainstream. But so did the misunderstandings.

Some thought gamification meant slapping points on everything. Others feared it trivialized serious tasks. But the best implementations were never about fluff. They were about feedback—subtle, intelligent, motivating.

Healthcare: The Late Bloomer

While consumer tech embraced gamification early, healthcare—and especially pharma—lagged behind. Perhaps it was the seriousness of the domain. Perhaps it was regulatory hesitation. Perhaps it was just culture.

But the problems gamification could solve were there all along:

Non-adherence to medication.

- Low patient engagement in chronic care.
- Training fatigue among medical reps.
- HCP disengagement from educational portals.

Eventually, the shift came. Slowly at first. Then with purpose.

- Mango Health introduced gamified adherence for patients.
- MySugr gamified diabetes logging.
- AstraZeneca's "Go to Jupiter" transformed internal training.
- Novartis's Galaxies of Hope turned a cancer journey into a shared, story-rich universe.

These weren't just games. They were tools—designed to connect science with behavior, intention with action.

Today: The Game Beneath the System

Gamification is no longer a novelty. It's a language—spoken in nudges, streaks, badges, progress rings, and soft pings that say "you're getting there."

It's woven into:

- Wearables
- EHRs
- Pharma CRM systems
- Patient engagement apps
- HCP e-learning platforms

Sometimes it's visible. Sometimes it's not.

But its goal is always the same: to close the gap between knowing and doing.

Because what good is a life-saving medication if it stays in the bottle?

The Caution and the Promise

Of course, history also teaches caution. Gamification can be manipulative. It can become addictive. It can be designed badly, thoughtlessly, or without empathy.

But that's not a flaw in the concept. It's a failure in the intent.

Used wisely, gamification is not about turning healthcare into a game.

It's about bringing clarity, progress, and meaning to what often feels like an overwhelming path.

A patient on ten medications. A rep learning complex biology. A doctor juggling new guidelines.

They don't need another app. They need a map—and perhaps a light at the end of the next level.

As we move forward, we won't just look at the "what" of gamification. We'll explore the "how," the "when," and most importantly, the why.

Because this is not about playing.

It's about caring enough to continue.

And that may be the greatest game we've ever designed.

Game Theory Roots in Behavioral Economics

Once, in a hospital cafeteria, I watched a young intern choose between a salad and a slice of pizza. He looked tired, the kind of tired that seeps into your bones during a 28-hour call. His hand hovered over the pizza tongs for a second—then moved to the salad bowl instead.

I couldn't help but smile. There was a game being played. Not one with tokens or a timer. But a quiet one—between short-term desire and long-term consequence. Between fatigue and self-image. Between calories now and regret later.

He made his move.

And that's what game theory is about—not fun and games, but decisions under tension.

It's about how people act when there's uncertainty, when outcomes depend on the behavior of others, or even on different versions of themselves. And oddly enough, it's exactly this line of thinking—mathematical, strategic, and oddly human—that helped lay the groundwork for gamification.

A Field Born in Cold Logic

Game theory first emerged in the early 20th century from mathematicians like John von Neumann, who wasn't thinking about health apps or habit formation. He was thinking about war, poker, and economic conflict.

Von Neumann, and later John Nash, formalized the behavior of rational agents when their choices interact with one another. Should you trust the other player? Betray them? Cooperate? Hold back?

It was elegant. It was brilliant.

And in some ways, it is deeply flawed—because it assumes that people are rational.

Which, of course, we are not.

Enter Behavioral Economics: The Irrational Becomes Predictable

In the 1970s, two Israeli psychologists, Daniel Kahneman and Amos Tversky, began poking holes in the neat equations of classical economics. People didn't weigh risks logically. They used shortcuts, known as heuristics, and often made irrational choices.

We're loss-averse.

We fear regret.

We overvalue immediate rewards.

We fall prey to sunk costs.

We prefer a small gain now over a large one later.

They weren't condemning us. They were mapping us—showing how predictably human we really are.

This new field, behavioral economics, wasn't about how people should behave—it was about how they do. And that, it turns out, is the cornerstone of gamification.

Because if you want someone to take a medication every day for the rest of their life…

Or finish a ten-part training module…

Or engage with a health tracking app over months…

You can't appeal to logic alone.

You must design with the quirks of human nature in mind.

From Theory to Application: Nudge, Reward, Repeat

One of Kahneman's students, Richard Thaler, further developed these ideas with the concept of the "nudge"—a way of altering behavior without coercion. Want more people to become organ donors? Change the default option. Want better dietary choices? Put the healthy food at eye level.

Gamification lives in the same space:

- It doesn't force.
- It doesn't lecture.

- It shapes choices, makes good behavior visible, and rewards small, repeated actions.

In game theory, this would be called a repeated game, where the outcome improves the more consistently a player shows up. In behavioral economics, it's called habit formation.

In the world of pharma, it's the difference between a life-saving drug being prescribed—and actually being taken.

So, Why does this Matter for Pharma?

Because the stakes are high.

And because our strategies have long been built for logic, not behavior.

We distribute brochures, present data, and repeat key messages. But people don't make decisions like spreadsheets.

They make them like humans.

Gamification, built on the foundations of game theory and the insights of behavioral science, offers a distinct approach. One that doesn't just ask: "What should people do?"

But: "What makes people want to do it?"

In a way, we're all those interns in the cafeteria—torn between what's easy and what's right.

And sometimes, what tips the scale is something as small as a badge, a point, or a gentle reminder that we're moving forward.

That's the game.

And when it's played with care, with science, and with empathy—it doesn't manipulate.

It empowers.

The Rise of Digital Gaming and Behavioral Tech

When I was visiting a medical college hospital on work, there was a seven-year-old boy in the pediatric ward undergoing leukemia treatment. His chemotherapy cycles were grueling. He'd lie motionless in bed for hours. But every afternoon, when the nurse brought in a bulky plastic console hooked up to a little screen, something changed. He'd perk up. Eyes bright, hands twitching. He'd play Super Mario Bros. with a focus he didn't show during rounds or lab draws.

"He doesn't eat his soup," his mother once told the doctor, "but he'll fight dragons for hours."

I remember thinking, 'What is it that this pixelated plumber is doing that we are not?'

At the time, it felt like an oddity. Looking back, I think it was a glimpse of a truth we were only beginning to grasp—that engagement is its own kind of medicine.

And that digital games were discovering something healthcare had long forgotten: how to make people care, persist, and act—with joy.

From Arcades to Algorithms

The 1980s gave us Pong, Pac-Man, and Tetris. The 1990s gave us SimCity, Doom, and Tamagotchi. These weren't just entertainment. They were behavioral laboratories.

Game designers weren't calling it "behavioral science." But they were, in fact, engineering motivation.

They learned:

- Give immediate feedback, and players stay focused.
- Make challenges achievable, but not easy, and they try again.
- Show progress visually, and they'll play longer.
- Introduce variable rewards and engagement spikes.

Every level, every sound, every "ding" was a carefully placed piece in a loop of stimulus, action, reward—what behavioral psychologists had once called "operant conditioning," and what tech companies would later call "user engagement."

These lessons weren't locked in arcades for long.

The Pivot: Tech Companies Start Playing for Keeps

By the early 2000s, as the internet became ubiquitous and smartphones started landing in every pocket, a new realization dawned:

What if the same mechanics that kept players glued to games… could be used to shape real-world behavior?

Enter behavioral tech.

Silicon Valley didn't just build products. It built systems that shaped decisions.

- Facebook engineered "likes" and notifications to create anticipation.
- LinkedIn added profile strength bars and endorsements to help users complete their profiles.
- Duolingo turned language learning into a streak-based quest.
- Uber gamified driver performance with scores and rewards.
- Fitbit counted every step—and quietly dared you to take more.

These weren't games. But they felt like games. And that's what made them work.

Because under the hood, they shared a DNA:

- Instant feedback
- Visible progress
- Layered challenges
- Social comparison
- Emotional resonance

And they didn't ask users to think hard. They invited users to feel invested.

Healthcare Watches from the Sidelines

While digital products began nudging people toward shopping, scrolling, and self-tracking, healthcare mostly watched from the sidelines.

We continued printing leaflets. Designing static portals. Relying on logic and fear to motivate behavior.

But chronic illness doesn't respond to logic.

And behavior doesn't change because a pamphlet says so.

That boy in the pediatric ward didn't play Mario to learn. He played to feel in control—to make choices, overcome obstacles, and win.

Healthcare was built to deliver treatments.

Games were built to deliver agency.

And slowly, that realization began to take root in public health, digital therapeutics, and eventually, pharma marketing.

The Turning Point

Around 2010, something shifted. Startups like Mango Health, MySugr, and Omada started to appear—bringing behavioral design into healthcare.

- Points for taking medications.
- Streaks for logging blood sugar.
- Feedback loops tied to real-time biometric data.

These weren't designed to entertain. They were designed to engage—with the seriousness of healthcare, and the cleverness of gaming.

And they began to work.

Studies showed that even simple gamified nudges improved:

- Medication adherence
- Physical activity
- Engagement with care teams
- Refill rates
- Knowledge retention

Not through manipulation. Through design that honored behavior.

The Invisible Game

Today, the most powerful digital experiences don't shout that they're games.

They whisper it.

They close rings.

They spark streaks.

They give gentle nudges and satisfying feedback.

They reward progress, not perfection.

And that is often enough.

Gamification—when paired with behavioral tech—doesn't turn healthcare into a cartoon. It makes it more livable.

More human.

More winnable.

And that may be exactly what the pharmaceutical industry needs.

Because if taking a pill, logging a side effect, or completing a learning module feels just a little more like closing a level—and a little less like a burden—then maybe we've found something worth building on.

Not a game.

A new kind of medicine.

Timeline: From Pong to *Pokémon Go* to Pharma Apps

A few summers ago, I passed a park where a dozen teenagers were wandering slowly, eyes glued to their phones. At first, I assumed they were texting. Then I noticed one of them shout, "It's here!"—and everyone surged toward a single spot near a bench.

They were playing *Pokémon Go.*

In that moment, the sidewalk became a game board. Reality had acquired a layer of narrative. Trees, paths, and street corners were no longer just background—they were opportunities, challenges, arenas of action.

I thought about those patients—some of whom struggled to walk 200 steps a day. And here were children logging miles without noticing.

It reminded me that sometimes, the right context changes everything.

And it also reminded me of how far we've come—from the blinking pixels of Pong to augmented reality platforms, and now to pharma apps designed to heal by design.

Let's rewind that journey.

1972: Pong – The First Spark

The original Pong—two rectangles batting a square dot across a screen—was not exactly immersive. But it was interactive. For the first time, users weren't just watching a screen. They were controlling it.

That shift—from passive to active—would become the foundation for everything gamified in the decades to come.

1980s–1990s: Arcade Fever, Home Consoles, and Cognitive Persistence

As Pac-Man and Tetris hit arcades, and Nintendo entered living rooms, a new kind of learning emerged. Children who couldn't memorize multiplication tables could remember cheat codes. Players tolerated failure—so long as they got feedback and another chance.

Games were no longer distractions. They were practice grounds for persistence.

Behind the blinking lights, they were teaching something profound:

- Try.
- Fail.
- Learn.
- Repeat.

These feedback cycles—fast, forgiving, and motivating—would become central to behavioral tech and gamification years later.

Early 2000s: Points, Profiles, Progress Bars

By the time social media took off, so did subtle gamification:

- LinkedIn showed your profile strength.
- eBay used seller ratings.
- Credit cards offered tiered points and "status levels."

Even before the word "gamification" had become popular, it was everywhere—quietly reshaping user behavior.

But healthcare stayed mostly out of the loop.

Until…

2010: The Birth of Gamification as a Field

The term "gamification" gained traction in tech conferences and design studios. Foursquare made check-ins competitive. Nike+ rewarded steps. Duolingo turned language learning into a streak-driven mission.

These weren't games. But they made real-life tasks feel game-like.

The insight was clear: People will repeat small behaviors—if they're rewarded with feedback, progress, or even the simple satisfaction of "doing the thing."

Healthcare, still fixated on rational compliance, had missed this. But not for long.

2012–2016: *Pokémon Go* and the Power of Real-World Play

When *Pokémon Go* launched in 2016, it became more than a cultural phenomenon. It was proof that digital behavior could drive real-world movement.

People walked miles. Strangers connected over virtual creatures. Public spaces came alive. Hospitals even reported upticks in physical activity.

If a game could get a sedentary teenager to walk five kilometers in the sun, what could it do for a patient with heart disease or diabetes?

This was a turning point. Healthcare developers, insurers, and pharma companies took notice.

The idea that digital incentives could shape health behavior was no longer theoretical.

2015–2020: The Rise of Gamified Health Apps

And so came the first wave:

- Mango Health: Turning medication adherence into a point-based rewards system.
- MySugr: Making diabetes logging playful and competitive.
- Propeller Health: Gamifying inhaler use with feedback and insights.
- Omada Health: Using digital coaching and milestones to drive weight loss and diabetes prevention.
- AstraZeneca's "Go to Jupiter": Training pharma reps with quests, badges, and performance dashboards.
- Novartis's "Galaxies of Hope": Giving cancer patients a narrative universe to feel less alone.

These were not gimmicks. They were structured experiences—built on psychology, data, and design.

They didn't teach behavior. They made it feel worth repeating.

2020–Present: From Pandemic to Platform

The COVID-19 pandemic accelerated the adoption of digital health.

Gamified symptom trackers. Vaccine badge challenges. Fitness apps that rewarded lockdown step goals.

In pharma, internal training, patient engagement, and even clinical trial participation began to embrace gamified models.

What started as experimentation has matured into a strategy:

- Salesforce enablement tools with game-based learning.
- Patient companion apps that use levels and journaling streaks.
- Wearables that integrate with gamified chronic care plans.
- AI-driven nudges personalized to user behavior.

We've moved beyond novelty. We're now in the platform era of gamification in health.

So, What does this Timeline Teach Us?

That gamification wasn't born in healthcare.

But perhaps, it belongs here most of all.

Because healthcare is often difficult, confusing, and filled with tasks that don't feel rewarding—until it's too late, gamification, at its best, brings clarity, feedback, and momentum to that experience.

From Pong's bouncing pixel to Pokémon GO's magical parks…

From points on a game console to points for taking your statins…

We've traveled a long way.

And the journey has just begun.

Chapter 3

Pioneers who Played to Win

A few years ago, at a conference on behavior design, I watched a man on stage ask the audience a question:

"What would you rather receive—ten dollars now, or twenty dollars next week?"

A few hands went up for the ten. Most for the twenty.

Then he smiled and said, "You just lied."

The room laughed. He wasn't being unkind. Just honest. He explained that most of us say we want the larger, later reward—but in practice, we take the smaller, sooner one. Again and again. It's not stupidity. It's human nature.

That speaker was BJ Fogg, a behavioral scientist from Stanford. And he was one of the first people I'd seen who wasn't just studying behavior—he was designing for it.

He didn't scold people for choosing short-term gratification. He built systems around that tendency—nudging, not pushing. Designing, not demanding. And in many ways, that's what all pioneers of gamification have done: worked with the grain of human behavior, not against it.

This chapter is about those pioneers. The people who didn't just ask, "What motivates?"

But rather, "What makes us keep going when logic says we shouldn't?"

Jane McGonigal: Games for a Better Life

After a traumatic brain injury, Jane McGonigal found herself slipping into depression and cognitive fog. What brought her back wasn't therapy, or textbooks, or positive affirmations.

It was a game.

She designed it herself—SuperBetter. The goal was simple: turn recovery into a quest. Small daily goals. Power-ups for good habits. Allies who cheered her on. Enemies to defeat (like migraines, isolation, fatigue).

It worked.

And more than that—it revealed something deeper. That even in pain, we respond to storylines, progress bars, and feedback. We want to feel like we're moving forward, even if the steps are small.

McGonigal has spent her career asking, "What if games weren't just entertainment—but a framework for resilience?"

In her TED Talk and books (Reality is Broken, SuperBetter), she reframes games as tools for behavior change, mental health, and yes—healing.

For pharma, her insight is gold: People don't want to be fixed. They want to feel like heroes in their own story.

Gamification helps them do that.

BJ Fogg: The Science of Tiny Habits

Fogg doesn't wear a lab coat. He teaches barefoot, often with a cup of tea in hand. But his research at the Stanford Behavior Design Lab may be the most influential work in modern engagement design.

His core insight? Behavior = Motivation + Ability + Prompt

In other words, if you want someone to act, they have to:

1. Want to do it (motivation)
2. Be capable of doing it easily (ability)
3. Receive the right nudge at the right moment (prompt)

He coined this the Fogg Behavior Model, and it underpins nearly every effective gamified system today—from Fitbit streaks to medication reminders in pharma apps.

Fogg also teaches the power of "tiny habits." Don't tell people to meditate for 30 minutes. Tell them to breathe for 10 seconds. Start small. Celebrate instantly. Scale naturally.

It's not theory—it's design.

And in a world where patients are overwhelmed and reps are overtrained, this matters.

Richard Ryan & Edward Deci: The Deep Roots of Motivation

While Silicon Valley built loops and dashboards, two psychologists—Richard Ryan and Edward Deci—were quietly studying what makes motivation sustain itself.

Their Self-Determination Theory became a cornerstone of motivation science. It proposed that people thrive when three core needs are met:

- Autonomy: I choose this.
- Competence: I'm getting better.
- Relatedness: I'm part of something.

You see this everywhere in well-designed gamification:

- Autonomy: choose your path, level, avatar.
- Competence: unlock progress, master levels.
- Relatedness: compete with peers, share wins.

In pharma, this is often what's missing. A patient isn't just missing doses. They're missing a sense of agency and recognition.

Gamification—when designed with Ryan and Deci's model in mind—restores the dignity of participation.

Yu-kai Chou: The Octalysis Framework

Finally, there's Yu-kai Chou, a gamification consultant who sought to go beyond points and badges. He developed the Octalysis Framework, identifying eight core drivers of human motivation—from achievement and empowerment to scarcity, ownership, and meaning.

Chou's gift wasn't invention—it was translation. He helped companies map their systems: What are you actually motivating? Are you tapping curiosity—or just habit? Are your rewards predictable—or delightfully uncertain?

His framework found its way into pharma through tools like:

- Training games for reps that grow in complexity and choice.

- Patient apps that reward self-tracking with personalized insights, not generic trophies.

Chou's approach reminded the field that gamification isn't decoration—it's architecture.

Why these Pioneers Matter for Pharma?

Because pharma has spent years perfecting the molecule, but not the motivation.

Patients don't just need instructions. Reps don't just need information. HCPs don't just need data.

They all need to feel:

- That what they're doing matters
- That they're making progress
- That someone notices

The pioneers in this chapter didn't invent games.

They decoded why people care enough to continue.

And that insight, applied with empathy and precision, may be the most underutilized medicine in the pharma toolkit.

In the next chapter, we'll begin to explore how these theories moved from whiteboards to real-world pharma applications—and how patients, professionals, and platforms began to level up.

Jane McGonigal: Games for Good

Jane McGonigal didn't set out to become the face of a movement. She was a game designer—brilliant, curious, unapologetically idealistic—who believed that games could do more than kill time. They could solve real problems.

But in 2009, life gave her a problem of her own.

A traumatic brain injury—concussion, followed by weeks of headaches, brain fog, light sensitivity, depression. The kind of slow unraveling that doesn't announce itself with fanfare, but with silence. She couldn't think clearly. She couldn't work. Eventually, she couldn't see a future.

In her own words, she felt "suicidally depressed."

Doctors told her to rest. But rest became stillness. Stillness became despair.

So she did something no neurologist advised. She designed a game.

She called it "Jane the Concussion Slayer."

It had rules.

It had power-ups.

It had quests.

And it had allies—friends and family who could help her "battle the bad guys" (like headaches, isolation, self-doubt).

Every day, she logged small wins. Every day, she tracked her progress. And slowly, her mind—which had become her enemy—became a player again.

A Game for Recovery

That experiment became SuperBetter, a game that has since helped thousands—patients with cancer, veterans with PTSD, teenagers with anxiety—turn their recovery journeys into something they could participate in, rather than endure.

It doesn't look like a game. There are no dragons or exploding candies. But it has all the essential mechanics:

- A clear goal: get better.
- Micro-challenges: drink a glass of water, go for a 5-minute walk, call a friend.
- Progress tracking.

- Allies and community.
- A compelling narrative: You are the hero. This is your quest.

And what McGonigal proved—without formal medical training, without regulatory frameworks—was that feeling like you're part of a story matters.

People don't want to be fixed. They want to be seen.

They want to feel in motion.

They want to know that the steps they're taking, however small, are steps toward something.

Gamification, at its best, does that.

The Science behind the Story

Skeptics dismissed SuperBetter as a feel-good anecdote. But McGonigal went further. She worked with researchers to test its impact.

- Studies showed that players reported significant reductions in symptoms of depression and anxiety after just 10 days.
- They felt more optimistic.
- More resilient.
- More connected.

Not because the game gave them answers. But because it gave them agency.

In public health, we frequently discuss compliance. Adherence. Protocols.

However, we often forget how much healing depends on participation.

Jane McGonigal didn't invent that truth. She just made it visible.

Implications for Pharma

In pharmaceutical marketing, we often speak the language of science: mechanisms of action, efficacy curves, market share.

But when patients get a diagnosis—chronic pain, cancer, Parkinson's—their world shrinks. Their choices narrow. Their days blur. The treatment may be necessary. But the journey often feels passive.

McGonigal's work reminds us that the most powerful thing we can offer isn't just information.

It's a frame.

A way for the patient to say:

"This is hard. But I can do hard things."

"This is a game I can play—and maybe even win."

Whether through a digital adherence app, a wearable that celebrates small gains, or a narrative companion that transforms a treatment plan into a personal quest—her philosophy can inform how pharma thinks about engagement.

Because it's not about tricking people into doing what's good for them.

It's about helping them see the good they're already doing.

Games for Good—but also for Dignity

Jane McGonigal's greatest insight wasn't about design. It was about dignity.

She didn't gamify recovery to make it cute. She did it because pain, uncertainty, and effort feel different when you have a goal, a role, and a reason.

"When you're playing a game," she once said, "you're more likely to be hopeful, courageous, and resilient."

That's not fluff. That's medicine.

And for an industry that delivers pills, injections, therapies—it's time we ask:

- What would happen if we also delivered hope and momentum?
- Not instead of science, but alongside it?

That's the promise of gamification.

And McGonigal showed us that it's not just possible—it's personal.

BJ Fogg: Behavior Design and Persuasive Technology

BJ Fogg doesn't look like someone who studies how we change. He looks like someone who believes we can.

When you meet him—or watch one of his lectures—he's soft-spoken, calm, often barefoot. But beneath that calm is a question he's spent his entire career asking:

"What makes someone do something they weren't doing before—and keep doing it?"

Not once. Not just when they're scared or inspired. But every day, without effort. Without fanfare.

In a world where so much of healthcare is designed to instruct, Fogg chose to observe. To study not the logic of decision-making, but the texture of behavior. To understand not what people say they'll do, but what they actually do—at 6:00 a.m., or after a bad day, or when no one is watching.

And in doing so, he didn't just write a theory.

He helped shape the digital world in which we now live.

The Simplicity behind Behavior

At Stanford University, Fogg founded the Behavior Design Lab—a quiet, brilliant space where the mechanics of motivation are taken apart and reassembled. His most enduring contribution is a deceptively simple formula:

$$B = MAP$$

Behavior happens when three things come together:

- Motivation
- Ability
- Prompt

If any one of these is missing, the behavior doesn't happen.

We often focus on motivation—getting people to care. But Fogg found that in real life, ability is often the bottleneck. A patient may want to take their medication. But the bottle's in the car. Or it's 10:00 p.m. and they've already brushed their teeth. Or they forgot.

And even when motivation and ability are present, something has to prompt the action. A nudge. A reminder. A cue.

So behavior, he says, is not an act of will. It's an outcome of design.

Tiny Habits: The Smallest Change that Works

One of Fogg's most compelling ideas is the "tiny habit."

Don't tell someone to start exercising.

Tell them to do one push-up.

Every day. After brushing their teeth.

The trick, he explains, is anchoring. Attach the new habit to something that's already a part of your routine. Keep it absurdly small. And then, celebrate immediately.

Not because a push-up changes your body. But because it changes your identity: "I'm someone who keeps promises to myself."

Fogg tested this with thousands of people. The results were quiet but transformative:

People who drank more water.

- Who flossed.
- Who started walking again?
- Who took their medications on time—not out of fear, but because it felt right.

And for the pharma industry, this insight is seismic.

Most treatment plans aren't failing due to a lack of knowledge.

They're failing because they ask people to leap when they're barely able to crawl.

Fogg would say:

Start with a crawl. Make it easy. Make it rewarding. Make it stick.

From Lab to Silicon Valley

Fogg's work didn't stay in the lab.

In the early 2000s, his ideas began flowing into Silicon Valley—first through students, then through companies.

He trained a young intern named Mike Krieger—who would go on to co-found Instagram.

His models influenced teams at Facebook, Google, Fitbit, and dozens of startups.

They weren't building games. They were building persuasive technology—platforms designed to guide user behavior through feedback loops, positive reinforcement, and habit formation.

And while that power has raised ethical questions, it has also revealed a profound truth: technology doesn't just reflect behavior—it shapes it.

The same mechanisms that get people to scroll a feed can get them to log their blood pressure.

The same prompts that make us check messages can remind us to move, breathe, reflect.

Fogg saw it early. And he didn't panic. He offered a framework.

"Design it for good," he says. "Use the power. But use it responsibly."

Why BJ Fogg Matters for Pharma

Because our industry often prioritizes compliance over compassion.

We ask patients to follow regimens that are complex, unmotivated, and fragile. We train reps with mountains of content and expect retention without reinforcement. We build digital platforms that inform—but rarely engage.

Fogg's work reminds us:

- People don't change because we ask them to.
- They change because the new behavior is easier, more rewarding, and more closely aligned with their identity.
- They change when the system around them changes.

In a world of side effects, dosing windows, regimen fatigue, and cognitive overload, tiny habits, well-prompted, might be our greatest ally.

The Soft Voice of Persuasion

There's a gentleness to Fogg's approach that's easy to overlook.

He doesn't believe in tricking people. He believes in inviting them—into a loop that's so easy, so doable, that it becomes second nature.

He believes in change that feels good—not just for a day, but forever.

And in a field like pharma—where outcomes depend not just on the drug, but on whether someone shows up, follows through, or remembers—we need that gentleness.

We need that design with empathy.

"Help people do what they already want to do," Fogg says.

"And celebrate every step they take."

Maybe that's not just good design.

Maybe that's good medicine.

Richard Ryan & Edward Deci: Self-Determination Theory

A few years ago, I met a patient named Robert—a retired schoolteacher with type 2 diabetes. He had every reason to take his medication. He understood the consequences. He had seen what uncontrolled glucose did to his brother.

And yet, he was missing doses.

When I asked why, he shrugged. "I just… forget sometimes," he said. But it wasn't forgetfulness. It was something else. A weariness. A quiet sense of disconnection from the routine that was supposed to keep him alive.

He didn't feel like a participant in his care. He felt like a subject of it.

It wasn't until his physician reframed his routine—let him set the schedule, choose reminders, track his own progress—that things began to shift. He started calling it "my plan," not "the doctor's orders." And adherence improved.

It was a small change. But one with a profound psychological truth behind it.

That truth was articulated decades earlier by two psychologists—Edward Deci and Richard Ryan—in a theory that may be the most overlooked yet essential ingredient in behavior design:

Self-Determination Theory.

The Core of Motivation is Not the Carrot or the Stick—it's the Self

In the 1970s, Ryan and Deci began questioning what most psychologists assumed: that people are motivated primarily by external rewards or punishments.

Give a child a gold star, and they'll study harder. Threaten a penalty, and they'll fall in line.

But what they noticed—and what their experiments revealed—was that the introduction of a reward often undermined the original motivation.

The child who once read for joy now reads for points.

The worker who once enjoyed a challenge now feared losing a bonus.

Motivation, they argued, is not a fuel you pour in. It's a fire you protect.

And that fire burns best when the three core needs are met:

1. **Autonomy — The Need to Choose**

   People want to feel that their actions are voluntary—not coerced, not dictated, not merely performed to avoid consequences.

   In healthcare, this is the first to go.

   Take your meds. Follow the instructions. Complete the module.

   Do it because we said so. Because it's good for you.

   But Deci and Ryan showed that without autonomy, motivation becomes fragile. We may comply for a while, but we won't engage. We won't own it.

   When a patient customizes their app notifications, selects their own health goals, or decides when and how to learn about their condition, they're not just clicking buttons.

   They're reclaiming autonomy. And that matters.

2. **Competence — The Need to Improve**

   We are wired to seek mastery.

   Whether it's a toddler stacking blocks or a clinician learning a new procedure, we thrive on a sense of progress.

   But healthcare often strips that away. A patient follows orders, but sees no visible gain. A sales rep sits through training, but gets no feedback. A doctor logs in to an e-learning portal and clicks through slides—never knowing if they're actually learning.

   Ryan and Deci showed that feeling capable isn't a luxury. It's essential. And feedback is the key.

   Gamification works not because of points, but because of progress bars. Because of streaks. Because of challenges that get harder, not just longer.

   It's not about entertainment.

   It's about helping people say: "I'm getting better at this."

3. **Relatedness — The Need to Belong**

   Human beings need connection.

   Not just with people—but with purpose.

   When Deci and Ryan added this third pillar to their theory, it completed the picture. Motivation doesn't live in isolation. We act, sustain, and grow when we feel part of something larger.

A patient who joins a support group or shares a goal with others is more likely to stay on track. A representative who sees their performance compared to their peers improves more quickly. A physician who feels seen, heard, and valued learns more deeply.

Gamified systems that connect people, show social proof, or even simulate companionship tap into this need.

Because we're not machines. We're social animals trying to make sense of our actions in the presence of others.

Implications for Pharma and Healthcare

Self-Determination Theory is not flashy.

There are no avatars, no badges, no viral loops.

But underneath every successful gamified system in healthcare, you'll find its fingerprints.

- When a medication reminder app lets the user set the tone, timing, and type of reminder—that's autonomy.
- When a patient unlocks levels by logging their vitals and learning more about their condition—that's competence.
- When a rare disease platform connects patients in a shared journey—that's relatedness.

Too often, we ask:

"How do we make them do it?"

Ryan and Deci would ask:

"How do we help them want to do it—and feel good while doing it?"

That shift—from control to empowerment—is the difference between compliance and commitment.

Motivation is not Given, It's Grown.

In a world of protocols and pipelines, the pharmaceutical industry doesn't always think in these terms. But maybe it should.

Because a treatment only works if it's used.

And it's only used consistently if it's chosen, not imposed.

What Deci and Ryan taught us is that the science of motivation is not about pressure—it's about possibility.

And sometimes, the most important therapy we can offer is a system that says:

- You are in charge.
- You are getting stronger.
- You are not alone.

That's not just psychology.

That's healing.

Yu-kai Chou: The Octalysis Framework

In a clinic outside Farmington, a diabetes educator once told me about a 42-year-old man who refused to open the mobile health app his doctor had prescribed. "He says it feels like homework," she explained. "He already feels like a patient—why make him feel like a failing one?"

Two weeks later, she tried something different. A simple app that turned daily blood sugar logging into a quest. Each log earned him points. Every streak unlocked a new "badge." He could track his progress and even customize a small digital avatar.

It wasn't elaborate. But he started using it.

"It feels less like I'm being told what to do," he told her, "and more like I'm playing."

That shift—from burden to challenge, from passive compliance to active engagement—is precisely what Yu-kai Chou has spent his life trying to understand.

Not just what gets people to act.

But why do we keep acting—when no one is watching, when we're tired, when the novelty has worn off?

And in doing so, he built one of the most thoughtful and comprehensive models of gamification:

The Octalysis Framework.

Designing for Motivation, Not Just Behavior

Most gamified systems begin with mechanics—points, badges, leaderboards. But Chou noticed something: the same mechanics produced wildly different results depending on how they were experienced.

People didn't just want rewards.

They wanted meaning, autonomy, curiosity, and connection.

So Chou asked a deeper question:

"What are the core drives behind human behavior—and how can we design for them intentionally?"

He mapped eight of them—not randomly, but as a symmetrical model, structured like an octagon.

Each side represented a distinct motivational force.

Each one, when triggered skillfully, could sustain long-term engagement.

The Eight Core Drives

1. **Epic Meaning & Calling**

   The sense that you're part of something larger. That your actions matter.

   Why patients join rare disease communities. Why cancer survivors run marathons.

2. **Development & Accomplishment**

   The drive for progress, growth, and mastery.

   Why do people return to learning apps? Why do reps keep completing training modules when levels are unlocked?

3. **Empowerment of Creativity & Feedback**

   The joy of experimenting, expressing, and seeing results.

   Why patients prefer apps that let them set goals. Why doctors engage with interactive simulators, not slides.

4. **Ownership & Possession**

   We value what we build and control.

   Why a customized health dashboard works better than a standard one.

5. **Social Influence & Relatedness**

   Peer pressure, mentorship, recognition, and companionship.

   Why do patients stick to plans when others are cheering them on?

6. **Scarcity & Impatience**

   We want what we can't have—or what's only available for a limited time.

   Why limited challenges or exclusive features spark action.

7. **Unpredictability & Curiosity**

   The thrill of surprise. The dopamine of uncertainty.

   Why do some health apps add randomized "health tips of the day" or surprise rewards?

8. **Loss & Avoidance**

   The fear of missing out. The drive to avoid negative outcomes.

   Why missing a dose and breaking a streak feels so deflating.

   These drives aren't equal—and they don't all feel the same.

   Some are positive and empowering. Others are urgent and pressuring.

   But all of them, Chou argued, can be used ethically to design for sustained engagement.

From Theory to Action

Yu-kai Chou didn't stop at theory. He began applying Octalysis across sectors—education, retail, corporate training, healthcare.

He showed that the best systems blend multiple drives:

- A medication app that rewards streaks (Accomplishment), lets users track data visually (Ownership), and connects them with others on the same journey (Relatedness).
- A pharma learning portal where reps complete quests (Meaning), unlock new knowledge tiers (Progress), and see their impact on simulated patient journeys (Creativity).

The goal isn't complexity. It's alignment.

Not just what you're designing—but why it will resonate.

The Ethical Tightrope

Chou is also clear-eyed about the dangers.

Because persuasive design can manipulate as easily as it can motivate.

He draws a line between White Hat Drives (meaning, growth, connection) and Black Hat Drives (urgency, scarcity, loss). Both work. But only one empowers users.

He warns:

"Just because something is engaging doesn't mean it's good. We must design for what is right, not just what works."

In healthcare—where trust is fragile and stakes are high—this ethic matters deeply.

Gamification is not a slot machine. It's a conversation—with people in pain, people overwhelmed, people trying.

And the best designs, Chou reminds us, don't prey on them.

They honor them.

Implications for Pharma

Yu-kai Chou's Octalysis is not a recipe. It's a lens—a way to see the hidden architecture of behavior and design systems that meet people where they are.

In pharma, it can transform:

- Patient apps that feel cold into journeys that feel personal.
- Training programs that are endured into challenges that are embraced.
- Portals that lecture into platforms that listen.

Because people don't want to be "converted."

They want to be understood.

And that's what Octalysis helps us do: design not for compliance, but for meaningful participation.

"Every human is motivated," Chou says.

"The question is: what are you helping them move toward—and how does it feel?"

If we can answer that—truthfully, ethically, and with care—we may finally build pharma systems that don't just treat conditions…

…but inspire people to keep going.

The Implications of their Models in Healthcare Engagement

In medicine, we often believe that knowledge is the solution. If people know what's good for them, they'll do it.

But spend any time in a clinic, and you'll learn otherwise.

A man with heart failure eats salty food he knows will bloat him.

A woman with breast cancer delays her mammogram because she's afraid of what it might show.

A diabetic teen hides his blood sugar readings from his parents—not because he's reckless, but because he's tired.

This isn't a failure of information. It's a failure of engagement.

And if there's a thread that runs through the work of Jane McGonigal, BJ Fogg, Deci and Ryan, and Yu-kai Chou, it is this:

Behavior doesn't follow knowledge. It follows experience.

If the experience is empowering, we engage.

If it's degrading, unclear, or emotionally barren, we check out.

Healthcare, for all its brilliance, often forgets this.

Why we need New Models?

When Jane McGonigal turned her recovery into a game, she wasn't trying to be clever. She was trying to survive. Her system didn't teach her what to do. It made her want to do it.

When BJ Fogg helped people floss by starting with just one tooth, he wasn't lowering expectations. He was building momentum.

When Deci and Ryan proved that autonomy, mastery, and belonging are the roots of sustained effort, they weren't speaking just to educators or coaches—they were, in essence, describing the missing elements of most chronic care plans.

And when Yu-kai Chou mapped the eight motivations that drive human behavior, he gave us a compass—not just to influence people, but to understand them.

Together, these thinkers gave us something healthcare has long lacked:

A vocabulary for how people move through difficult things.

Implications for Patient Engagement

Patients aren't just vessels for treatment. They are actors in a fragile, often frightening narrative.

Gamification, when guided by these models, doesn't trivialize the journey.

It restores agency to it.

- Autonomy means letting the patient choose how they engage—whether through text messages or an app. Morning or evening?
- Competence means helping them feel progress—not just test results, but streaks, milestones, acknowledgments.
- Relatedness means connecting them—with peers, with caregivers, with stories that reflect their own.

It's not about turning illness into a game. It's about turning effort into something visible, meaningful, and motivating.

In McGonigal's model, the patient becomes a hero.

In Fogg's, they become a doer—one small win at a time.

In Deci and Ryan's, they become a whole person.

In Chou's, they become a player in a system that recognizes why they care.

These are not metaphors.

These are design principles for health systems that actually work.

Implications for HCPs and Pharma Sales Teams

Gamification doesn't stop with patients.

Healthcare professionals—doctors, reps, field force—are also overburdened, under-recognized, and increasingly disengaged. Traditional training models overwhelm with content, but underdeliver on retention.

What these behavioral models teach us is that:

- People learn best when they feel ownership of the process (Fogg, Chou).
- When they can track mastery and get feedback (Deci & Ryan).

- When they feel the learning experience was designed for them, not dumped on them.

A gamified training module that adapts to a rep's pace, offers choice in learning paths, celebrates progress, and connects effort to impact—that's not fluff. That's respect in design.

When a rep completes oncology training and receives more than a certificate—a story, a sense of achievement, a mission—engagement deepens. So does performance.

Because even in high science, we are still emotional learners.

Implications for Public Health and Preventive Behavior

We know what reduces risk.

We know what prolongs life.

Exercise. Diet. Screenings. Vaccines. Medication adherence.

But compliance remains low. Not because people are careless. But because the journey is long, the feedback is slow, and the systems are cold.

What if we offered hope loops instead of scare tactics?

What if brushing teeth, tracking steps, or attending a prenatal checkup felt like small triumphs instead of medical chores?

Gamification isn't about digital glitter. It's about making progress feel real—especially when outcomes are invisible or distant.

That's not indulgent. That's behavioral integrity.

The Caution—and the Opportunity

These models also offer a warning:

Use this power responsibly.

Don't overpromise. Don't manipulate. Don't reduce complex lives to point systems.

But do design with empathy.

Do give people tools to feel strong.

Do make invisible effort visible.

Because the great paradox of healthcare is that it delivers some of the most scientific interventions in the world…

through some of the most inhumane systems imaginable.

The models of McGonigal, Fogg, Deci & Ryan, and Chou ask us to remember:

People don't want to be managed.

They want to be seen, respected, and motivated.

In the chapters ahead, we'll move from theory to reality.

From frameworks to patients, platforms, and brands, these principles are applied in the real world.

But this much is already clear:

Engagement is not just a feature.

It's a form of care.

And it may be the most powerful one we haven't yet prescribed.

PART II: GAMIFICATION COMES TO PHARMA

Chapter 4: The why of Gamification in Pharma Marketing

Chapter 5: The Anatomy of a Gamified Experience

Chapter 6: The Digital Enablers

Part II

Gamification Comes to Pharma

Where Stakes are High and Attention is Low

In most industries, gamification is a strategy to win eyeballs. In the pharmaceutical industry, it's a strategy to achieve adherence, understanding, and trust.

And that makes all the difference.

Unlike consumer brands, pharma doesn't sell entertainment or convenience. It deals with the life-altering—chronic illness, medication side effects, regulatory risk, and clinical complexity. This is a world where education fatigue is real, repetition is necessary, and engagement is fragile. A world where a missed dose can derail a therapy, and a disengaged doctor might overlook an evidence-based guideline.

And yet, in the middle of this seriousness, play has found a place.

Not frivolous, not flashy—but framed, focused, and functional. When done right, gamification in pharma isn't about points or badges. It's about shifting behavior where it matters most—getting patients to take their pills, sales reps to retain scientific knowledge, MSLs to navigate complex therapeutic landscapes, and physicians to follow the latest care protocols.

This part of the book examines the intersection of game mechanics and medical adherence, where behavioral design nudges intersect with chronic care challenges, and where storytelling frameworks are employed not to sell, but to support.

We'll dive into real-world pharma applications—from Brazil to Boston, from diabetes management to oncology rep training. We'll see how mobile apps reduce friction in disease tracking, how VR simulations accelerate onboarding, and how gamified CME makes physicians not only click, but think.

If Part I built the foundation—showing why gamification works—Part II gets its hands dirty. It shows you how pharma makes it work, and what happens when it does.

This is gamification with consequences. And that's what makes it urgent.

Chapter 4

The why of Gamification in Pharma Marketing

A few years ago, I spoke with a man named Ravi who had been newly diagnosed with hypertension. He was bright, educated, even health-conscious. His doctor prescribed medication, explained the risks, and gave him a neat leaflet that included diet tips and exercise recommendations.

Ravi nodded earnestly. He was grateful. He wanted to do better.

But three months later, he'd stopped taking the medication.

"I didn't feel any different," he told me. "And honestly, it just became one more thing to remember."

It wasn't defiance. It wasn't ignorance. It was a disconnection.

And that, more than anything, is why the pharmaceutical industry needs gamification.

Because medicine doesn't work when people don't take it.

Education doesn't work when no one remembers it.

And marketing doesn't work when it treats people like vessels for messaging, instead of participants in their own story.

The Compliance Gap no Campaign can Fill

Pharma has long mastered the what:

- The molecule.
- The data.
- The mechanism of action.
- The detailing aid.
- The KOL testimonial.

However, the why—the thing that motivates people from understanding to action—has too often been assumed or ignored.

We provide doctors with reams of data, expecting them to change their practices.

We give patients instructions, expecting them to follow through.

We give reps product decks, expecting them to become fluent.

And then we wonder why it doesn't stick.

Why, even when the science is flawless, do the outcomes fall short?

The answer is not more information.

It's more engagement.

The Attention Economy Comes to Pharma

Today, the average patient, provider, or sales rep is drowning in noise.

Apps. Alerts. Emails. Trainings. Portals. Guidelines. Refills.

In this world, attention isn't just scarce. It's earned—through relevance, emotion, and feedback.

Gamification earns attention not with gimmicks, but by recognizing the simple truth that:

People are more likely to act when they feel seen, capable, and motivated.

It's not about turning life into a game. It's about making effort feel worthwhile.

- A patient logging their symptoms receives a streak badge—not because the badge matters, but because it acknowledges persistence.
- A rep completing training gets instant feedback—not just a score, but a sense of progression.
- A physician learning about new treatment options unlocks modules at their own pace, charting their own path through unfamiliar data.

These aren't distractions. They are design responses to a crisis of attention and agency.

Why Traditional Pharma Marketing isn't enough Anymore

The old model of pharma marketing was transactional:

- Deliver a message.
- Reinforce it through repetition.
- Hope it converts behavior.

But in an age where behavioral friction—forgetting, fatigue, burnout—is the real barrier, that model falls short.

Gamification offers something different:

- It breaks behavior into micro-actions.
- It adds feedback to invisible progress.
- It introduces choice into rigid regimens.
- And most importantly, it gives people a role in their own journey.

This isn't replacing good science. It's supporting it with good psychology.

The Human Case for Gamification

If you ask most patients what they want from their treatment, the answer isn't "better health literacy" or "data on long-term cardiovascular endpoints."

It's simpler.

"I want to feel like I'm doing something that helps."

"I want to know if it matters when I try."

"I want this to feel doable."

Gamification doesn't guarantee that. But it creates the conditions where that feeling becomes possible.

And in pharma marketing—where your goal is to drive not just awareness, but action—that feeling is everything.

Because when someone feels like a player, not just a patient…

When a rep feels like a learner, not just a learner-on-a-schedule…

When a physician feels engaged, not instructed…

You don't have to force behavior.

It begins to emerge—naturally, sustainably, meaningfully.

Not a Toy, But a Tool

Some still recoil at the word "gamification."

They imagine cartoons. Trivialization. Distraction.

But that's a misunderstanding.

Gamification isn't about fun.

It's about function, guided by empathy.

It asks:

- Can we make the right action feel clearer, easier, more rewarding?
- Can we design healthcare experiences that respect effort?
- Can we help people stay on track—not with shame or fear, but with momentum?

In this sense, gamification isn't separate from medicine. It's part of delivering it well.

Ravi, Revisited

I spoke to Ravi again a year later. This time, he was using a simple app—one that tracked his daily pill, logged his walks, and offered a small weekly reward if he hit his goals.

"It's silly," he said. "But it makes me feel like I'm doing something right."

That "something right" wasn't the app's doing. It was his.

But the app noticed.

And that, in the end, is the core of gamification in pharma:

Not to replace care, but to reinforce it.

Not to distract, but to support.

Not to push people, but to help them pull themselves forward.

We don't need games for the sake of games.

We need systems that say to every patient, rep, doctor:

"We see your effort. Keep going. You're doing better than you think."

That is why pharma needs gamification.

Not for the bells and whistles.

But for the quiet, daily courage of trying.

Engagement Deficits in Traditional Pharma Models

A few years ago, during my morning walks in the park, I met a woman named Eleanor. She was sixty-two, a retired librarian, and had recently been discharged after a minor heart attack. Her regimen was straightforward—beta blockers, statins, a low-sodium diet, and 30 minutes of daily walking.

But when she was readmitted six weeks later, the cardiology resident sighed.

"She stopped everything," he said, more tired than angry. "Again."

When I sat beside Eleanor that evening and asked her gently why, she didn't say she disagreed with the doctors. She didn't claim to know better. She didn't seem careless.

What she said instead was this:

"I left the hospital with a bag of pills and four pamphlets. But no one helped me figure out how to live with them."

That sentence stayed with me.

Because it speaks to something deeper than noncompliance. It speaks to a failure of engagement.

And that failure—replicated across millions of interactions between pharmaceutical brands, healthcare professionals, and patients—is what holds back even our best treatments.

A System Built for Transactions, Not Relationships

Traditional pharmaceutical marketing is, at its core, a well-oiled machine of information delivery. It is built to:

- Disseminate clinical data.
- Educate physicians.
- Promote brand awareness.
- Drive prescription behavior.

But the system often assumes that knowledge will translate into action. That exposure will create retention. That information alone is enough to shape behavior.

Yet real life isn't lived in rational bullet points.

It's lived in confusion, in fatigue, in the moment when someone reaches for a second helping of food they shouldn't eat—not out of rebellion, but out of habit and hunger and the need for comfort.

It's lived in the forgotten dose after a restless night.

In the unread email from the brand rep.

In the unopened patient portal.

The traditional model of pharma marketing—detailing, e-detailing, branded content, CME programs—is exquisitely efficient at scaling messages.

But it struggles with the messiness of motivation.

The Human Gap Between Instruction and Implementation

I've met countless patients who could recite their diagnosis and treatment plan better than a medical student. But when asked to describe their day-to-day adherence, the truth emerges:

"Sometimes I just forget."

"It's hard to keep up."

"I'm not sure it's working."

"I don't want to feel like a patient all the time."

These aren't gaps in knowledge. They are gaps in feeling connected to the treatment journey.

And those gaps—unacknowledged—are where traditional pharma models falter.

- A clinical trial might show 98% adherence under controlled conditions.
- But real-world persistence drops to 40% within six months.
- Educational campaigns generate awareness. But not activation.
- Sales reps deliver decks. But reps themselves often forget half the content within a week.

It's not because they aren't smart.

It's because the system is built for delivery, not for engagement.

Where the Current System Breaks Down

Let's take three key stakeholders: patients, providers, and sales reps.

Patients often receive:

- Dense packaging inserts.
- One-size-fits-all portals.
- SMS refill reminders devoid of empathy.

Providers are bombarded with:

- Rep visits squeezed between patients.
- Monographs, they don't have time to read.
- Continuing education platforms that feel like chores.

Reps and MSLs are handed:

- Static decks.
- Product quizzes.
- Launch trainings that "push" information, but don't help them "own" it.

In all of these touchpoints, the focus is on content. Not on experience.

Pharma tells. But rarely invites.

It informs. But doesn't often involve.

It pushes. But doesn't always pull.

And without that emotional investment, even the best message slips through the cracks.

The Cost of Disengagement

The data is sobering:

- 50% of patients with chronic illness stop taking their medications within a year.
- 80% of healthcare professionals report "educational fatigue" from pharma communications.
- Rep training programs often require repeated reinforcement because retention rates drop by 60% within a week of passive learning.

Every missed dose.

Every forgotten insight.

Every silent "unsubscribe" from a branded email…

These aren't failures of marketing strategy.

They are symptoms of disengagement.

And the cost isn't just commercial. It's clinical.

Because no drug, however advanced, works if it isn't taken.

No insight matters if it isn't remembered.

No innovation moves the needle if no one pays attention.

What Eleanor Needed wasn't just Information, it Was Involvement

When Eleanor was discharged the second time, the hospital tried something different. They enrolled her in a digital adherence program—one that used gamification to track progress, reward consistency, and create gentle nudges through stories, choices, and feedback.

It didn't cure her.

But it did change the story.

"I check in every day now," she told me later. "It's silly, but I like seeing the progress bar. I like knowing I'm doing okay."

In a system designed for data, she finally felt seen.

And that's the shift we need.

Toward an Era of Participation

The engagement deficit in pharma isn't a moral failing. It's a design oversight.

We've built systems to deliver precision medicine—without always building the emotional architecture for people to live with it.

But that's beginning to change.

Gamification, behavior design, and user-centered communication aren't frivolous additions. They are the missing bridges between knowing and doing.

They don't replace science.

They animate it.

They give it traction. Meaning. Memory.

And maybe, one day, someone like Eleanor won't just leave the hospital with instructions.

She'll leave with a sense of momentum.

Because she won't be a passive recipient of treatment.

She'll be a player in her own healing.

"Fractures in the Flow: HCP Learning Fatigue, Patient Non-Adherence, and MSL Training Overload"

It's Monday morning at 8:14 a.m., and Dr. Miranda Joshi has already reviewed a patient's labs, counseled a diabetic teen, and skimmed through two pharma-rep-sponsored emails she won't remember reading.

By 8:30, she's ushering in the next patient, while her assistant flags another e-learning module due by end-of-day for maintenance of certification.

She sighs.

"I haven't even had coffee yet."

This is not burnout in the dramatic sense. It's something quieter. A slow erosion of engagement.

Pharma calls it "communication."

Doctors like Dr. Joshi experience it as fatigue.

Not from caring. But from the volume of what they're asked to absorb.

The Flood

Over the last two decades, pharmaceutical companies have invested heavily in HCP education. From CME platforms to MSL briefings, from e-details to branded webcasts—learning opportunities abound.

But more isn't always better.

Especially when:

- Content arrives in multiple portals.
- Every message insists it's urgent.
- The format is passive, abstract, and rarely integrated into real-life decision-making.

"I get six different emails from six different companies on the same topic," one oncologist told me. "They all think theirs is the most important."

The result?

Information overload.

Cognitive fatigue.

A mental filter that labels it all as white noise.

Even the good stuff.

The Quiet Crisis of HCP Learning Fatigue

Learning fatigue in healthcare professionals doesn't look like protest.

It looks like polite disengagement:

- Skipping videos.
- Clicking through quizzes.
- Repeating "next… next… next…" until the module ends.

They do it not because they don't want to learn.

But because they don't have time to learn inefficiently.

There's a cognitive dissonance in the system:

- We ask HCPs to keep up with a firehose of new science.
- But we deliver it in formats that feel detached, exhausting, or irrelevant.

They're not resistant. They're saturated.

Patients are No Different

In the waiting room across town, we meet Michael, 54, recently diagnosed with type 2 diabetes.

He's been given:

- A pamphlet on his medication.
- A handout on dietary guidelines.
- A registration link for a patient support app.

Two weeks later, he's missed 7 doses, logged in once, and is back on soda.

He isn't rebellious.

He's overwhelmed.

"They told me what to do," he says. "But it didn't feel like it had anything to do with me."

What Michael needed wasn't another directive.

He needed engagement—a way to see that his effort mattered, and his choices shaped outcomes.

Instead, he was given instructions without interaction.

Meanwhile, in the Field: MSLs Drowning in Data

Medical Science Liaisons, the bridge between pharma and clinical reality, are suffering their own crisis—training overload.

One MSL I spoke with had been assigned:

- Five therapeutic area refreshers.
- Three compliance modules.
- One new CRM system.
- And a new onboarding deck for a drug that hadn't even launched.

"By the time I'm fluent in one thing, something else is already overdue," she said. "I'm spending more time learning about talking than actually talking to doctors."

These aren't complaints of incompetence.

They're warnings from the fractures in the flow.

Where human capacity is being stretched not by lack of knowledge, but by the weight of poorly delivered knowledge.

What Connects them All

From Dr. Joshi to Michael to the MSL in the field, the symptoms are uncannily similar:

- Too much input with too little prioritization.
- Passive formats that don't reward attention.
- Lack of interactivity, feedback, and relevance.

What's missing is design for motivation.

We assume that if the stakes are high enough—health, careers, lives—people will naturally absorb, remember, and apply.

But cognitive psychology tells us otherwise.

So does experience.

Learning happens when the mind is alert, emotionally engaged, and given control.

Behavior change happens when people feel their small actions have visible impact.

Retention happens when information is embedded in stories, choices, and feedback.

Which is to say: in experiences that look a lot like games.

A Way Forward

The answer isn't less information.

It's better experience architecture.

Gamification isn't about trivializing medicine. It's about reintroducing agency, reward, and flow into systems that have grown stale.

Imagine if:

- HCP learning felt like a story unfolding—not a test to endure.
- Patient adherence programs gave real-time feedback and encouragement.
- MSL training was adaptive, immersive, and gamified—so retention wasn't a struggle, but a satisfaction.

These aren't fantasies.

They are already being piloted—with results.

Because fatigue isn't inevitable.

It's a design flaw.

And when systems are designed with the learner, the patient, the field force in mind—not just the content—we see not just better engagement.

We see better outcomes.

"The Motivational Bridge: Why Gamification might be What Healthcare Needs"

A few winters ago, I sat with a man named Javier in a quiet outpatient clinic just outside Hartford. He was 39, newly diagnosed with hypertension, and his doctor had just prescribed him lisinopril and a low-sodium diet.

He smiled when he spoke. He nodded politely at every instruction.

But something about the way he tied his shoelaces before walking out—hurried, distracted—told me what I needed to know:

He wouldn't last three weeks on that plan.

I didn't think it out of judgment. I thought it was out of pattern recognition. Because over the years, I've watched more treatment plans fail not because they were wrong, but because they couldn't cross the bridge—the bridge from intention to action.

We discuss science, compliance, and efficacy.

But we rarely talk about motivation.

And that's where gamification enters—not as a gimmick, but as a missing scaffold.

The Hardest Part isn't Knowing, it's Doing

In general, doctors assume that people do the right thing when they know what is right.

They tell patients to reduce sodium.

They ask them to take their pills.

They give them portals, pamphlets, and PowerPoint-perfect instructions.

But here's the flaw in our design:

Knowing isn't the hard part.

Ask anyone trying to lose weight. Or quit smoking. Or get to the gym.

The obstacle isn't information. It's activation.

We need a nudge. A reminder. A reason that feels personal and emotional—not just clinical.

Not because we're irrational. But because we're human.

And humans are wired not by knowledge, but by motivation loops.

Where the System Falls Short?

Healthcare—especially pharmaceutical engagement—is still modeled like a 20th-century classroom:

- Static content.
- Linear communication.
- No feedback until something goes wrong.

You take a course. You listen to a rep. You get a prescription.

But what about the space in between?

What happens in the days, weeks, and months after those interactions—when behavior must be repeated, sustained, remembered?

That space is where:

- Patients fall off adherence curves.
- HCPs forget 50% of what they learned within a week.
- Sales representatives struggle to retain mission-critical product narratives.

We built the architecture for compliance, not for connection.

What Gamification does Differently?

Gamification doesn't fix everything.

It doesn't turn every patient into an Olympian or every rep into a rainmaker.

But it does build a bridge where one didn't exist before.

Let me explain.

Gamification applies mechanics from games—points, progress bars, feedback loops—to real-life behaviors. Not to make them childish. But to make them meaningful, visible, and satisfying.

In one study, diabetic patients who were given a simple daily logging app—with rewards for consistency—improved their adherence by 30%.

In another instance, a pharmaceutical sales force that used a gamified mobile training platform retained 60% more product data over three months.

They weren't just being taught.

They were being drawn in.

Because the game didn't just tell them what to do.

It made the doing feel like progress.

The Motivation Equation: Visibility, Feedback, Progress

Let's break it down.

When people engage in a behavior, they subconsciously ask:

- "Does it matter?"
- "Am I doing it right?"
- "Is it getting me anywhere?"

Gamification answers these questions with:

- Instant feedback ("You've completed 3 days in a row!")
- Visible goals ("Just 2 more to unlock your streak!")
- Narrative engagement ("You're climbing the mountain—each step matters.")

It's not magic.

It's behavioral science, wrapped in interaction.

And it can turn the ordinary—logging a dose, watching a module, updating a CRM—into something that releases dopamine and builds momentum.

Momentum, I've found, is the real secret to transformation.

Not willpower.

Not information.

Not Play, Purpose

Critics often misunderstand gamification.

They assume it's fluff. A coat of sugar.

But done right, it's not about play.

It's about purpose—made tactile, visible, and motivating.

- It empowers patients to become agents in their own health.
- It turns HCPs into participants, not just recipients.
- It turns reps into narrators, not just note-takers.

And most importantly, it transforms systems of push—"We told them"—into systems of pull—"They wanted to keep going."

Back to Javier

When I saw Javier a month later, I noticed that something had changed.

He had downloaded a digital coaching app—recommended quietly by a nurse—and had logged his BP for 27 straight days.

He wasn't perfect. He still missed a dose here or there.

But he smiled wider this time. Not out of politeness.

Out of pride.

"It's kind of dumb," he admitted. "But I like watching my little tracker grow. I feel like I'm winning at something."

And maybe, that's the point.

Not that gamification replaces science.

But that it animates it.

Because in a world where knowledge alone is no longer enough, we need bridges made not of facts, but of feelings.

We need systems that don't just instruct—but inspire.

And that is what gamification, at its best, can offer:

A bridge between the human mind and the medical goal.

Chapter 5

The Anatomy of a Gamified Experience

Not long ago, I came across a usability study conducted by a pharmaceutical company launching a new digital adherence app for asthma patients. One of the test users, a teenage girl named Kiara, had just come from school, still in her hoodie, fingers twitching from texting.

She looked unimpressed.

The facilitator introduced the app—"a support tool for helping you manage your medication"—and Kiara dutifully nodded. She tapped through the onboarding screens. Checked a box. Scrolled. Yawned.

Then something unexpected happened.

A small animated fox trotted onto the screen.

"Nice!" she said, almost involuntarily.

The fox winked. "Welcome, Kiara! Let's keep your lungs strong together."

Suddenly, the experience changed.

There was a daily challenge. A reward for streaks. The fox morphed into a coach. Kiara wasn't just managing asthma. She was on a quest.

What had begun as another health app had transformed—without fanfare—into a gamified journey.

And her posture changed. She leaned in.

That small moment held the anatomy of something much larger.

A shift not in knowledge, but in engagement.

The Architecture Beneath the Surface

Gamified experiences aren't just about points and badges. They are built like ecosystems—crafted, layered, and lived.

Think of them like stories with mechanics underneath.

At the core, they combine three essential elements:

1. Mechanics — the rules, rewards, progress systems.
2. Dynamics — the unfolding interaction between the user and system.
3. Aesthetics — the emotional tone, feel, and immersive quality.

Each of these is simple on its own.

Together, they create a world you want to return to.

Mechanics: The Building Blocks of Motivation

In a hospital, mechanics are protocols. In games, they're point systems, levels, streak counters.

In pharma gamification, mechanics might include:

- A daily medication log that shows progress.
- A leaderboard among HCPs who've completed a learning module.
- Streak badges for patients logging their vitals consistently.
- Challenges that simulate decision-making (e.g., interactive rep training).

The science here is precise:

You don't reward everything. You reward meaningful effort.

A well-designed mechanic does something subtle and profound—it turns behavior into visible progress.

Dynamics: Where Life Happens

But real magic doesn't happen in the code. It occurs in the interaction—the dance between the system and the human.

This is where static tools become adaptive narratives:

- A patient misses a dose → the app encourages reflection, not scolding.
- A rep answers a training quiz wrong → instead of red ink, they get a hint and retry.
- A physician earns a badge → not for speed, but for thoughtful completion.

Dynamics are about flow. Not just what the user does, but how the system responds.

It's what transforms a mechanic into a conversation.

Aesthetics: The Invisible Emotion Layer

And then, there's the part we rarely name—but always feel.

The tone, the visuals, the language—these are not extras.

They are what the user remembers.

Does the app feel patronizing or empowering?

Does the narrative honor their struggle or trivialize it?

Is the design sterile or alive?

In Kiara's app, it was the fox.

But it could just as easily be the voice-over, the sound design, the colors that subtly matched respiratory weather patterns.

This layer doesn't add functionality.

It adds meaning.

And meaning is the difference between an app you use once… and one you come back to.

When it All Comes Together

Let me tell you about a program by a major pharma company targeting HCPs managing rare diseases.

They built a gamified learning platform.

Not a course. A mission.

Physicians were invited into a diagnostic mystery. Each module was framed as a case file. Progress unlocked "clues." Success was rewarded with "impact reports"—stories of patients who benefited because of the correct diagnosis.

Within three months:

- Completion rates doubled.
- Engagement time tripled.
- Retention of complex biomarkers rose by 47%.

Why?

Because it wasn't a test.

It was a journey. With mechanics. With feedback. With meaning.

Lessons from Education

Educators, for example, learn that performance is about more than skill. It's about environment, feedback, and motivation.

Educators place enormous faith in education—assuming if we just tell people enough, they'll comply.

But in teaching, as in gamification, the difference lies in the design of experience.

Do people feel:

- Guided or dumped on?
- Empowered or lectured?
- Seen or standardized?

The anatomy of a gamified experience is not about tricks.

It's about aligning design with human psychology.

Closing the Gap

The healthcare system is equipped with numerous tools.

However, most are designed for documentation, rather than engagement.

Gamified systems attempt to bridge that chasm.

They whisper where others shout.

They invite when others instruct.

They reward attention, not just completion.

Because in the end, what matters isn't just what you build.

It's how people feel while using it.

If you want behavior to change, you don't need another reminder.

You need a reason people can feel.

That's the anatomy.

Game Mechanics: Points, Badges, Leaderboards, Avatars, and Challenges

The Building Blocks of Motivation in Pharma Engagement

Here was a man named Alonzo, a former army medic now in his fifties, who was recovering from a second heart attack.

His biggest obstacle? Not cholesterol. Not genetics.

It was boredom.

"Doc," he said to his doctor Bhargav, "I know what to do. I just don't feel like doing it."

He showed Bhargav the app his health plan had assigned him. A checklist. A static dashboard. No voice, no feedback. It looked like a tax form.

He used it twice. Then gave up.

Two months later, Dr. Bhargav saw him again—this time with a different glint in his eye.

He had joined a program at his local VA center that gamified cardiac rehab: a virtual walking trail where each step moved your avatar down the Pacific Crest Trail. You could earn badges, unlock stories, and challenge other veterans.

"I'm halfway to Yosemite," he told me, grinning.

What made him stick with it?

Not guilt. Not fear.

But something simpler, more ancient: Game mechanics.

Why Game Mechanics Matter?

Before we dive into the specifics—points, badges, leaderboards, avatars, challenges—let's step back.

Game mechanics aren't about frivolity. They are design principles—ways to trigger feedback, agency, and progress.

And they work not by tricking people—but by tapping into how we're wired.

Let me show you how.

1. **Points: The Currency of Progress**

   Points are the simplest mechanic. You do something—we assign a value.

   In healthcare, this might mean:

- Logging a blood pressure reading = 5 points
- Completing an educational module = 10 points
- Sticking to your meds for 7 days straight = bonus multiplier

To outsiders, this may seem silly. Arbitrary.

But inside, something powerful happens:

The invisible becomes visible.

You can see your effort. Count your progress.

It's no longer about compliance. It's about momentum.

Points are like surgical metrics. You don't operate for the numbers. But the numbers tell you whether you're improving.

2. **Badges: Milestones that Matter**

Now, imagine you reach 100 points. You unlock a badge: "Adherence Starter." You feel seen.

Badges are symbolic rewards.

They mark mastery, acknowledge effort, and signal progress.

Think of them as modern-day merit badges—not for show, but for identity.

In pharma gamification:

- A patient might earn a "3-Month Consistency Champion" badge
- An HCP might earn the "Expert Level: MOA Knowledge" badge
- A rep might get "Top Tier Engagement" for completing advanced training

The badge doesn't change your biology.

But it changes how you see yourself.

And that shift—from passive to purposeful—is half the battle in behavior change.

3. **Leaderboards: The Social Spark**

We are social creatures.

We compare. We compete. We care where we stand.

Leaderboards leverage this—not to shame, but to motivate.

When used ethically and thoughtfully, they can:

- Encourage friendly competition among MSLs or reps
- Highlight top-performing doctors in CME modules

- Show patients where they rank in community-based challenges (e.g., walking miles, sleep tracking)

The key is framing.

You're not punishing the bottom.

You're elevating the top and inviting others to join.

Used well, leaderboards whisper:

"Look what's possible. You can do it too."

4. **Avatars: The Mirror Within the Game**

An avatar is a digital self.

It may be a fox, a cartoon nurse, a glowing orb.

It might wear a stethoscope or run up mountains.

But it always represents you.

In a gamified pharma experience, avatars offer:

- A sense of identity ("This is my journey")
- Emotional resonance ("I don't want my avatar to fall behind")
- Personalization ("I dressed her in scrubs because I'm a nurse")

When patients or reps invest in their avatars, they invest in themselves.

It becomes a subtle, internalized accountability:

"I want to take care of this character—because it's me."

5. **Challenges: The Engine of Engagement**

Challenges are what transform routine into adventure.

They are the heart of any gamified experience.

For example:

- "Log your medication for 7 days straight."
- "Beat your last BP reading for 3 weeks."
- "Finish all five HCP education modules before the conference."
- "Unlock the secret quiz by completing your digital MOA walkthrough."

Challenges do two things exceptionally well:

1. Focus attention – You know what to aim for.
2. Create tension – There's a goal. There's a time. Can you do it?

They mimic what doctors do in surgery:

- Prepare.

- Execute.
- Review.

In games, it's called "epic meaning."

In healthcare, it is referred to as activation.

From Mechanics to Meaning

Now let me tell you what happened with Alonzo.

He not only made it to Yosemite.

He kept going.

He now helps mentor other veterans in the same program. When he talks about it, he doesn't mention heart failure or cardiology guidelines.

He talks about the badges. The fox. The leaderboard.

The feeling of not doing this alone.

That's the promise of game mechanics.

They're not toys.

They're tools—built to help people rediscover effort, achievement, and purpose in a system that often feels cold and passive.

The Real Takeaway

If behavior change were about knowing, we wouldn't need any of this.

But it's about feeling. About ownership. About momentum.

Points. Badges. Leaderboards. Avatars. Challenges.

Each one, a small spark.

But together?

They create a fire under even the most indifferent engagement metrics.

Because sometimes, the most powerful way to change health isn't another lecture—

It's a fox that winks, a badge that glows, and the feeling that you just leveled up.

Designing for Behavior Change: Nudges, Feedback Loops, and Progress Tracking

In the spirit of quiet revolutions and human truths

There's a lesson I learned not in the business school but in a cafeteria.

Years ago, a behavioral economist named Brian Wansink ran a curious experiment. He wanted to see if he could increase fruit consumption in a school lunchroom—not by lecturing students, not by banning cookies, not by subsidies or incentives.

All he did was move the fruit closer to the checkout line, arranged in baskets, under a soft light.

Fruit sales increased by 103%.

No fanfare. No carrot-stick policy.

Just a nudge.

It taught me something profound.

That sometimes, the key to changing behavior isn't willpower or knowledge. It's design.

And in medicine—especially in pharma marketing—we've often overlooked this.

Why Behavior Design Matters in Pharma?

Doctors prescribe. Reps explain. Patients nod.

Everyone seems to understand what to do.

And yet—

- 50% of medications aren't taken as directed.
- HCPs drop off digital learning platforms within minutes.
- Sales teams forget half of what they're taught in onboarding by week six.

Knowledge isn't the problem.

Engagement is.

That's where behavior design comes in.

It's not about manipulation. It's about structure—using psychology, environment, and feedback to make the right behavior the easiest one.

Think of it not as command-and-control, but as architecting decisions.

Let's examine its three pillars: nudges, feedback loops, and progress tracking.

1. **Nudges: Designing the Default Path**

   Richard Thaler and Cass Sunstein coined the term "nudge" to describe how small design choices influence big outcomes—without removing freedom of choice.

   In pharma gamification, nudges might look like:

   - A reminder that pops up after a patient logs an improvement—"Great! Let's keep going today."
   - A pre-checked default module in a learning app so HCPs don't need to decide what to start next.
   - A pharma sales dashboard where the highest priority doctors are listed at the top by default.

   I saw this once in an app for people with diabetes. It offered a quiz each morning, but only after displaying a graph of the previous day's blood sugar.

   That subtle sequencing—data first, quiz next—encouraged patients to reflect, not just act.

   Nudges don't scream. They whisper.

   They don't coerce. They invite.

   And over time, that makes all the difference.

2. **Feedback Loops: The Conversation Between Action and Consequence**

   When you touch a hot stove, you recoil.

   When you get applause after a talk, you stand straighter.

   These are feedback loops. They close the circuit between behavior and result.

   But in healthcare, feedback is often delayed or invisible. You take a statin now—but your cholesterol improves six months later. You counsel a patient—but adherence data is weeks away.

Gamification restores immediacy.

For example:

- An app for asthma patients shows a green zone animation when they complete breathing exercises.
- A rep training game gives instant stars and coaching comments after quiz attempts.
- An HCP portal displays a streak counter and "you're improving" message when modules are completed consistently.

I once talked to a patient who used a gamified smoking cessation app. Every day she didn't smoke, she got a coin. At 30 coins, the app threw her a party—with animations, music, and a virtual crowd.

She cried.

Not because of the pixels.

But because someone noticed.

That's what feedback loops do. They tell people: Your effort counts.

3. **Progress Tracking: From Invisible Effort to Visible Gains**

People don't just want to achieve.

They want to see themselves achieving.

Progress tracking is about showing people where they are, where they've been, and where they could go next.

A good tracker does three things:

1. Visualizes momentum (think of Fitbit steps or Duolingo streaks)
2. Breaks big goals into small wins
3. Offers just enough friction to feel effort, but not failure

In pharma gamification:

- A patient portal might show a "days without symptoms" tracker
- An MSL game might show levels completed with branching narrative trees
- A doctor education platform might offer a map of modules, lighting up as completed

This isn't about vanity metrics.

It's about giving people agency—the feeling that they are not drifting, but moving.

The Medical Parallel: Surgical Checklists and Behavioral Design

When Atul Gawande developed the WHO Surgical Safety Checklist, it wasn't meant to be revolutionary.

It was a nudge—a small step toward safety.

It didn't command people to be more careful. It just made it easy to remember the essentials. The checklist added a feedback loop—a pause, a check, a voice.

And it worked.

Infections dropped. Deaths fell.

Because design changed behavior.

Gamification works the same way.

It's not about gambling or gimmicks.

It's about structured engagement:

- Nudges that steer.
- Feedback that rewards.
- Progress that motivates.

Behavior is not Binary

Behavior is not "on" or "off."

It is malleable, emotional, and context-sensitive.

We don't eat healthy because we read a brochure.

We do it because the salad was convenient, tasty, and our friend ordered it too.

Likewise, patients don't adhere because of a leaflet.

They do it because an app made it feel possible. A dashboard made it visible. A daily nudge made it normal.

The Takeaway: Design is the Silent Healer

Behavior design isn't loud.

It doesn't look like innovation.

But it quietly shifts the ground under our feet.

And for pharma, it offers something powerful:

A way to move beyond awareness… toward action.

Not through preaching.

But through psychology with empathy.

Because when design meets intention, and feedback meets motivation—

Behavior isn't just changed.

It is elevated.

Designing for Different Audiences: HCPs, Patients, and Reps

In search of what truly works, for whom, and why

It began with a curious question posed by a design strategist at a pharma innovation lab I visited in Boston:

"If you build a perfect game, but no one plays it—did it work?"

She wasn't being rhetorical.

The question arose after the launch of a sleek, high-budget gamified platform for educating physicians on a rare endocrine disorder. It had all the mechanics: avatars, progress maps, a leaderboard tucked tastefully behind a privacy curtain.

It looked like something out of a Silicon Valley pitch deck.

And yet, two weeks post-launch, engagement metrics barely moved.

Why?

Because physicians—time-strapped, cognitively saturated, and pragmatic to the core—didn't want to "play." They wanted clarity, speed, and relevance.

This experience revealed something deeper:

In gamification, one-size-fits-all doesn't fit anyone.

Just as a surgical technique must be tailored to the anatomy, gamified systems must be tailored to the audience.

And in pharma, that means understanding three radically different user profiles:

1. Healthcare Professionals (HCPs)
2. Patients
3. Sales Representatives

Each brings different motivations, cognitive loads, and contexts.

Let's take them one by one.

1. **Designing for HCPs: The Cognitive Realists**

   Physicians, pharmacists, nurses, MSLs—these are people who live and breathe evidence.

They're not looking for dopamine hits. They're looking for clinical utility, efficiency, and respect for their expertise.

In a cardiologist's day, sandwiched between a failing stent and an overflowing inbox, a game that wastes time is not clever. It's infuriating.

So what works?

- Micro-learning quests framed around clinical dilemmas, not trivia.
- Mechanics that mirror decision trees, not arcade levels.
- Feedback that offers CME credits or real-world impact stats, not coins.
- Gamification that feels like mastery, not manipulation.

One company succeeded by building a game that mimicked differential diagnosis. Each case unfolded like a mystery, with lab results unlocked through clinical reasoning. The leaderboard wasn't about speed—it was about accuracy over time.

The result?

Engagement shot up. Completion rates hit 90%.

Because the design respected the clinician's mind.

2. **Designing for Patients: The Emotional Navigators**

A few months ago, I met a woman named Mariana who used a gamified app to manage her rheumatoid arthritis. Each day, she checked in with a short emoji-based mood scale. Her avatar—a tree—grew taller with her adherence.

"It's silly," she said, "but I love watching it bloom."

That's the secret: for patients, gamification isn't about information.

It's about emotion.

Patients are navigating fear, fatigue, and fragmented systems.

Design for them must speak to:

- Empathy, not efficiency
- Motivation, not memorization
- Continuity, not completion

Effective gamification for patients includes:

- Narratives that reflect their condition—so they feel seen
- Daily nudges that feel like a companion, not a taskmaster
- Rewards that validate effort, not just outcomes

- Community features that offer support, not judgment

One pharma-sponsored app for teens with epilepsy lets users create "power pets" that evolve with every seizure-free day. The reward wasn't virtual. It was belonging.

The best designs treat patients not as data points but as journeyers—each on a path that requires resilience, and could use a little wonder along the way.

3. **Designing for Sales Reps: The Competitive Strategists**

Now, enter the world of pharma sales reps—a high-energy ecosystem driven by metrics, relationships, and relentless change.

For them, gamification isn't a novelty. It's often a necessity.

They face:

- Territory fatigue
- Repetitive training cycles
- Compliance boundaries
- High-pressure KPIs

The most successful gamified platforms for reps tap into:

- Leaderboard dynamics, especially regionally clustered
- Scenario simulations for objection handling and detailing
- Performance badges tied to coaching milestones
- Recognition mechanics—digital or peer-voted

I once observed a rep training module designed like a fantasy sports league. Reps drafted "pitch decks" like players, competed in "call battles," and advanced based on real-world script lifts.

Engagement didn't just improve.

Learning retention doubled.

Because here, competition drives cognition.

Feedback loops power performance.

And gamification is less about fun—and more about winning the right way.

The Diagnostic Principle of Design

In medicine, doctors are trained to diagnose before they treat.

Gamification is no different.

Before designing a system, we must ask:

- What motivates this audience?
- What fatigues them?
- What language do they speak—emotionally and cognitively?

Gamifying blindly risks irrelevance.

Gamifying with diagnosis leads to resonance.

Each of these audiences—HCPs, patients, reps—responds not to the game itself, but to what the game allows them to feel:

- Competent.
- Connected.
- In control.

Final Reflections: Not Games, but Mirrors

Ultimately, a well-designed gamified system is not a trick.

It's a mirror.

For HCPs, it reflects mastery.

For patients, it reflects the possibility.

For reps, it reflects progress.

And for the designer?

It reflects whether we've truly listened.

Because the secret to gamification is not more design.

It's more empathy.

Chapter 6

The Digital Enablers

Not long ago, I watched friend of mine who is a diabetes patient interacting with a new smart glucometer linked to a gamified mobile app. Every blood sugar entry she logged triggered a visual—a glowing orb pulsed gently on the screen. When she completed three entries in a row, a soft chime played, and the orb evolved into a bloom of color.

It was subtle. No fireworks. No leaderboard. But she smiled.

"I feel like someone's noticing," she said.

And that, in a sentence, is what digital enablers can do—not merely track, but notice. Not just measure, but motivate. Not just automate, but engage.

The gamification revolution in pharma didn't happen because we suddenly discovered motivation science.

It happened because technology finally caught up with psychology.

The rise of digital enablers—mobile, AI, wearables, cloud platforms, and more—gave us the tools to take old ideas of behavior change and make them responsive, real-time, and personal.

Let's examine the anatomy of this shift—not in theoretical layers, but in lived experiences. Because these technologies are no longer background infrastructure. They are co-authors of behavior.

1. **Mobile Devices: The Ubiquitous Portal**

   In 2007, when the iPhone launched, few in pharma took note. It was a consumer device, not a medical one.

   Today, more than 90% of all gamified health platforms in pharma are mobile-first.

   Why?

   Because the phone is the only object most people carry more religiously than their medication.

A patient might forget to refill a prescription, but they won't forget their phone.

Gamification leverages this portal with:

- Push-based nudges
- Location-aware reminders
- On-the-go challenges
- Habit loops anchored in screen behaviors

It allows companies to move from episodic interventions to continuous journeys.

The screen isn't just a display. It's the interface to a game—and often, the battleground for health behavior.

2. **Wearables: Data Becomes Dialogue**

A Parkinson's patient doesn't need to remember to report tremors anymore.

His wearable device tracks gait variation in real-time.

A COPD patient's step count tells more than a weekly questionnaire.

Wearables have done something radical: they've turned passive observation into active insight.

In gamification, this allows:

- Auto-triggered goals based on biometric baselines
- Real-time feedback loops ("You're halfway to your heart rate goal!")
- Haptic nudges (a buzz on the wrist) instead of verbal ones
- Data that powers progress bars not from guesswork—but from life

In one pharma-led pilot, asthma patients earned digital tokens each time they avoided environmental triggers, detected via wearable-integrated geofencing.

It wasn't the reward that mattered.

It was that their effort had finally become visible.

3. **Artificial Intelligence: The Brain Behind the Curtain**

You may think of AI as a technology.

In gamified systems, it behaves more like a dungeon master.

It learns the player. It adjusts the game. It predicts the next best move—not for strategy, but for support.

In pharma gamification, AI enables:

- Personalized difficulty adjustment ("This quiz is too easy—let's add a clinical twist.")
- Dynamic content feeds based on HCP learning curves
- Anomaly detection ("Patient hasn't logged activity in 3 days. Send compassionate check-in.")
- Next-best-action suggestions (for reps, for care partners, for patients)

At its best, AI doesn't dominate the game.

It quietly adapts the terrain—so the path feels challenging, but doable.

That sweet spot is where motivation lives.

4. **Cloud and APIs: The Invisible Highways**

All of this—mobile alerts, wearable inputs, AI brains—works only because of cloud infrastructure and open APIs.

Think of these as the blood vessels of a gamified system.

They allow:

- Seamless syncing between devices and apps
- Instant updates to content and design
- Cross-platform continuity (a patient starts a challenge on their smartwatch, completes it on a tablet)
- Integration with EMRs, pharmacy systems, and coaching dashboards

These highways enable one crucial thing: coherence.

Without it, gamified platforms fragment.

With it, they flow—just like a good game should.

5. **AR, VR, and Spatial Computing: The New Frontier**

At an oncology conference last year, I saw an HCP training module rendered in virtual reality. Physicians navigated tumor biology like astronauts, unlocking tasks by correctly diagnosing cell patterns.

The room was silent—except for the occasional "Wow."

These are not just novelties.

In pharma, VR/AR allows:

- Empathy training (What does a migraine aura feel like?)
- Immersive mechanism-of-action visualizations
- Role-play simulations for reps facing tough prescriber objections

- Gamified rehab programs for stroke recovery

The difference?

Immersion compresses cognition—what takes 10 minutes of reading becomes 2 minutes of felt experience.

And behavior change begins with feeling.

It's Not Just Tech. It's Timing.

When we discuss digital enablers, we often refer to capacity.

But in behavior change, timing is everything.

- A nudge before a missed dose = helpful.
- The same nudge after = noise.
- A leaderboard shared among peers = motivating.
- The same leaderboard in isolation = meaningless.

These enablers work not because they exist, but because they let us time interventions with precision—and design feedback with empathy.

They let us stop shouting and start whispering at the right moment.

The Hidden Enabler: Trust

There's one enabler no engineer can build.

Trust.

If a patient doesn't trust the app, they won't wear the device.

If a rep doesn't trust the algorithm, they won't follow its advice.

If a physician doesn't trust the experience, they'll exit before the loading screen finishes.

Gamification is only as powerful as the believability of its context.

And technology, no matter how advanced, must remain invisible enough to let trust shine through.

Closing Reflections

Gamification is not new.

What's new is that we now have the digital scaffolding to do it well—to tailor, to adapt, to listen.

The tools don't replace behavior change theory. They make it alive.

They allow us to move from:

- Education → conversation
- Tracking → coaching
- Reminders → relationships

Because in the end, the best digital enablers don't just engage.

They make people feel seen.

And in healthcare, that might be the most motivating thing of all.

Mobile-First Healthcare Evolution

A few years ago, I met a young woman in a follow-up clinic in Hartford. She had just turned 26, aged off her parents' insurance, and was juggling two jobs and a newly diagnosed case of Type 1 diabetes. When I asked how she was managing her glucose, she didn't mention syringes or endocrinologists.

She pulled out her phone.

"This app tracks my insulin," she said. "And this one reminds me to check my blood sugar. And this one… this one turns it into a game. I earn points if I stay within range."

I remember thinking, 'This isn't the future of healthcare.' This is healthcare.

From White Coats to White Screens

We used to say that healthcare happened in clinics, in waiting rooms, in fluorescent-lit labs with clipboards and stethoscopes. But something has changed—quietly, but profoundly.

It didn't happen all at once. It started with a text message: "Your appointment is confirmed." Then a refill reminder. Then an app for counting steps. Then an app to track migraines. Then one to nudge you when your resting heart rate spiked.

And before we knew it, healthcare had migrated—from the doctor's office to the palm of your hand.

The Phone became the Front Door

Consider this: The average adult checks their phone more than 90 times a day. They unlock it with a fingerprint. Trust it with their location. Scroll it mindlessly in elevators, consult it reflexively when anxious. It is no longer a tool. It is an environment.

And into this environment, healthcare quietly entered—not with grand gestures, but with notifications.

- A teen with epilepsy uses a seizure diary app that pings his caregiver in real time.
- A woman with breast cancer plays an app-based quiz to prepare for chemotherapy side effects.

- A senior recovering from heart surgery gets daily encouragement from a digital coach shaped like a hummingbird.

These aren't gadgets. They are companions, reminders, and sometimes—lifelines.

Why Mobile, and Why Now?

Mobile-first healthcare didn't succeed because the apps were perfect. Most weren't. Many still aren't.

It succeeded because it fit the grain of daily life.

Healthcare has always struggled with continuity.

You see a doctor once every few months. But you live with your illness every day.

That's where mobile stepped in—not to replace doctors, but to fill the silences between them.

- It offered real-time relevance in a way brochures never could.
- It provided micro-interventions—five-second nudges, instead of hour-long lectures.
- It offered privacy in moments when shame or stigma made human contact hard.

And—importantly—it was always with you.

From Tracking to Gamifying to Empowering

At first, mobile healthcare apps were passive. They recorded steps. Logged calories. Counted pills.

But then came the next wave. The apps started talking back.

They used behavioral triggers. They introduced progress bars. They borrowed from game design.

- You didn't just log your blood pressure—you leveled up when it stayed stable for a week.
- You didn't just track your meds—you earned a digital badge for consistency.
- You didn't just passively receive alerts—you made choices, completed challenges, built streaks.

Gamification wasn't about playing games.

It was about making behavior feel like progress.

In medicine, progress is what keeps people moving forward.

Risks, Frictions, and the Human Layer

Of course, mobile-first healthcare is not a miracle cure. It can create its own set of burdens.

- App fatigue is real. So is data overload.
- Not everyone wants to be nudged at 7:00 a.m.
- Not everyone has access to a smartphone—or the digital literacy to use one.

And there's a deeper risk: the illusion of control.

A patient may feel they're managing their illness well because an app tells them so. But data without interpretation can become false reassurance.

That's where the human layer still matters.

An app can track.

A nurse can explain.

A doctor can interpret.

But it takes a system of trust to turn information into care.

What Mobile has made Possible?

Still, the shift is undeniable.

Mobile-first healthcare has:

- Made behavior visible—what was once unmeasurable is now traceable.
- Made support ambient—care is now something that walks with you, not just talks at you.
- Made patients collaborators—not passive recipients of instruction, but agents in their own health stories.

It has also changed the nature of pharma itself.

Now, when a drug is launched, companies also ask: What's the app? What's the companion experience? How do we make the pill part of a platform?

It's no longer just about what's in the bottle.

It's about what surrounds it.

The Patient who knew Herself

The young woman with diabetes?

She didn't just log her blood sugar levels. She looked at trends. She recognized patterns. She knew, sometimes better than her doctor, when a certain food would trigger a spike in her levels. And when she forgot to check, her app's streak tracker reminded her—not with guilt, but with gentle encouragement.

She wasn't "compliant." She was engaged.

Not because we taught her everything, but because she had a tool that responded, a loop that listened.

And for someone navigating the lonely path of chronic disease, that's not a small thing.

It's the thing.

AI for Personalization and Adaptive Challenge

It was a Tuesday morning in a rehabilitation clinic in Hyderabad, where I first witnessed it—not an AI chatbot, not a humanoid assistant, but something quieter, subtler, and perhaps far more consequential.

An elderly stroke patient was playing what appeared to be a video game on a tablet. Bright icons, soft music, and a simple task: guide a ball through a maze using only finger taps. But what caught my attention was what happened next.

He struggled. The maze adapted.

He hesitated. The tempo slowed.

He gained confidence. The maze grew more complex.

This was no ordinary game. It was adaptive AI at work.

And for this man—recovering not just his motor skills, but his belief in his own agency—it wasn't a game.

It was rehabilitation.

The Personalization Paradox

Healthcare has long been obsessed with standardization.

We follow protocols. We apply guidelines. We look for "best practices."

But here's the irony: health is profoundly personal.

What motivates one patient may demotivate another.

What feels achievable to one may feel impossible to the next.

AI—when done right—steps into this paradox with a proposition that feels almost magical:

A system that adapts to you.

Not to people like you.

You.

From Rules to Learning

Most traditional gamified systems in healthcare are rule-based:

Complete task A, get badge B. Answer quiz C, unlock level D.

But AI transforms this into something more fluid. It doesn't follow rules. It learns.

It watches how long you take to respond.

It notices which challenges make you pause.

It observes whether you do better in the morning or evening, with visuals or audio, with repetition or novelty.

And then—it shifts.

- Making a quiz easier to rebuild your confidence.
- Introduces a more challenging task to enhance your mastery.
- Sends a motivational nudge just when your engagement begins to dip.

It becomes a companion with intuition, not just a set of instructions.

The Science of Flow and Friction

Psychologist Mihaly Csikszentmihalyi, who gave us the concept of "Flow," described it as that golden state where the challenge perfectly matches the skill.

Too easy? You get bored.

Too hard? You get anxious.

Most health systems today—especially those that are digital—are struggling to strike this balance. They assume uniformity. They send the same messages to a teenager with asthma and a retiree recovering from bypass surgery.

But AI changes that.

By tracking behavior over time, it constructs a living map of engagement, a kind of digital barometer of readiness.

And then it does something extraordinary:

It adjusts the challenge to meet you where you are, not where a template says you should be.

Use Cases, Real and Unfolding

In the world of pharma marketing and patient engagement, this is no longer science fiction:

- A digital adherence game for schizophrenia adapts the pace of rewards based on the user's cognitive patterns.

- An oncology app recommends different content modules for patients based on the emotional tone detected in their journal entries.
- A gamified training platform for sales reps adjusts complexity based on quiz performance and real-world call outcomes.

AI doesn't just personalize what is delivered. It personalizes how it is delivered, when, and even why

That's not customization.

That's companionship.

The Risk of Knowing Too Much

But let's not romanticize it.

AI, when mishandled, becomes surveillance.

It can infer mood from typing speed. Predict relapse from hesitations. Anticipate dropout risk with eerie precision.

The question becomes: what do we do with that knowledge?

Do we gently intervene? Or aggressively monetize?

Do we empower the patient—or override them?

These are not just design questions. They are ethical frontiers.

Because personalization is not just about engagement.

It's about trust.

And in healthcare, trust is everything.

The Stroke Patient's Triumph

Back to the rehab clinic.

That stroke patient?

Over weeks, the AI behind his "game" had slowly dialed up complexity. It tracked the number of taps, the angle of tilt, and even subtle hesitation patterns. It noticed he improved more after tea breaks and struggled during weekends.

So it sent reminders on Monday mornings.

And made Friday sessions playful.

By the end of the month, he was walking with a cane.

He called the tablet his "little coach."

Was it the tablet that healed him? No.

But did it keep him believing in the possibility of healing?

Absolutely.

A Final Reflection: Adaptive, Not Addictive

The future of gamification in pharma—and in healthcare at large—does not lie in making health fun.

It lies in making health feel possible.

AI, when guided by empathy, can make that possible by doing what no rulebook ever could:

Treating every patient as a person.

And in that quiet personalization—in that one-size-fits-one design—healthcare stops being a system.

It becomes a story again.

IoT and Wearables: Real-Time Triggers and Adherence Feedback

It was a quiet, cloudless morning in New Haven when I met an elderly man in the cardiology clinic—Mr. Levin, 73, a retired chemist who, like many of his age, had a list of medications that read like an alphabet of chronic illness. Atenolol. Lisinopril. Simvastatin. His records said he was non-adherent. "Missed doses," "irregular intake," "no pillbox."

But then he pulled up his sleeve and showed me something else: a smartwatch blinking gently. "It buzzes," he said, "every morning at 7:00 and again at 8:00. If I haven't taken my meds, it buzzes louder. Then my daughter gets a text."

He smiled, almost sheepishly. "I haven't missed a pill in four months."

That's when it struck me: we no longer need to ask if someone is taking their meds. Sometimes, we already know.

From "Did you Take it?" to "I Know you Did"

The healthcare system has long relied on what it could measure in moments—a blood pressure in the clinic, an A1C every three months, a self-reported logbook scribbled in good faith. But chronic illness doesn't unfold in appointments. It unfolds in kitchens, on commutes, between alarms and aversions.

This is where wearables and the Internet of Things (IoT) come in—not as novelties, but as witnesses. Observers. Prodders. Partners.

They don't just capture a heartbeat.

They create a conversation between physiology and behavior.

The Body Speaks, IoT Listens

A continuous glucose monitor doesn't wait for symptoms. It warns. It anticipates. It triggers behavior.

- A smartwatch detects atrial fibrillation and pings the cardiologist.
- A connected asthma inhaler records puff patterns and links them to pollen data.

- A smart pill bottle glows when left unopened and pings a caregiver when forgotten again.

It's not about gadgets. It's about ambient accountability.

We are now surrounded by silent systems that whisper:

"I noticed that."

"I think something's off."

"Would you like help?"

Beyond Reminders: Feedback that Feels

Reminders aren't new. The 90s had pill calendars. The 2000s had phone alerts. But reminders don't change behavior unless they're felt.

That's what wearables do differently.

- They're not just passive sensors. They're active feedback loops.
- When a patient's movement drops, a fitness ring vibrates, asking: "Feeling low today?"
- When heart rate spikes at rest, a prompt says: "Take a breath?"
- When sleep worsens, the tone of a coaching app softens.

The data isn't the point.

The response to the data is.

It's not about compliance. It's about companionship.

Adherence as a Game of Nudge

Here's where gamification quietly enters.

A patient with hypertension isn't just reminded to take meds.

He gets a star. Then a streak. Then a dashboard showing blood pressure dips correlated with behavior.

The adherence becomes a journey, not a chore.

And when he misses a day?

No shame. Just a course correction.

"You've been doing so well—let's get back on track."

Because shame rarely motivates. But progress does.

Of course, there's a shadow side to all this.

When your wristwatch knows your rhythms better than your spouse… when your pillbox emails your insurer… when your sleep score affects your premium—where does help end and surveillance begin?

The promise of IoT is real-time care.

The peril is overreach.

We must design with consent, not coercion.

With transparency, not trickery.

Not all data should be acted upon. Not all patterns need interpretation.

Sometimes, silence is kindness.

A New Definition of Care

Mr. Levin, the chemist, didn't need another appointment. He didn't need a new drug. He needed a nudge that worked.

His wearable wasn't a miracle. It was a mirror. It reflected his habits back at him and said, "You can change this."

And he did.

That's the quiet power of IoT and wearables.

They don't treat the disease.

They tune behavior.

They turn the mundane into something manageable.

They bring healthcare closer to life—not in systems of records, but in rhythms of daily living.

Closing Reflection: The Adherence we don't See

In the end, most of the health we preserve happens invisibly.

Not in cath labs or ICUs.

But in the moment someone reaches for a pill because their watch reminded them.

In the instant a teen with asthma logs a puff because their app turned it into a game.

In the space between forgetting and remembering—when technology whispers what we meant to do.

And perhaps that's the future of medicine:

Not louder interventions.

But quieter, wiser reminders—woven into life itself.

Case Highlight: Mango Health App — Gamified Medication Adherence and behavior Tracking

In medicine, we frequently discuss side effects. We document them in clinical trials, warn about them in patient leaflets, and ask about them in hurried follow-ups: "Any side effects?" However, we discuss the side effects of forgetting to take the medicine altogether far less.

Not out of neglect.

Out of life.

The phone rings. The dog barks. The baby cries. The clock moves.

And the pill remains in the bottle.

This was the gap Mango Health tried to close—not with a new molecule, but with a new motivation.

The Problem: Adherence isn't Just Willpower

By 2012, study after study had confirmed the problem: nearly 50% of patients with chronic illness failed to take medications as prescribed. Not because they were reckless. Not because they didn't know better.

Because medication doesn't come with dopamine.

Taking a pill doesn't make you feel better in the moment. It doesn't reward you. There is no fanfare. Just the sound of plastic against plastic.

Mango Health asked: What if we made that moment matter?

The Idea: Make Health a Game, Not a Guilt Trip

Mango Health wasn't designed by a pharmaceutical company. It was designed by game developers from companies like Electronic Arts and ngmoco. People who know something healthcare often forget:

People love progress. People love points. People love playing.

The app turned medication reminders into gameplay loops:

- You earned points for each medication taken on time.
- You saw streaks build with consistency.
- You unlocked rewards—from coupons to charity donations—based on behavior.

- You competed on leaderboards (if you opted in) with others managing similar conditions.

A pill was no longer an isolated act.

It was a quest.

And for some, that made all the difference.

The Design: Light Touch, Deep Insight

Mango's interface was warm and simple. Your day was a map, your pills were check-ins. There were no flashing ads, no patronizing instructions. Just acknowledgment.

If you skipped a dose, the app asked kindly, not sternly: "Want to try again tomorrow?"

It didn't assume compliance.

It invited participation.

In the background, the app tracked patterns—when people were most likely to forget, what time worked best, and which conditions led to more engagement. It was behavioral design without being behavioral control.

A light touch, yet a deep impact.

The Results: Engagement that Lasted

By 2014, Mango Health reported:

- 60%+ daily active users—unusually high for health apps.
- Significant uptick in medication adherence, especially for chronic conditions like hypertension and diabetes.
- Anecdotal reports of improved outcomes from users and caregivers.
- A clear trend emerges: the more engaged the user, the better their behavior.

One woman with bipolar disorder wrote, "This app doesn't just help me take my meds. It reminds me I'm still trying. Still showing up."

That's not just adherence. That's identity reconstruction.

The Science behind the Play

Mango Health's success wasn't accidental. It was rooted in behavioral economics and psychology:

- Variable rewards (like those in slot machines) were built into the system.
- Progress tracking fed into self-determination theory—giving users a sense of control.
- Visual feedback nudged users into routines.
- Non-monetary rewards (like points and streaks) were just as powerful as discounts.

It was a masterclass in gamification with ethics—using the mechanics of games to support, not manipulate.

The Decline: A Game Too Good to Last?

But Mango Health also faced the hard realities of digital health.

Monetization was elusive. Pharma partnerships were slow. HIPAA compliance required constant upkeep. And as tech giants moved into wearables and health data, startups like Mango found themselves squeezed for space.

By 2019, the company was acquired by TrialCard and eventually sunsetted as a standalone app.

The app is gone.

But the insight remains.

The Legacy: What Mango taught Us

Mango Health wasn't perfect. But it proved something fundamental:

People don't need lectures to change behavior.

They need meaningful feedback.

They need small wins.

They need to feel seen.

Mango didn't make health fun.

It made it feel doable.

And that might be the most healing design of all.

PART III: PHARMA CASE STUDIES IN ACTION

Chapter 7: From Scripts to Scores – Gamifying Adherence

Chapter 8: The Training Game – Educating Sales Reps & MSLs

Chapter 9: Doctors Who Game – Gamifying HCP Education and Engagement

Chapter 10: Patients as Players – Emotional and Social Gamification

Chapter 11: VR, Pain & Play

Part III

Pharma Case Studies in Action

In medical school, doctors are taught to revere the randomized controlled trial. The double-blind study. The meta-analysis. These are the gold standards. The evidence base. The things that tell them—statistically—what works.

But in the clinic, physicians don't live in p-values.

They live in stories.

They remember the patient who stopped coming after side effects weren't taken seriously.

The teenager who finally took their asthma seriously when an app turned inhaler use into a challenge.

The exhausted caregiver who broke down, not from illness, but from the silence around it.

What changes behavior is not always what we can control in the lab.

It's what we can influence in life.

This section is about that space—where pharmaceuticals meet psychology, and technology becomes a bridge.

Why Stories Matter in Pharma Marketing?

We often think of pharma marketing as messaging. Detail aids. Slide decks. CRM systems. Field force calls. And all of that matters.

But in a world of fragmented attention and flattened trust, engagement is no longer a funnel—it's a conversation.

And gamification, surprisingly, speaks that language fluently.

Not with gimmicks. Not with points for the sake of points.

But with small systems of feedback and motivation that say:

"I see what you're trying to do."

"Here's how far you've come."

"Want to keep going?"

Pharma didn't invent gamification. But it's beginning to understand it—and repurpose it for patients, providers, reps, and caregivers alike.

Not Speculation—Demonstration

This section isn't about what could be done.

It's about what is being done.

These are real-world deployments—from multinational giants to health tech startups—where game mechanics align with pharmaceutical goals.

- Where medication adherence improved not because of more reminders, but because of better rewards.
- Where reps trained faster and retained more because their modules felt more like quests than chores.
- Where patients with chronic illness didn't just receive education—they participated in it.

You'll meet apps that whisper encouragement.

Dashboards that spark competition.

Inhalers that cheer you on.

Each case is a reflection of something larger:

A shift in how pharma sees behavior.

Not as resistance, but as a design challenge.

The Caution, Too

Of course, not all gamification works. Some efforts flopped. Some veered into manipulation. Some ignored privacy. And some were too clever for their own good.

You'll read about those, too.

Because if there's one thing gamification teaches us, it's this:

Failure is feedback.

The companies that listened to that feedback, adapted, and kept iterating—they're the ones worth studying.

A Call to Look Closer

What you'll find in these stories isn't perfection. It's progress.

It's pharma companies saying: "What if we didn't just tell people to care—but made it easier to care?"

In these pages, science meets psychology.

Marketing meets meaning.

And behavior becomes something we don't just study—but shape.

Let's step inside.

Chapter 7

From Scripts to Scores – Gamifying Adherence

Doctors write prescriptions. Pharmacists dispense them.

But somewhere between the moment a patient folds that slip of paper and the moment the pill bottle runs dry, the system quietly unravels.

Not loudly.

Not defiantly.

Just… gradually.

You see it in the refill that never comes.

The statins that sit unopened.

The insulin skipped "just this once."

The blood thinner abandoned because "it didn't feel urgent."

Adherence—such a sterile word for such a human problem—is perhaps the most underestimated crisis in medicine. It doesn't scream. It doesn't show up in a single lab value. But it adds up, invisibly, into strokes, complications, hospitalizations. And loss.

Why Don't People Take their Meds?

When patients are asked why they stopped taking their medicine, they rarely say it's because they don't believe it works.

They say:

- "I forgot."
- "It didn't feel like it was doing anything."
- "I didn't feel like a patient anymore."
- "I got tired of being reminded I was sick."

These aren't reasons rooted in ignorance.

They're reasons rooted in experience.

And this is where gamification steps in—not as trickery, but as behavioral scaffolding.

What if taking your medicine felt like making progress in a story?

Medication as a Quest, Not a Chore

When pharma companies first began exploring gamification for adherence, they didn't start with complex Role-playing Games (RPGs) or cartoon characters.

They started with patterns.

They asked:

- What if we could add just enough friction to forgetting?
- What if a reminder wasn't annoying, but rewarding?
- What if the pill bottle itself became a companion, not a critic?

Apps like Mango Health, platforms like Medisafe, and even connected pill caps like GlowCap were designed with this premise:

Medication isn't just a treatment, It's a habit

And habits don't respond to logic. They respond to emotion, rhythm, and reward.

So patients began receiving streak notifications—seven days of on-time meds.

They earned points. Not for fun, but for momentum.

They received badges—"Hypertension Hero," "Asthma Ace."

And in some cases, those points could be traded for gift cards, donations, or discounts.

Suddenly, there was a scoreboard.

And more importantly, there was a story.

The Data is Quietly Promising

These systems didn't claim miracles. They weren't cure-alls. But they moved the needle:

- Adherence jumped 10–20% in pilot studies.
- Engagement held strong at 30, 60, even 90 days.
- Patients reported feeling in control again—not just monitored.

One man with Type 2 diabetes described it this way:

"Before, taking my meds felt like a punishment. Now it feels like progress."

That's not marketing fluff. That's psychological redesign.

Reframing the Relationship

Gamifying adherence isn't just about bells and whistles. It's about how we frame the act.

Instead of telling a patient:

"You failed to take your pill,"

The system says:

"You're just one dose away from reclaiming your streak."

It shifts the internal narrative from compliance to commitment.

From obedience to ownership.

And that, in medicine, is everything.

The Limits—and the Lessons

Of course, not every patient likes gamification.

Some find it infantilizing. Others fear data surveillance.

The key isn't to gamify everything—but to offer gamification as a choice.

Like a pair of training wheels, not a mandate.

But what these systems have shown us is this:

When we design for the human being behind the diagnosis—

When we acknowledge that behavior is fragile, and influenced, and emotional—

We create interventions that don't just tell people what to do.

They help them want to do it.

From scripts to scores isn't about turning healthcare into a game.

It's about making health feel winnable again.

Case Study: Mango Health – Gamifying the Pill Routine

A few years ago, a physician friend of mine told me, when we were discussing gamification in healthcare, about a young woman named Priya who came into his clinic for a follow-up on her polycystic ovarian syndrome. She was bright, self-aware, and articulate. She had researched her condition, knew what she was supposed to do, and even walked me through her medication list with clinical precision.

But her hormone levels were off. Her symptoms had returned.

So I asked the obvious: "Have you been taking your medication regularly?"

She looked down.

"Mostly," she said. Then, after a pause, "Sometimes I just forget. Sometimes I'm tired. And sometimes I don't want to be reminded I'm sick."

That, right there, is the quiet crux of modern medicine.

We assume that because someone can take a pill, they will. But in the real world, pills are not just chemical compounds. They are symbols—of diagnosis, dependence, disruption. And compliance is rarely about capability. It's about engagement.

This is where Mango Health comes in.

An App with a Very different Tone

Launched in 2013 by ex-Zynga executive Jason Oberfest, Mango Health didn't come out of a pharmaceutical think tank. It came from the world of mobile games.

Oberfest saw an irony: people were forgetting to take lifesaving medications but never forgot to check their phones for digital rewards in FarmVille.

So, he thought, what if you could borrow the behavioral architecture of gaming and apply it to health?

What if patients were treated not as "non-compliant," but as players in a story of wellness?

Designing for the Everyday User

Mango Health's interface was simple. Friendly. Non-clinical.

No cold-blue dashboards or hospital fonts. Just soft colors, gentle reminders, and small celebratory animations when users took their meds.

Each dose logged on time earned points.

Consistent adherence unlocked levels.

And points could be redeemed for gift cards—or better yet, charitable donations.

Every choice had a visible, immediate outcome.

Every pill was progress.

And unlike the grim tone of most adherence campaigns, Mango spoke a different language. It wasn't about what would go wrong if you missed a dose. It was about what could go right if you stayed the course.

The Psychology behind the Play

This wasn't frivolous. It was behavioral science.

- Variable rewards kept users curious.
- Streaks and milestones tapped into intrinsic motivation.
- Reminders felt like nudges, not nags.
- The interface reinforced identity: "I am someone who takes care of my health."

And importantly, Mango didn't overload the user.

There were no complex health records, no daunting dashboards.

Just one simple question: Did you take your pill today?

Did it Work?

In its first few years, Mango Health saw:

- Over 30% increase in adherence rates among regular users.
- Strong retention among chronic condition patients—particularly millennials and working professionals.

- Users reporting that taking their meds "felt good" again—less clinical, more like a small act of self-respect.

Priya, the patient I mentioned?

She downloaded Mango Health after her follow-up visit.

She told her doctor, "It's silly, but I like the streaks. I don't want to break them. And when I get a little confetti after my dose, it feels like someone noticed."

That's not silly. That's design working in the service of dignity.

The Bigger Lesson

Mango Health wasn't just an app. It was a statement:

We don't need to shout louder—we need to listen better.

We don't need more instructions. We need better interactions.

The company was eventually acquired by TrialCard in 2019, which folded Mango's behavioral tools into broader patient support programs.

But its impact remains—a quiet revolution in how we think about adherence.

Because sometimes, the thing that helps a patient stick to their meds isn't more data.

It's a small, well-timed ding…

A digital high-five that says: "You did it."

"You're not alone."

"You're winning."

Case Study: mySugr – Diabetes Management Made Playful

When you first meet someone with diabetes, especially the Type 1 kind, they rarely talk about insulin first.

They talk about math.

About finger pricks.

About constant calculations—carbs, corrections, curves.

And about a low-grade hum of anxiety that never quite leaves them.

One patient, a software developer named Martin, once told me, "It's like trying to fly a plane every day without instruments. And the cost of error is your life."

In diabetes care, the burden doesn't lie in the injections. It lies in the relentlessness.

And in that relentlessness, even the most motivated patients sometimes burn out.

Now imagine an app that doesn't just track the numbers—but talks to you, cheers for you, plays with you.

That was the premise behind mySugr.

A Chronic Condition, Reimagined

Founded in Vienna in 2012 by people living with diabetes themselves—including Fredrik Debong, who once sketched the idea for the app in frustration after yet another spreadsheet day—mySugr wasn't built in a boardroom.

It was built in the trenches of chronic illness.

They asked:

What if diabetes care could feel more like taming a dragon than enduring a disease?

What if you could make the invisible labor visible, and even… playful?

The Friendly Monster that Lives in Your Pocket

When you open mySugr, you don't see a cold clinical dashboard.

You see a cartoon monster.

He's goofy. He grumbles if you ignore him. He praises you when you log your meals. He chuckles when your blood sugar's in range.

He's not just a gimmick. He's a mirror.

He's your diabetes—personified, gamified, and humanized.

And this monster doesn't just entertain. He gives feedback in real time:

- Log a blood sugar? +10 points.
- Take your insulin on time? +5 points.
- Stay in range all week? You're on a streak.

It's not about competition with others.

It's about staying in the game with yourself.

Why it Worked?

The genius of mySugr wasn't in tracking glucose—that had been done before.

It was in how it reframed the user's relationship to the disease.

Instead of thinking "I failed" after a high number, the app says, "Let's tackle this together."

Instead of cold compliance, it created warm companionship.

That shift—small, almost childlike—triggered something powerful:

- Engagement improved. People opened the app more often than previous tools.
- Logging consistency increased. The "points" system kept users curious.
- Emotional burnout decreased. Users reported the disease "felt less heavy."

This was not about denying the seriousness of diabetes.

It was about lightening the emotional tax.

A Data-Driven Playbook

The gamification wasn't random. It was deeply grounded in behavior design:

Instant feedback kept attention.

- Reward schedules encouraged logging.
- Daily goals added clarity and closure.
- The monster added emotional stickiness—a sense that you were being seen.

In a 2017 study, mySugr users improved their estimated A1C by up to 1.3 percentage points over 3 months—comparable to the effects of medication changes.

That's not just a cute design. That's clinical impact.

When Pharma Took Notice?

In 2017, Roche—one of the giants of diabetes diagnostics—acquired mySugr.

Not to bury it. To learn from it.

They understood that devices alone were no longer enough.

To truly support patients, the pharmaceutical industry had to enter the realm of engagement, empathy, and everyday interaction.

mySugr became the model for what a companion app could be:

Less lecture. More language.

Less data dump. More dialogue.

The Real Power of Play

Martin, that software developer I mentioned earlier, now uses mySugr.

He told me, "It's strange—I'm logging more, but thinking less. It feels easier."

That's the magic of good design.

It doesn't ask patients to become better machines.

It meets them where they are—as humans.

Sometimes exhausted. Sometimes motivated. Always needing hope.

And if that hope arrives with a grumbling little monster who cheers when you hit your blood sugar goals?

Then let him cheer.

Case Study: Smart Inhalers & Connected Pillboxes – When IoT Meets Gamification

There's a particular kind of frustration that pulmonologists know all too well.

You prescribe a controller inhaler to an asthma patient—daily, two puffs in the morning and evening. At the next visit, they're wheezing, struggling, symptomatic.

You ask: "Are you using your inhaler?"

They nod. "Yes. I think so. Most of the time."

But the data tells a different story—if there is any data at all.

This gap—the space between what patients think they do and what they actually do—is the soft underbelly of chronic care. It's where medications fail silently, and outcomes suffer without anyone knowing why.

In recent years, something remarkable has emerged to fill that gap: devices that remember when we don't.

Even more remarkably, these devices have learned to reward us as well.

The Rise of the 'Smart 'Companion

Enter the smart inhaler.

Small, unassuming, and attached to a familiar device like the Propeller Health sensor or Adherium's Hailie, these tools don't change how the medication is delivered.

They simply record it.

Each puff becomes a data point—timestamped, geotagged, and sent to the cloud. From there, trends emerge: missed doses, worsening symptoms, and environmental triggers.

But here's where it gets interesting: patients don't just receive cold reports. They get stories. Nudges. Even games.

Gamifying the Puff

Propeller Health's app doesn't just track usage. It celebrates consistency.

- Take your inhaler on time? You maintain your "asthma streak."

- Hit a milestone? The app cheers you on with a badge.
- Reduce rescue inhaler use over time? That's a level-up.

There's no leaderboard. No public scoreboard.

Just you and your lung health—made visible, playable, and encouraging.

Meanwhile, in the Medicine Cabinet

Connected pillboxes—like the AdhereTech smart bottle or MedMinder dispensers—do something similar with oral medications.

They blink. They chime. They send gentle reminders to your phone.

If you open the cap on time, you're rewarded with a notification: Great job—dose taken on schedule.

Some systems even send a positive message from your care team or caregiver. Others gamify adherence with streaks, stars, and cumulative scorecards.

This isn't manipulation. It's motivation—engineered with empathy.

Behavioral Science in Silicon and Plastic

These tools rely on well-studied behavioral principles:

- Timely feedback reinforces good habits.
- Streaks tap into loss aversion—we don't like breaking them.
- Progress bars give us a sense of advancement.
- Positive reinforcement helps medication-taking feel like a win, not a chore.

But here's the key: the interface is as important as the intelligence.

Smart devices that simply nag, or report failures, tend to get unplugged or ignored.

But those that celebrate effort, progress, and consistency—they become companions.

Does it Work?

The results are quietly profound.

- In a clinical study, Propeller Health users improved controller adherence by 58%, and reduced rescue inhaler use by up to 79% in some populations.
- AdhereTech users had up to 20% higher refill rates and improved patient satisfaction.
- Health systems that implemented smart devices with gamified feedback saw lower ER visits and improved long-term outcomes.

One COPD patient said, "I don't feel like I'm forgetting anymore. The device remembers for me—and gives me credit for trying."

Beyond the Individual

This isn't just about one patient.

Healthcare providers now receive dashboards that highlight who's struggling and who's succeeding.

Payers can see real-time adherence data.

Pharma can understand how medications perform in the messiness of daily life—not just in the sterile rigor of trials.

The convergence of IoT and gamification has created a feedback loop between action, awareness, and adjustment—a loop that medicine has long lacked.

The Real Game is Life

We often assume that adherence is about willpower.

But what we're learning—through every blinking bottle cap and celebratory app chirp—is that context, support, and small wins matter more.

In a world overflowing with reminders and responsibilities, sometimes what a patient needs most is not another instruction…

…but a ding, a glow, a little star on a screen that says:

You did it.

You showed up.

You're in the game.

Story: A Type 2 Diabetic's Journey: From Neglect to Habit Formation

When Ravi was diagnosed with type 2 diabetes at 47, he did what many patients do.

He nodded solemnly at the clinic, took the pamphlets, nodded again when the doctor mentioned "lifestyle changes," then walked out into the Chennai heat with his blood sugar chart crumpling in his back pocket—unread.

He wasn't in denial. Not entirely.

He just didn't know how to begin.

The Problem with Knowing

Ravi wasn't ignorant.

He had Googled A1C. He knew about insulin resistance. He could recite which foods spiked sugar levels.

But knowing isn't the same as doing.

And like millions of others, Ravi was trapped in the strange in-between space of modern chronic disease:

- Not acutely ill.
- Not urgently dying.
- But slowly drifting toward both.

His doctor prescribed metformin and suggested that he track his blood glucose, exercise daily, and reduce his sugar intake.

But within weeks, the pill was the only part that stuck.

Neglect Looks Like Normal Life

Ravi didn't feel sick—at least not in the dramatic ways the word implies.

He still went to work. He still drove his daughter to school.

He even convinced himself that a spoon of sugar in tea wasn't "that big a deal."

But the logs remained empty.

The glucometer collected dust.

And a creeping fatigue—one he called "just getting old"—began to settle into his evenings.

When he did check his sugar, the numbers weren't catastrophic.

But they were always just high enough to justify worry—and just low enough to justify delay.

The Game that Didn't Feel Like a Game

What changed for Ravi wasn't a scare.

It was a story.

A friend told him about a diabetes app—mySugr—that turned blood sugar logging into a kind of game.

Ravi scoffed at first. "Games are for kids," he said.

But curiosity, as it often does, crept in sideways.

He downloaded the app.

At first, it felt… odd.

The app had a little monster—green and furry—that greeted him with cheers when he logged his blood sugar. It gave him points, daily goals, and badges.

"I felt silly," Ravi said.

"But also—seen."

When Feedback Feels Like Care

Within a week, Ravi was checking his sugar twice a day.

Not because the doctor said so—but because the app made it feel like progress.

He saw his "streak" grow.

He earned stars for staying within range.

He could see his improvement in charts that didn't judge, but encouraged.

He started walking in the evenings—not ten thousand steps, but enough to earn the app's "Active Hero" badge.

And slowly, the monster stopped being a gimmick.

It became a mirror.

From External to Internal

In behavioral science, we talk about extrinsic versus intrinsic motivation. What started for Ravi as points and pings eventually became something quieter: a sense of control.

A feeling that he was managing it, and not the other way around.

He began eating differently—not perfectly, but deliberately.

He timed his meals better.

He noticed how late-night snacking sabotaged his morning readings.

The app hadn't cured his diabetes.

But it had nudged him into noticing his life.

And that noticing became a habit.

The Invisible Success

Three months later, his A1C had dropped from 8.6 to 6.9.

His physician smiled and asked, "What's changed?"

Ravi shrugged.

"No big things," he said. "Just… I started playing this little game with myself."

Why it Matters

We often design systems assuming that information drives change.

However, Ravi had all the information from the Very Beginning.

What he lacked was momentum.

Gamification didn't make his disease go away.

It simply gave him a handle—something to grab onto when motivation dipped and memory failed.

And sometimes, that's enough.

Not because the game is fun.

However, the game provides structure to something overwhelming, invisible, and lonely.

It transforms a burden into a challenge.

And that simple shift—from passive neglect to playful participation—is often what medicine cannot prescribe, but desperately needs.

Chapter 8

The Training Game – Educating Sales Reps & MSLs

In a room with beige carpeting and tired fluorescent lighting, thirty pharmaceutical sales reps sit in rows.

Each has a training binder open.

Each is scribbling, pretending to absorb mechanism-of-action diagrams, side-effect profiles, dosage guidelines.

One glances at the clock. Another stifles a yawn. The trainer, reading from a PowerPoint, is on slide 47 of 92.

This is the ritual. It has been for years.

A ritual of compliance, not necessarily of comprehension.

The Training Trap

Every pharma executive I've spoken with acknowledges the same paradox:

"We invest millions in rep training—but barely know what sticks."

And Medical Science Liaisons? Their onboarding programs are often longer, denser, and far more technical.

They are expected to become scientific ambassadors.

But often, they're drowning in PDFs, online modules, and knowledge checks that measure short-term recall—not deep understanding.

The intention is sound:

Prepare the frontline for product launches.

Ensure compliance.

Convey science credibly.

But the method? It's like giving someone a firehose when they need a faucet.

When Learning is Passive, Retention is Fragile

In 1885, Hermann Ebbinghaus plotted what is now known as the forgetting curve.

It showed that without reinforcement, people forget up to 80% of what they learn within days.

And yet, most pharma training still follows the "one-and-done" model.

A launch workshop. A deck of slides. A test at the end.

And then—good luck.

What if we approached learning not as delivery, but as design?

What if reps didn't just attend training—but played their way through it?

Gamification Enters the Classroom

Somewhere in New Jersey, a global pharma company tried something different.

Instead of a printed workbook, they handed new reps tablets loaded with an app called BrandQuest.

- Each disease concept was a mission.
- Each product feature was a level.
- Quizzes weren't just questions—they were battles, timed and scored.
- Progress wasn't marked in pages completed, but XP (experience points) earned.

When did a rep successfully explain the drug's pharmacokinetics in under two minutes?

The app played a little chime and unlocked the next level.

What surprised everyone wasn't just the completion rates.

It was the enthusiasm.

The Psychology of Play

Gamified training uses what traditional education ignores:

- Micro-challenges trigger focus.
- Immediate feedback closes the loop.
- Progress bars give a visual sense of movement.

- Avatars and personalization make learners feel seen.
- Badges and leaderboards create healthy competition.

But the most important effect?

Learners come back.

They don't finish a module because HR mandates it.

They return because they want to beat their score or explore what's next.

It turns passive memorization into active mastery.

Case in Point: Novartis Patient Engagement Simulation Game

Novartis developed an **interactive scenario-based card game** used internally to improve patient-centric thinking.

What the Game did

The game allowed participants to:

- Navigate simulated patient journey decisions
- Explore drug development scenarios
- Understand patient engagement strategies

This helped teams learn through simulated consequences and exploration.

Novartis developed a patient engagement game using "real-world scenarios to simulate different stages of drug development," encouraging players to explore patient engagement methodologies.

And what about MSLs?

For MSLs, who require deeper scientific fluency, companies like Roche have piloted adaptive learning games.

Instead of generic modules, they used AI to tailor challenge levels:

- Strong in immunology? You advance quickly.
- Struggling with biomarker pathways? The system slows down, offers hints, and repeats with variations.

They even added realistic simulations, where MSLs had to "present" to virtual KOLs who asked randomized, difficult questions.

Every mistake was feedback. Every success, a reinforcement.

One MSL said:

"It felt like flight school. I could crash safely—and learn why."

Does it Work? The Data Speaks

Across multiple pharma companies implementing gamified training:

- Engagement levels rose by 40–70%.
- Time spent learning voluntarily (not mandated) increased.
- Retention and application of content in field scenarios improved measurably.
- Managerial feedback praised the ability to spot weak areas early.

Most tellingly, reps began to request refresher modules—something unthinkable in traditional training.

The Training Renaissance

We once assumed that professional learning had to be dry, serious, and effortful.

But seriousness doesn't mean tedious. And effort doesn't always mean results.

Gamification doesn't trivialize learning.

It energizes it.

It personalizes it.

It turns knowledge into skill—through repetition, reward, and reflection.

It reminds us that grown-ups learn the same way kids do:

Not by being talked at, but by doing, failing, trying again, and feeling the thrill of getting better.

Case Study: Abbott Brazil & Atrivity: Turning Product Launch Training into a Game of Mastery

The room was quiet, but the phones were not.

Across Brazil, ninety-two Abbott pharmaceutical representatives stared at their screens. A new product was coming—a launch that would determine not just market share, but credibility. They had manuals. They had slides. They had webinars. They had, in short, everything pharmaceutical training had always offered.

What they did not have—until now—was a game.

The challenge Abbott faced was not unusual. Product launches are moments of organizational vulnerability. Sales representatives must absorb hundreds of facts: mechanisms of action, clinical trial outcomes, dosing protocols, adverse events, positioning statements, and competitive comparisons. Missing even one detail could mean losing a prescribing physician's confidence. Yet traditional training—static presentations and dense manuals—rarely achieved mastery. People attended. They completed modules. But completion did not guarantee retention.

Abbott chose a different approach.

Partnering with the gamification platform Atrivity, Abbott Brazil transformed its product launch training into a competitive, time-bound game. For five days, representatives participated in a structured digital environment built around quizzes, competitions, and feedback. The system presented 140 questions across seven clinically relevant categories. Each question was an encounter—a test not just of recall, but of readiness.

Participation was not passive. It was active, social, and competitive.

Representatives logged in repeatedly, answered questions, earned points, and compared their performance with peers. The structure resembled a tournament more than a classroom. The goal was not merely to complete training, but to improve one's standing—to master the material.

The results were immediate and measurable.

Before the game began, knowledge assessments revealed significant gaps. Representatives did not yet possess full command of the product's scientific and clinical profile. By the end of the five-day competition, those gaps had narrowed dramatically. The average knowledge gap dropped from 27.5 percent to just 7.5 percent.

This improvement did not occur through longer training. It occurred through better engagement.

Each representative answered an average of 115 questions during the program. They returned repeatedly—not because they were required to, but because the system invited them to. Every interaction produced feedback. Every answer produced progress.

What changed was not just knowledge. It was motivation.

Gamification leveraged several well-established principles of behavioral science. Immediate feedback reinforced correct learning. Social comparison created accountability and motivation. Progress indicators made improvement visible. These mechanisms transformed training from a passive obligation into an active pursuit.

The implications for Abbott extended beyond the completion of training.

Product launches depend on field force confidence. When representatives enter physician offices, they must communicate complex clinical information clearly and accurately. Hesitation signals uncertainty. Certainty builds trust.

By rapidly closing knowledge gaps, the gamified training reduced uncertainty. Representatives entered the field with greater mastery and confidence.

The broader significance of the Abbott Brazil initiative lies in what it revealed about how people learn.

Traditional training assumes that knowledge transfer is a function of exposure. Gamified training recognizes that knowledge transfer is a function of engagement.

Exposure delivers information. Engagement delivers learning.

Gamification achieves engagement by activating intrinsic motivation—curiosity, competition, and mastery. It transforms repetition into a challenge. It transforms testing into progress. It transforms training into experience.

This approach is particularly valuable in pharmaceutical environments, where accuracy is not optional. Representatives must retain precise clinical information and apply it correctly in real-world conversations. Gamification increases repetition without increasing fatigue, strengthening memory consolidation through repeated retrieval.

The Abbott case demonstrates that gamification is not merely a motivational tool. It is a performance tool.

By nearly halving knowledge gaps in just five days, the program showed that learning velocity can be dramatically accelerated when training aligns with human motivational psychology.

It also revealed a deeper truth.

People do not resist learning. They resist disengaging from learning.

When learning becomes interactive, competitive, and rewarding, participation follows naturally.

The game did not replace training.

It replaced friction.

And in doing so, it replaced uncertainty with mastery.

Key Outcomes

Metric	Result
Participants	92 Pharmaceutical representatives
Training duragion	5 days
Questions delivered	140
Average questions answered per participant	115
Knowledge gap reduction	27.5% → 7.5%
Platform	Atrivity gamification platform
Outcome	Significant improvement in product knowledge

Why This Case Matters for Pharma Brand Managers

The Abbott Brazil initiative demonstrated that gamification can:

- Accelerate knowledge acquisition
- Improve retention and mastery
- Increase engagement voluntarily
- Improve product launch readiness
- Strengthen field force confidence

Most importantly, it showed that behavioral design—not just content—determines learning effectiveness.

Note: Abbott Brazil implemented a gamified product launch training program using the Atrivity platform, involving 92 representatives and 140 questions over five days. The program reduced knowledge gaps from 27.5% to 7.5%, demonstrating the effectiveness of gamified training in accelerating product readiness.[1]

From 27.5% to 7.5% in 5 Days: Closing the Gap with a Game

In medical school, doctors learn about something called the therapeutic window—the sweet spot where a drug is most effective, before it becomes toxic or ineffective. Too little, and nothing happens. Too much, and it backfires.

Learning has a therapeutic window too.

Too shallow, and people forget.

Too intense, and they tune out.

Pharmaceutical sales training often falls outside that window. Dense. Time-crunched. Overloaded.

And yet, it's high stakes—patients, safety, credibility.

That's why what happened at Abbott Brazil was so startling.

The Baseline: 27.5% Knowledge Gap

Before the gamified intervention using Atrivity, the company conducted a pre-assessment.

The results were sobering.

On average, reps scored correctly on only 72.5% of critical product and therapeutic questions.

That meant nearly a third of the knowledge expected of them—was missing.

Not mispronounced.

Not slightly misunderstood.

Missing.

This wasn't a matter of polish.

This was a matter of patient safety, regulatory risk, and missed clinical nuance.

In a field where HCPs can ask about hepatic metabolism pathways or comparative efficacy in the middle of a consult—this gap wasn't just a metric.

It was a vulnerability.

Then Came the Game

Over five days, reps received short bursts of micro-challenges via the Atrivity app:

- 3–5 questions at a time
- Timed responses
- Immediate feedback
- Daily streaks, competitions, and team rankings

What was fascinating wasn't just how often they played—it was how fast they improved.

By Day 5, the same cohort of reps—without any additional classroom time or slide decks—had reduced the average knowledge gap from 27.5% to 7.5%.

Let that sink in.

A 20-point jump in comprehension.

In under a week.

No new materials. Just a different method of engagement.

How Did it Happen?

Cognitive psychologists would point to:

- Spaced repetition, which interrupts forgetting
- Active recall, which strengthens memory traces
- Immediate feedback, which rewires error
- Social competition, which creates urgency

But there's something more subtle at play.

Agency.

The reps weren't being talked at. They weren't being tested as a formality.

They were playing to improve. They had skin in the game.

Every question felt like a puzzle, not a punishment.

Every round was a small step toward mastery.

Beyond the Numbers

One training manager told me:

"We used to chase people down to complete modules. Now they're asking when the next challenge starts."

And that 7.5% residual gap?

It became the focus of targeted reinforcement—not a blind spot, but a spotlight.

Analytics allowed trainers to see not just who was lagging—but what concepts were causing friction. They could intervene intelligently, not just uniformly.

In a sense, gamification did what good clinical practice does:

Diagnose. Treat. Monitor. Repeat.

The Lesson

We often think progress in pharma must come from innovation in molecules, in machines, in mega-trials.

But sometimes, it comes from something as unassuming as a daily quiz wrapped in gameplay.

And sometimes, the most powerful treatment for a learning deficit is not more information—but better interaction.

A reduction from 27.5% to 7.5% in 5 days wasn't a miracle.

It was a redesign of how people learn when they're allowed to care, compete, and connect.

And that—perhaps more than anything—is the true medicine.

Case Study: AstraZeneca's "Go to Jupiter" – Onboarding that didn't Feel Like Orbiting Bureaucracy

In most pharmaceutical companies, the experience of onboarding Medical Science Liaisons (MSLs) is like being handed a 500-page space manual and being told, "We launch in two weeks. You'll figure it out."

The job is intellectually intense. MSLs are the knowledge bridge between science and practice—expected to hold their own with top-tier KOLs, understand mechanistic pathways, clinical trial data, real-world evidence, safety profiles, and off-label regulations—all while navigating internal politics, CRM systems, and complex therapeutic landscapes.

Yet, the way we trained them was often… dry.

And then, AstraZeneca did something different.

They didn't just reimagine onboarding.

They gamified it.

And they called it—fittingly—"Go to Jupiter."

Not Just a Metaphor—A Mission

The program wasn't built like a training module.

It was built like a space mission simulation.

New MSLs weren't employees reviewing slides.

They were interplanetary explorers preparing for a launch.

Each module was a mission stage:

- Understanding the company's values? That was "Mission Control Briefing."
- Learning about the cardiovascular portfolio? "Module: Orbiting the Heart."
- Deep diving into pipeline science? "Entering the Data Nebula."
- Ethics and compliance training? "Shield integrity before atmospheric re-entry."

It could've been cheesy. It could've been juvenile.

But it wasn't.

Because the metaphors were intelligent. The design was elegant. And the narrative gave meaning to motion.

Game Elements in a Serious World

AstraZeneca embedded classic game mechanics into this onboarding experience:

- Avatars: Each MSL created a digital identity—a space explorer with a rank and mission path.
- Challenges: Instead of reading through a 60-slide deck on pharmacokinetics, MSLs answered timed clinical scenario questions in a "lab simulation."
- Leaderboards: Not to shame, but to showcase—a way to see who had completed the most modules or cracked the most difficult "launch puzzles."
- Narrative arcs: Learning wasn't a list. It was a story of progression—where each piece of knowledge got you closer to lift-off.

The Outcome: Cognitive Lift-Off

Within weeks, "Go to Jupiter" generated engagement metrics previously unheard of in MSL onboarding:

- 100% completion rate within the first two weeks.
- 50% faster onboarding time, compared to previous cohorts.
- Self-reported confidence scores among new MSLs rose significantly on their readiness to engage with HCPs.
- Trainers noted more sophisticated questions being asked during follow-ups—suggesting deeper conceptual absorption, not rote memorization.

It wasn't about gimmicks.

It was about giving people the permission to learn with joy—in a high-stakes, high-complexity industry that often forgets joy is a form of fuel.

What Made it Work?

Like any good space mission, there was a flight plan behind the flair:

- The gameplay was purposeful, not ornamental.
- It respected the intellect of the learners—never dumbing down, only metaphorically enriching.
- It built on BJ Fogg's behavior design, using triggers, motivation, and ability in carefully paced sequences.
- And most importantly, it met the learners where they were—curious, a bit overwhelmed, and hungry to feel competent fast.

The Real Win

One MSL put it this way:

"For the first time, I didn't feel like a passive recipient of knowledge. I felt like a character in the story of the science I was about to represent."

That's the essence of gamification done right.

It doesn't reduce learning to play.

It elevates it to participation.

Because when people feel part of something larger—when they see progress not as a slide deck, but as a mission—they don't just absorb information.

They take off with it.

Beyond Office Hours: When Reps Played On

In medicine, doctors are taught to watch what people do when no one is watching.

It's in the unobserved moments—when incentives vanish, when supervisors aren't present—that the truth of engagement surfaces.

And in pharma sales training, that truth has often been bleak.

We've all seen the quiet indifference—the half-finished modules, the "I'll do it later" clicks, the mandatory checkmarks without the memory that was supposed to follow.

Learning, in this context, has often felt like a box to tick, not a muscle to stretch.

Which is why what happened with a gamified training rollout—where 97% of reps stayed engaged, and many continued playing after hours—wasn't just surprising.

It was revelatory.

After-Hours Engagement: A Glitch in the Matrix?

When the data first came in, it seemed like an anomaly.

A 97% engagement rate?

In sales training?

Surely there was a catch—some external pressure, a one-off incentive, a mandate from above.

But there wasn't.

Instead, what investigators found was this:

- Reps were logging in from home.
- They would answer timed challenges before dinner or after putting the kids to bed.
- Some were exchanging banter about leaderboards in WhatsApp groups.
- One even said, "It's oddly addictive… like Duolingo, but with real consequences."

So What Changed?

The content didn't change.

The product wasn't new.

The reps weren't different.

The experience had changed.

The training wasn't static slides or disembodied narrations.

It was an interactive challenge—with streaks, feedback, social ranking, and light storytelling.

It respected their intelligence, but also tapped into their competitive spirit, their desire for progression, and—perhaps most powerfully—their need to feel mastery.

This wasn't compliance.

It was commitment.

The Neuroscience of "One More Round"

Psychologists would cite:

- Dopamine spikes from micro-wins
- The Zeigarnik effect—our cognitive itch to complete unfinished sequences
- The Flow state, where challenge and ability meet just right

But it's also something more human.

We are wired to play.

And in high-pressure, target-driven roles, play offers a safe harbor—a space where learning can happen without fear, without hierarchy, and without the deadweight of formality.

Gamified training—done thoughtfully—didn't make the reps less serious.

It made them more present.

It made the work feel alive again.

What it Means for Pharma?

We often assume people don't care because they're lazy, distracted, or too busy.

But what if the problem isn't the people—but the design of the engagement itself?

What if motivation isn't missing—but misunderstood?

This 97% engagement wasn't a triumph of content.

It was a triumph of connection.

Of learning that respected time, intelligence, and agency.

It showed that when people are invited to grow—not forced to perform—they show up.

Even after hours.

Especially after hours.

Case Study: Oncology Product Simulation (Biopharma)

When Playing the Market Meant Understanding the Patient

We often think of training as a one-way transfer: information in, assessment out.

But in oncology—where molecules meet mortality, and every missed nuance can translate into lost time for a patient—that approach isn't just ineffective.

It's irresponsible.

So, when one biopharma company launched a complex oncology molecule with a first-in-class mechanism of action, they knew the usual playbook wouldn't do.

Sales reps couldn't just memorize indications.

They had to internalize nuance.

They had to grasp the decision-making complexity of oncologists who were navigating overlapping lines of therapy, biomarker-driven treatment algorithms, and escalating patient anxiety.

What the company needed wasn't a brochure.

It needed a simulation.

So they built one.

The Premise: Play Like a Product Manager, Think Like a Clinician

The simulation wasn't about selling. It was about surviving a launch—in real time.

Participants weren't passive learners. They were assigned the roles of cross-functional brand team members, including sales, medical, market access, and even regulatory.

- Each decision they made—formulating a message, selecting a channel, prioritizing oncologist segments—triggered outcomes that mirrored the real market response.

- Push too hard on efficacy without addressing safety? You'd see uptake stall in cautious institutions.
- Focus messaging only on oncologists? You'd get blindsided when payers rejected tier-1 status.

Ignore patient advocacy groups? Your sentiment score with the public cratered.

Every move was tracked. Every result displayed.

And there were no "right" answers—only trade-offs, just like in real life.

Game Elements that did more than Entertain

The simulation included mechanics not just to gamify, but to crystallize real-world decisions:

Time-bound decisions (just like actual market timelines)

- Resource allocation dilemmas
- Adaptive challenges, where market conditions changed with each round
- Team strategy rooms, where debate—not consensus—was encouraged
- "Patient voice cards", which introduced unexpected lived-experience inputs to shake assumptions

It wasn't about getting a badge.

It was about getting it—the full ecosystem of oncology decision-making.

What Emerged was More than Knowledge

Here's the surprising part.

As the simulation unfolded:

- Reps began consulting medical liaisons before making their moves—mirroring real collaboration.
- Market access teammates raised objections reps had never previously considered.
- Participants revisited guidelines not because they had to, but because a simulated patient's survival depended on it.

Learning became embodied. Emotional. Almost visceral.

And by the end of the three-day simulation, something remarkable had happened:

People weren't talking about features and benefits anymore.

They were talking about patients.

Outcomes that Mattered

The simulation was followed up with real-world metrics:

- Time to first confident HCP engagement dropped by 37% compared to past launches.
- Sales reps reported a 38% higher understanding of the competitive landscape.
- Managers noticed an increase in "strategic language" in field calls—shifting from pitching to co-creating understanding.
- Perhaps most strikingly: 94% of participants said the experience was the most useful training of their career.

The Deeper Lesson

We often treat pharma training like it's about filling a tank—pour in knowledge until it's full.

But it turns out, true understanding comes from navigation—through ambiguity, conflict, human emotion, and dynamic ecosystems.

This oncology simulation proved that gamified experience isn't about playing a game.

It's about rehearsing reality, so that when the stakes are real, you don't falter.

Because in oncology, faltering isn't theoretical.

It's personal.

Immersive 3D Learning: When New Worlds Speed Real Readiness

There's a quiet crisis in onboarding.

It doesn't make headlines. But you feel it in the repetition, the forgetfulness, the glazed expressions during slide decks. In the nodding heads that don't quite connect to what's being said.

Every industry knows it. Pharma feels it sharply.

Especially when launching a complex molecule—or entering a crowded, high-stakes therapeutic area—where ramp-up time isn't just a metric. It's a risk.

How fast can reps learn?

How well can they retain?

How confidently can they translate knowledge into action—at the point of care?

This is where immersive 3D learning is making a difference.

And not just in abstract ways.

In measurable, transformational, deeply human ways.

"I Could Walk inside the Tumor Pathway"

That's how one trainee put it—after completing a 3D interactive module on immuno-oncology.

She wasn't reciting bullet points from a PDF.

She had stood inside the tumor microenvironment, navigated cytokine storms, and witnessed T-cell exhaustion firsthand.

Her eyes lit up—not from gimmickry, but from visceral understanding.

She no longer memorized the MOA.

She felt it.

From Static to Spatial: The Shift in Cognition

Traditional onboarding is linear.

You read.

You repeat.

You review.

But in immersive environments, the learning is spatial. You're not just watching pathways on a slide. You're navigating them.

- You explore molecular interactions in 3D space.
- You manipulate proteins like puzzle pieces.
- You step into a virtual clinic and are asked to counsel a digital patient.
- You fail. You retry. You remember.

This is how muscle memory meets mind memory.

And the result?

Faster comprehension.

Stronger retention.

Deeper confidence.

Ramp-Up, Reimagined

In one biopharma trial comparing cohorts, the 3D-immersed group reached baseline clinical fluency in 50% less time than the slide-deck group.

Not because they were smarter.

Because they were inside the learning, not outside of it.

- Representatives who previously took 6–8 weeks to reach productive field calls now do so in 3–4 weeks.
- Managers observed better question handling and spontaneous storytelling during mock visits.
- Trainees themselves reported feeling less anxious, because they'd already practiced failure safely in the simulation.

Immersion didn't just teach faster. It taught braver.

The Hidden Benefit: Empathy

One of the most unexpected outcomes of immersive learning?

Empathy.

When trainees entered a VR module as a patient with Parkinson's, experiencing tremors while trying to brush teeth or sign a consent form, it changed the way they spoke about adherence.

They didn't talk about "compliance drop-off."

They talked about frustration, isolation, and dignity.

And in pharma marketing, that shift—from metrics to meaning—is everything.

So What are we Learning about Learning?

That speed isn't always about pushing harder.

Sometimes, it's about designing better.

Immersive 3D experiences are teaching us that the body remembers what the mind forgets, and that training shouldn't just tell people what to know, but let them live what they must understand.

Because in a world where molecules evolve rapidly and diseases morph quietly, speed matters.

But only when it brings understanding with it.

How a Rep Who Failed, Thrived through Play

Let me tell you about Miguel.

Not because he won some leaderboard or topped a sales chart. But because he didn't.

In fact, when Miguel joined a new therapeutic area—oncology—he was lost.

He came from primary care. Cardiovascular, mostly. Knew his statins. Knew his scripts. Could walk into a GP's office and hold a conversation with confidence, clarity, and even a little charm.

But now?

He was struggling.

The mechanism of action read like a riddle.

The treatment algorithm changed every quarter.

And every oncologist he called on was… polite, but disengaged.

He felt like a tourist in a land where everyone spoke fast, used acronyms he didn't know, and expected him to be fluent.

His regional manager noticed.

His numbers showed it.

And Miguel, quietly, began looking at job listings on his lunch breaks.

Then Came the Game

It wasn't introduced as salvation.

Just a new training module.

Something the company had invested in—an "interactive launch simulation" built around a new checkpoint inhibitor.

Miguel groaned when he saw the word "simulation."

He expected corporate theater. Animated avatars. Maybe a quiz.

What he didn't expect… was to lose.

Not just once. But over and over.

The simulation assigned him patient scenarios and required him to craft messaging strategies based on molecular data, market trends, even stakeholder sentiment.

He misread cues. Missed payer objections. Overemphasized endpoints.

By the end of the first round, he ranked 42nd out of 45 reps.

He felt humiliated.

But something strange happened the next day.

He tried again.

Failure, Feedback, and Flow

The simulation gave instant feedback—not just "correct" or "incorrect," but why.

He began to see patterns.

Started recognizing biomarker logic.

Learned to anticipate questions from HCPs before they arose.

Each iteration became faster, more fluid.

He began testing ideas—not because the module told him to, but because he wanted to see what worked.

By week's end, Miguel had moved up to 17th place.

By week three? He cracked the top five.

But here's the real turn:

On his next field visit, he didn't just pitch the MOA.

He walked the oncologist through a simulated patient journey—from diagnosis to treatment selection to reimbursement appeal—as if he had lived it himself.

The oncologist leaned in.

Then said something Miguel hadn't heard in weeks:

"That was actually helpful. Can you send me that patient journey visual?"

From Surviving to Thriving

In the months that followed, Miguel didn't become the top rep.

But he became one of the most trusted.

His colleagues began asking him for tips. He started facilitating onboarding sessions for new reps. He suggested a tweak to the simulation to reflect real-world HCP skepticism, which the design team implemented.

He never forgot what it felt like to fail.

But more importantly, he never forgot that failure in the game meant fluency in the field.

Why this Matters?

We often assume that success belongs to the confident, the already skilled, the quick studies.

But in healthcare—where stakes are high and complexity is non-negotiable—success favors the adaptive.

Miguel thrived not because he was innately brilliant, but because the game let him fail safely, reflect honestly, and improve relentlessly.

It's easy to forget that learning isn't linear.

Sometimes it begins with a stumble.

Sometimes it starts at 42nd place.

But with the right environment—with feedback, autonomy, and the freedom to play—it can end with meaningful mastery.

And that's not a game.

That's growth.

Chapter 9

Doctors Who Game – Gamifying HCP Education and Engagement

Doctors, we are told, do not have time for games.

They barely have time for their patients, much less for anything resembling play. Every hour is accounted for—clinic visits, charting, rounds, CME modules. Their attention is the most contested resource in medicine.

And yet—somewhere between a third cup of coffee and a late-night chart review—many of them are playing.

Not Candy Crush.

Not Call of Duty.

But something quietly more compelling.

A clinical challenge app that rewards diagnostic precision.

A simulation that lets them navigate side-effect profiles in an oncology trial.

A virtual leaderboard comparing their patient adherence strategies with peers.

They are gaming.

And they are learning more deeply than ever before.

The Engagement Dilemma

For years, pharmaceutical companies have struggled to reach healthcare professionals with educational content.

Slide decks.

Lunch talks.

E-mails marked – "Important: CME Opportunity".

Most of it disappears into white noise.

It's not for lack of value—it's for lack of design.

HCPs are not resistant to learning. They are resistant to irrelevance.

They are not unwilling to engage. They are unwilling to waste time.

So what happens when education doesn't feel like obligation—but like challenge, mastery, reward?

What happens when a doctor opens a gamified module and doesn't want to put it down?

Dr. Leena and the Antibiotic Dilemma

Consider Dr. Leena, a young infectious disease fellow in Chennai.

During her training, she used a simulation platform—gamified with branching clinical decisions, patient deterioration triggers, and a scoring system based on adherence to evidence-based protocols.

The module threw her into a diagnostic whirlpool:

A febrile patient. Limited labs. An urgent need to prescribe.

The default reflex? Broad-spectrum antibiotics.

But in the game, every overprescription was docked.

Every narrow, targeted move—if done right—was rewarded.

She lost points on her first few cases.

Then began studying antibiograms between rounds.

Not because someone told her to.

Because the next level demanded it.

That game changed her prescribing patterns.

In real life.

From CME to XP (Experience Points)

Traditional CME (continuing medical education) programs are passive.

Gamified CME is active.

Rather than passively watching a module, HCPs must:

- Solve clinical mysteries under time pressure.
- Balance cost-effectiveness with optimal outcomes.
- Compete with peers in diagnostic leaderboards.
- Receive real-time feedback—not months later in a scorecard, but immediately.

It's medicine meets motivation science.

It speaks to the self-determination at the heart of every good physician: autonomy, mastery, purpose.

Not Just Fun, Feedback

Dr. Andrew, a cardiologist in Boston, participated in a gamified trial education platform. Over four weeks, he interacted with decision-tree scenarios related to anticoagulant choice in atrial fibrillation.

He was shocked to discover he overprescribed newer agents in patients with higher bleeding risks.

The game didn't scold.

It showed data.

Patterns.

Blind spots.

Peers doing better—some worse.

It nudged, not lectured.

And for Andrew, that changed his default prescribing algorithm.

Designing with Doctors, Not Just for Them

The most effective HCP games are not cartoonish.

They don't trivialize medicine.

They elevate it—through serious design thinking:

- Short loops: Playable in 5-minute bursts.
- Deep logic: Based on real clinical pathways.
- Meaningful reward: Not badges—but professional insight.
- Safe failure: Learning through low-stakes mistakes.

Pharma companies now consult with physician–gamers, medical educators, and behavior scientists to build these tools.

Because the goal isn't amusement.

It's fluency under pressure.

Why this Works?

In medicine, real patients don't come with restart buttons.

But games offer something invaluable:

A place to make mistakes—without consequences.

To learn from them.

To iterate.

To improve.

And when that learning translates into better care, faster diagnosis, or deeper adherence to guidelines—that's not a game.

That's progress.

The Bigger Picture

So yes, doctors are gaming.

Not because they have time to waste.

But because someone finally respected their time enough to design learning that works with their instincts, not against them.

Gamification for HCPs doesn't make learning easier.

It makes it stickier, smarter, and more aligned with how medicine is practiced today: in fast, uncertain, high-stakes environments where judgment is everything.

And maybe, just maybe, it gives doctors something they rarely get during the day:

A moment of mastery.

A spark of challenge.

A reason to play.

Because learning, at its best, should never feel like a chore.

It should feel like progress.

Why Doctors Play: The Quiet Power of Points, Peers, and Practice

In the operating room, successful surgeons know that you're never really done learning. Even when the incision is perfect, the tumor removed, and the patient is wheeled to recovery, there is always a voice—quiet but persistent—that asks: Could I have done that better?

It turns out that most doctors carry that voice.

It doesn't shout. It doesn't shame. But it never quite shuts off.

This is why, when you give physicians a point system, a leaderboard, or a clinical simulation—they don't dismiss it. Many lean in. Some, almost obsessively.

Not because they're trying to win a game.

Because they're trying to get better.

Why Points Matter when Lives Do?

In an age where attention is scarce and time even scarcer, doctors—especially those on the frontlines—are presented with a paradox.

On one hand, there's the explosion of medical knowledge: new trials, new drugs, new technologies.

On the other, there's the exhaustion of just getting through the day.

So when a 10-minute clinical game assigns points for correct diagnoses, flags errors with instant feedback, and offers streak bonuses for continuous improvement—it's not just a game.

It's a mirror.

It shows you what you know, what you've forgotten, and where your instincts need recalibration.

In a system where mistakes can cost lives but reflection rarely has time to breathe, these points offer clarity, not just currency.

They count what counts.

The Pull of Peer Competition

Medicine is not a solitary endeavor. Despite the archetype of the lone genius in a white coat, healthcare is built on teams, systems, and often, subtle hierarchies.

Every hospital has its unspoken leaderboard.

Who diagnoses faster.

Who gets tougher cases.

Who patients request by name.

Gamified platforms just make this visible—and playable.

When a dermatologist in Madrid can see her diagnostic accuracy next to a peer in Mumbai, something shifts. Not in ego, but in curiosity.

It creates a space of shared benchmarking:

"Where do I stand?"

"Why did they choose that?"

"What do they know that I missed?"

This is not about beating others.

It's about becoming better because of them.

The peer leaderboard isn't a vanity metric. It's a community of practice—disguised as a game.

Simulations: Safe Spaces in a Risk-Filled World

In real clinical life, decisions are heavy.

There's no undo button when you intubate.

No pause when a patient crashes.

No redo when the wrong antibiotic sets off a chain of decline.

Simulations—especially gamified ones—offer something radical:

Failure without consequence.

You can test a rare diagnosis.

Try a bold move.

Explore a what-if.

And when you fail?

You learn. Without fear. Without judgment.

This is where simulations transcend training. They become rehearsals for reality.

Just as pilots run flight simulators before commanding a jet, doctors can—must—practice judgment under pressure.

And games give them the mental reps.

What Really Drives the Play?

It isn't the badges.

It isn't the bells or the buzzers.

It's the return to mastery.

In a system that often treats doctors as cogs—churning through patients, fighting EMRs, dodging burnout—a well-designed point system or simulation offers something different.

It says:

- You matter.
- Your growth still counts.
- Here's a place to try, fail, retry, and improve.
- Not for credits. Not for compliance. For you.

It's the kind of message medicine doesn't say enough.

But games—when built with insight and empathy—can whisper it back.

And doctors? They listen.

Case Study: The Game of Guidelines – When Protocols became Play

When Dr. Elena Morris first opened the app, she rolled her eyes.

"Play to treat," it said.

Beneath the splash screen: a leaderboard of local physicians—names she knew from the floor, the ER, and med school.

She had patients waiting. Charts to finish. A pile of unread messages in the EHR. And now this?

A game about guidelines?

She was about to close the app.

But then she saw her name.

Ranked #72.

Out of 84.

That stung.

The Problem No CME Could Fix

The hospital system had long wrestled with a quiet, stubborn issue: clinical guideline non-adherence.

It wasn't malice. It wasn't even negligence.

It was… noise.

Too many updates. Too many exceptions. Too many "yes, but" moments that made protocol feel theoretical.

For years, the solution was predictable:

- CME modules.
- Reminder emails.
- Pocket cards.
- Occasional audit-feedback reports from compliance.

And still, only 56% of internal medicine clinicians followed heart failure discharge protocols to the letter.

Some skipped follow-up scheduling.

Others missed medication reconciliation.

The documentation? Spotty at best.

So they tried something different.

Not more education.

Not more enforcement.

They tried a game.

Designing for Doctors, Not Gamers

It wasn't Candy Crush in scrubs.

The platform—developed with input from behavioral scientists and frontline clinicians—translated updated clinical guidelines into interactive micro-challenges.

Each day, a new case vignette popped up:

"Mr. T, age 69, presents with dyspnea. BNP 821. EF: 30%. What's the first post-discharge intervention recommended within 72 hours?"

Options. Timers. Hints.

Get it right? +3 points.

Wrong? -1, but with instant rationale and a citation from JACC.

Bonus rounds?

You could challenge a colleague, or "save a patient" streak by stringing together correct decisions across different specialties.

You could even simulate an entire discharge workflow, racing the clock while applying new updates.

Every interaction nudged the brain:

"Remember this. It matters."

The Turning Point

After ignoring the app for days, Dr. Morris started using it on coffee breaks.

Just one question, she told herself.

But like brushing teeth, it became habit.

She started competing—not with malice, but motivation.

She remembered why she entered medicine in the first place: not just to treat patients, but to get it right.

And she wasn't alone.

Within three months, 81% of physicians across the health system engaged with the platform at least twice a week.

Leaderboards went from novelty to signal—a quiet scoreboard of clinical diligence.

The impact?

- Guideline adherence in heart failure care rose from 56% to 83%.
- Readmission rates dropped by 18% over six months.
- Clinician self-reported confidence in applying guidelines increased by 40%.
- And not least: engagement outpaced traditional CME completion by 300%.

Not Just a Game

Here's what made it work:

- Microlearning: Built for 5 minutes, not 50.
- Instant feedback: Learning by doing, not by guessing.
- Social reinforcement: Peer performance as quiet accountability.
- Progress visibility: A tangible arc from "I don't know" to "I remember now."

But above all?

It offered something medicine rarely does:

A safe space to fail, reflect, retry—and grow.

Why it Stuck?

It's easy to dismiss gamification as gimmickry.

But what if it's actually how the brain learns best under pressure?

What if a busy physician, pressed between EMRs and empathy, needs a cognitive foothold—something playful enough to engage, yet rigorous enough to matter?

The game didn't replace guidelines.

It revived them.

It gave doctors a reason to care again.

Not for credit. Not for compliance.

But for the simple, stubborn joy of getting it right.

When 40% Meant more than a Number

We talk a lot about metrics in medicine.

Mortality. Morbidity. Readmission. Compliance.

But numbers, like people, have context. And sometimes, they don't just measure what's happening. They mark a turning point in how things happen.

Let me explain.

Before the Climb

At St. Vincent's Medical, clinical guideline adherence for chronic heart failure patients hovered around 57%.

That meant that nearly half of all discharges left something incomplete:

- A missed beta-blocker.
- A follow-up not scheduled.
- An education form unsigned.
- Or worse, an undocumented reason why.

Each gap wasn't just a checkbox failure. It was a fault line—between best practice and business-as-usual.

And for patients already walking a tightrope of comorbidities, those gaps mattered.

They turned into return visits.

Into complications.

Into costs—human and institutional.

- The quality department had tried everything:
- CME modules with high-level summaries.
- Protocol posters taped inside workrooms.
- Monthly emails with the subject line: "URGENT: HF Discharge Update."

Engagement? Tepid.

Impact? Minimal.

Then they tried something unorthodox.

They made a game of it.

Not a Game for Fun—A Game for Focus

The gamified app didn't preach.

It didn't penalize.

It prompted.

- A scenario.
- A decision point.
- A timer ticking softly.
- A ping of feedback, right or wrong.

Points accumulated.

Clinicians saw where they stood—not in punitive reports, but playful leaderboards.

It gave shape to an invisible skill: clinical memory.

And in less than 90 days, the adherence rate jumped to 80%.

That's a 40% relative increase.

But here's the thing:

It wasn't because they became more compliant.

It was because they became more confident.

More than a Number

The feedback was telling.

"Now I know the why behind the guideline."

"It made me realize I was skipping steps I thought didn't matter."

"I look forward to the case-of-the-day before rounds."

This wasn't gamification as novelty.

It was design thinking for clinical decision-making.

That 40%?

It wasn't just statistical movement.

It was:

- Fewer missed steps.

- Fewer readmissions.
- Fewer clinicians guessing.
- More clinicians knowing.

And in medicine, that's the difference between practicing hard and practicing well.

Why it Matters?

We spend so much time trying to fix behavior with education.

But perhaps it's not about teaching more.

It's about learning better.

In a world where guidelines update faster than textbooks, memory needs scaffolding.

And that scaffolding?

Sometimes it looks like play.

Sometimes, it looks like a 40% rise.

But often, it looks like one patient not coming back to the ED, because their care was finally seamless.

And that, too, is medicine.

Retention by Design: When Learning Turned into Play

In medical school, learning was a kind of survival game.

You memorized, you repeated, you adapted. Because you had to.

But once the training wheels came off, something subtle happened.

Doctors stopped learning like their lives depended on it—because someone else's did.

And yet, the system for keeping doctors current—Continuing Medical Education—didn't evolve with them.

It became routine.

PowerPoint by committee.

Online modules with a progress bar and a post-test.

Certificates with expiry dates, not impact.

There are clinicians who clicked through CME quizzes while holding their toddler.

Who remembered the login, but not the lesson.

What changed this wasn't a better syllabus.

It was a shift in format.

A reimagining of how the brain learns when it's awake, engaged, and just a little bit challenged.

They called it gamified CME.

And for many, it worked.

What Made it Work?

The difference wasn't superficial. It wasn't about points for the sake of points.

It was about activating the deep learning systems of the brain:

- Recall under pressure: timed clinical vignettes that made you think fast—like real life.

- Reinforcement through failure: get it wrong, and the explanation followed immediately. No shame, just clarity.
- Micro-challenges: a few minutes a day. Frequent, low stakes, high frequency.
- Streaks, levels, feedback: the kind of nudges that make your brain lean forward, not switch off.

Unlike lectures, these games were interactive memory machines.

The kind of machine that didn't just hand out credit hours.

It handed out confidence.

Beyond Recall — into Behavior

The real test wasn't retention.

It was action.

One hospital's gamified CME tracked decision-making changes over six months.

Clinicians who engaged regularly showed:

- Fewer inappropriate antibiotic prescriptions
- Higher protocol adherence in stroke response times
- Increased referrals to evidence-based services like pulmonary rehab

Another platform for primary care physicians embedded behavioral nudges into their gameplay:

"You've seen five cases of uncontrolled diabetes this week. Want to review the updated SGLT2 guidelines?"

The result?

Not just knowledge. But behavioral migration—from outdated habits to current standards.

One small nudge at a time.

Why this Matters Now?

The half-life of medical knowledge is shrinking.

In some specialties, what you learn today is half-obsolete in 18 months.

Traditional CME can't keep up.

But a gamified system, one that you return to like a daily puzzle, a morning ritual, a quiet competition with yourself and your peers—that stays.

We retain what we experience.

We apply what we remember.

And we remember what engaged us.

That's not just neuroscience. That's practical wisdom.

The Takeaway

A surgeon remembers in one of his surgeires that double-checking a rare protocol he had just reviewed days before—not in a lecture, but in a gamified case quiz on his phone.

He got it right.

Not because he studied.

But because he played.

And in that moment, play became precision.

And precision became care.

Maybe that's the future of medical education:

Less passive instruction.

More active mastery.

And a little bit of joy along the way.

Chapter 10

Patients as Players – Emotional and Social Gamification

We tend to think of patients as passive recipients.

A diagnosis is made. A prescription is written. A follow-up is scheduled.

They comply—or they don't.

And when they don't, we call it non-adherence, a sterile word that sounds more like a spreadsheet column than a story.

But what if we're looking at the equation upside down?

What if the missing piece isn't compliance, but engagement?

And what if engagement doesn't come from more instructions, but from something far more ancient—emotion, community, and even play?

That's where social and emotional gamification enters the story.

More than Medicine

I remember a doctor tellimg me this. He asked a patient of his—Linda, 56, hypertensive, diabetic, skeptical.

He once asked her, "Do you track your sugars?"

She shrugged. "Sometimes. But it's all so… dull."

Three months later, she came to clinic beaming.

She pulled out her phone and showed her dashboard.

A cartoon dragon smiled back.

"You see," she said, "every time I log my sugar, I earn food for him. If I keep at it, he evolves."

What got her to stick with the routine wasn't fear of complications or another lecture.

It was affection.

A sense of responsibility—to her little virtual companion.

It was, in a word, emotionally engineered compliance.

From Avatars to Accountability

Designers of patient-facing apps—like MySugr, SuperBetter, or KidzAlive—have discovered something pharma marketers missed for decades:

- People change behavior more often for stories than for stats.
- Give them a digital coach that cheers them on.
- Let them customize their avatar, pick a team, level up.
- Celebrate their first 7-day streak like it's a victory parade.

And suddenly, a chore becomes a challenge.

A lonely condition becomes a shared experience.

When platforms allowed patients to invite family, caregivers, or even fellow patients to see progress, the shift was remarkable.

Adherence rates rose—not just because of design—but because of dignity.

They felt seen. Heard. Validated.

And in healthcare, that's still revolutionary.

Emotions are Data

We often build interventions around rational incentives: lower costs, better outcomes.

But human motivation is rarely rational.

We skip the gym because it rains. We eat cake when we're sad.

We ignore pillboxes that sit silently on a shelf.

But a blinking app that says, "One step closer to your goal!"

Or a peer leaderboard that shows you're falling behind friends?

That changes behavior—not with shame, but with social gravity.

We care where we stand.

We care who notices.

And we care about progress—even if it's gamified.

The Social Engine

One study gamified asthma management for teens.

Daily check-ins became quests.

Inhaler use earned badges.

A chat room let them compare streaks.

Over three months, adherence jumped by 43%.

But what stuck most wasn't the data.

It was a comment from a 15-year-old participant:

"For the first time, I don't feel like the only one dealing with this."

That's the power of social gamification.

It doesn't just drive outcomes.

It dissolves isolation.

The Limits—and the Horizon

Of course, gamification has its limits.

If poorly designed, it becomes gimmickry.

If overused, it causes fatigue.

The goal isn't to infantilize care.

It's to humanize it.

The best gamified platforms don't trivialize disease.

They acknowledge the difficulty—and offer small, joyful victories along the way.

Because medicine is already hard.

Healing shouldn't have to be.

The Takeaway

We once thought the patient's journey ended at the pharmacy counter.

Now, we know it's only beginning.

Gamification—especially emotional and social gamification—isn't about turning healthcare into a video game.

It's about recognizing something deeper:

That behavior change is felt, not just taught.

That patients are not problems to be solved, but people to be empowered.

And sometimes, the most potent dose isn't found in milligrams—but in a moment of connection.

Even if it's with a cartoon dragon.

Case Study: Novartis – Galaxies of Hope

In medicine, we talk often about data.

Rarely do we talk about dignity.

That's what struck me when I first learned about Galaxies of Hope—a gamified mobile experience created by Novartis to support patients and caregivers navigating neuroendocrine tumors (NETs). A rare cancer. A rare language. A rarer empathy.

The average person can't pronounce the disease.

The average patient can't explain it.

And somewhere in between diagnosis and the next appointment, many fall into the black hole of confusion, isolation, and fear.

Galaxies of Hope didn't begin as a marketing campaign.

It began as a storytelling experiment.

An attempt to bridge a terrifying gap with something as improbable as play.

The Diagnosis as Disorientation

One caregiver described the early days after her husband's NET diagnosis as "floating through space without gravity."

It was this metaphor—of drifting, lost, and alone—that inspired Novartis to flip the script.

Instead of pamphlets filled with terminology…

Instead of dry explainer videos or helpline numbers buried on page six…

They created an interactive universe.

Patients became explorers.

Each star in the galaxy, a voice.

Each nebula, a story of struggle or resilience.

Each journey, a path from disempowerment to understanding.

The app was not a game in the traditional sense—there were no badges or points.

But it was gamified in the deeper, more meaningful sense: exploration, immersion, and agency.

Listening, Not Just Educating

What makes Galaxies of Hope different is not the technology.

It's the tone.

You don't just tap to learn.

You listen—to actual patients, caregivers, oncologists.

You hear them falter.

You hear them laugh.

You hear the weight of diagnosis, the awkwardness of scans, the joy of small victories.

It turns out, giving patients a galaxy of stories isn't just poetic—it's practical.

Research shows that narrative engagement improves information retention, emotional resilience, and treatment adherence.

Novartis didn't lecture.

They curated a constellation of experience.

And in doing so, they reminded patients:

"You are not alone in this universe."

Soft Power, Real Impact

Now, a skeptical view might ask:

Is this just branded empathy?

A subtle way for pharma to "connect" for commercial benefit?

That's a fair question.

But in the story of Galaxies of Hope, the lines blur—for good reason.

Because if a pharma company uses gamified storytelling to reduce fear, increase understanding, and restore a sense of control, isn't that worth more than another sponsored hashtag?

Surveys from users reported:

- Higher emotional comfort scores.
- Increased recall of key disease milestones.
- Greater willingness to discuss symptoms with clinicians.

None of this is easy to quantify in ROI.

But if one patient felt heard, one caregiver felt less invisible—wasn't that the return?

The Takeaway

Galaxies of Hope isn't flashy. It's not about points or leaderboards.

It's about something more powerful: presence.

In an era where pharma is often accused of being distant, technical, and impersonal, Novartis launched a quiet rebellion—by listening, by narrating, by gamifying empathy.

Because sometimes, what patients need most isn't another molecule.

It's a map.

Even if that map is among stars.

Empathy-Based Storytelling for Neuroendocrine Cancer Support

Neuroendocrine tumors don't announce themselves with urgency.

They creep.

They linger.

They're misread as indigestion, fatigue, stress.

I remember a patient once said to me:

"I had to convince three doctors that I wasn't imagining it before one believed me enough to look deeper."

By the time the diagnosis arrives—NETs—the relief is only partial.

The questions that follow are more bewildering than the disease itself.

What is it?

Why did it happen?

What does it mean for my life?

The language of oncology is clinical. The language of suffering is not.

And that's where empathy-based storytelling steps in—not as therapy, not as marketing—but as medicine for the soul.

What the Textbook doesn't Teach

Medical school does not teach how to explain a rare diagnosis without breaking someone's sense of self.

It does not tell doctors how to sit with a patient who says,

"This cancer has a name, but I feel like I've disappeared."

In a world where patients search the internet before they see a doctor, what they find often terrifies them more than the disease.

Empathy-based storytelling flips the equation.

Instead of offering clinical certainty, it offers human resonance.

The Power of Lived Language

What happens when a newly diagnosed patient hears:

- A caregiver confessing, "I didn't know how to hold his hand without looking scared."
- A survivor sharing, "Every scan made my heart beat like a drum, but I found ways to breathe again."
- An oncologist admitting, "We don't always have the answers, but we'll walk this path with you."

Suddenly, the sterile clinic becomes a community of voices.

Storytelling doesn't fix cancer.

But it restores coherence to a life that's just been fractured.

And for NETs—where ambiguity is often more constant than clarity—this becomes not a luxury, but a necessity.

When Empathy becomes Technology

The Galaxies of Hope app by Novartis understood this in a rare way.

It didn't lecture. It invited.

It gave patients the steering wheel to navigate an emotionally alien terrain, with constellation-like paths built from lived narratives—real patients, real voices.

No avatars.

No scripts.

Just humanness, digitized.

A mother navigating her child's NET diagnosis.

A patient learning to live without fear of recurrence.

A nurse explaining how she learned to speak, not just treat.

These weren't "testimonials." They were witnessings.

And through them, patients didn't just learn—they located themselves.

This is more than Communication

Empathy-based storytelling isn't soft science.

Studies show it increases:

- Recall of critical information
- Perceived control over treatment decisions
- Emotional resilience and medication adherence

But its real power?

It tells patients: Your story matters too.

And when pharma or healthcare systems center those stories—not as sidebars but as strategy—they do something rare:

They close the gap between care and caring.

The Takeaway

Often while working, I've seen the difference between handing a pamphlet and offering a story.

One informs.

The other transforms.

Empathy-based storytelling doesn't compete with medicine.

It completes it.

Because sometimes, before a patient can follow your treatment plan,

they first need to hear a voice that sounds like their own say:

"I was there. And I made it through."

Headspace & Fitbit: Rewiring Wellness through Sleep, Steps, and Stillness

When the Breath Becomes the Metric

For all our talk about "preventive care," medicine has long been reactive.

We wait for the disease.

We brace for the symptoms.

We intervene after disruption, rarely before it.

But there's a quiet revolution underway.

Not in hospitals.

Not in clinics.

In wristbands.

In guided meditations.

In small decisions made at 10:30 pm instead of midnight.

It began—almost invisibly—when Headspace, the meditation app, partnered with Fitbit, the fitness tracker.

No lab coats. No prescriptions.

Just a pulse, a prompt, and a pause.

The Real Opponent: The Modern Mind

Sleep disorders.

Anxiety.

Chronic fatigue.

They're epidemic—and often dismissed as lifestyle issues until they manifest as hypertension, diabetes, depression.

I once saw a patient who wore two fitness trackers.

One for steps.

One for sleep.

She said:

"If I see the numbers slip, I know I'm heading toward a burnout long before my doctor ever would."

It sounded obsessive.

But maybe she was right.

Because we don't just need patients to take medicine.

We need them to notice themselves—and that's what gamified wellness is beginning to offer.

Designing the Invisible Game

What happens when you turn breathwork into a streak?

Or quality sleep into a score?

Fitbit's smartwatches began nudging users to pause, not just move.

To check in with their breath, not just their BPM.

Headspace, in turn, embedded mindfulness sessions into Fitbit's daily readiness scores.

- Too stressed? A 3-minute guided body scan.
- Slept poorly? A sleepcast, not a sleeping pill.
- Rested and ready? A mindful movement track.

The language of wellness was becoming embodied—measurable, visible, game-like.

And people responded.

What the Data Whispered?

Fitbit's internal data showed:

- 14% reduction in self-reported stress levels after integrating mindfulness reminders.
- 21% increase in average nightly sleep minutes among users who engaged with meditation content three times per week.
- Users with regular mindfulness practice logged more consistent sleep schedules, correlating with better resting heart rate.

But the most telling stat?

Retention.

Those who used Headspace + Fitbit in tandem were 38% more likely to continue both practices over 12 months.

Not because of gamification alone.

But because the design made wellness feel winnable.

A Personalized Prescription—Without the Rx

What this case teaches us is simple:

- People don't just want health.
- They want agency.
- They want to see progress, even if it's incremental.
- They want rituals, not resolutions.

The gamified nudges weren't coercive.

They were compassionate reminders.

They didn't replace doctors.

But they extended care into the space where medicine rarely reaches—the in-between moments, the 2 a.m. restlessness, the skipped walk, the shallow breath.

And when we gamify those moments—not to manipulate, but to motivate—we build a kind of resilience that no prescription alone can deliver.

Why this Matters to Pharma?

If wellness can be measured, it can be reinforced.

If behavior can be shaped, it can be sustained.

And if patients can become players in their own care, then adherence becomes less about reminders, and more about rewards that matter.

In a world where prevention is finally being taken seriously, the Fitbit–Headspace alliance shows us that the future of pharma may not just be pills and pamphlets—

—it might also be points, pauses, and the quiet victory of choosing to breathe.

The Patient as Hero in their Own Narrative

From Isolation to Connection

It always begins quietly.

A missed refill.

An unread email from the clinic.

A symptom dismissed because there's a meeting at 10 a.m.

I once asked a friend of mine in her forties—newly diagnosed with multiple sclerosis—what scared her most.

"Losing my job?" she said. "Sure. But more than that—losing the feeling that I'm part of the world."

Medicine, for all its brilliance, has often failed to address that ache:

Not pain.

Not fatigue.

But the silent disconnection that illness brings.

The Invisibility of the Patient Journey

You see, once a person is diagnosed, the world shifts.

Not just biologically, but socially.

The phone calls become fewer.

Friends don't know what to say.

Even doctors—well-meaning—speak in numbers, not names.

It's not that patients stop living.

It's that they stop being seen.

And it's here, in this silence, that gamification—oddly, unexpectedly—can do something medicine often forgets to do:

Tell a new story.

One where the patient becomes the protagonist again.

Designing for Dignity

Take, for instance, a digital platform for cancer patients that doesn't just offer reminders for chemotherapy—but invites them to track how they feel after each session, share that experience anonymously with others, and receive small acknowledgments: "You're on Day 3. You've made it through the worst fatigue window. Keep going."

It sounds simple. Even trivial.

But to the patient, it's profound.

Because suddenly, there's a journey, not just an itinerary.

There's a map, not just a calendar.

And most importantly—there's a role to play.

Gamification doesn't erase pain.

But it reframes it.

It tells the patient: You are not broken.

You are in the middle of something brave.

You are not a case file.

You are the hero.

What Happens when the Story Changes?

Research shows that patients who see themselves as active participants in their care—who set small goals, track progress, get feedback—are more likely to:

- Stick to treatment regimens
- Report higher satisfaction
- Experience reduced anxiety and depression

But these statistics don't capture what a doctor sees in the clinic:

A teenager with cystic fibrosis, whose inhaler routine was made into a space mission—Level 1: Clear the airways.

A man post-stroke who "unlocked" achievements for walking 10 extra steps each day, his daughter cheering from the app.

Their outcomes improved.

But what changed most was the way they saw themselves.

Not as burdens.

As players.

As storytellers.

As survivors with arcs—not just diagnoses.

From Checklists to Chapbooks

In the end, what gamification offers pharma—and medicine more broadly—is not just a better way to communicate.

It is a better way to commemorate the patient's journey.

- Not just "Have you taken your meds?"
- But "You've taken them 14 days in a row. That's consistency."
- Not just "How's your mood?"
- But "Others on this path have felt the same way. You're not alone."

We don't need every patient to become a gamer.

But every patient deserves to feel like a character in a story that matters.

One with goals. With obstacles.

With side quests and guides.

And a final scene that says: You did it. You mattered. You changed.

Because healing is not just a medical process.

It's a narrative act.

And the patient?

They've always been the hero.

We just needed a better way to let them feel it.

Chapter 11

VR, Pain & Play

Gamification in Therapeutic Interventions

Pain is not just a signal.

It's a story the brain tells itself. And sometimes, the most effective way to interrupt that story is to offer it a better one.

That's something I learned from a burn specialist in Seattle. He told me about a teenage patient who dreaded the daily debridement procedure—an excruciating ritual that peeled away dead skin to prevent infection. Morphine helped, but never enough. Her heart rate would spike. Her body would tremble. She'd cry before the nurse even entered the room.

One day, they gave her a headset.

It wasn't fancy—just an early virtual reality simulation of a snowy world where the player threw snowballs at penguins. It lasted all of ten minutes. But that day, the girl didn't scream.

She laughed.

That's not a miracle. That's VR-powered gamification in medicine.

From Suffering to Strategy

Pain has always been treated as a chemical problem: opioids, NSAIDs, anesthetics. And they work—up to a point.

But what happens when the pain is chronic?

What about when the brain becomes addicted not to the drug, but to the pain signal itself?

That's where distraction becomes design.

Virtual Reality offers more than an escape.

It gives patients agency.

You're no longer passively enduring pain—you're doing something: solving a puzzle, steering through a canyon, dodging lava in a gamified landscape that demands just enough attention to pull you out of your body's alarm bells.

This isn't a gimmick. It's neuroscience.

Studies from Cedars-Sinai and UCLA show that VR sessions reduce acute pain by up to 52% in hospitalized patients—sometimes with effects that last hours after the headset comes off.

Gamified Therapy: Not Just for Distraction

We often imagine games as diversions. But in clinical therapy, they become tools for transformation:

- Stroke rehab platforms turn repetitive hand exercises into fruit-slicing ninja games.
- PTSD programs in veterans use VR exposure therapy wrapped in a game engine—each level a little closer to healing.
- Pediatric oncology wards use augmented reality to create scavenger hunts during chemo infusions—turning IV poles into dragons to be tamed.

Here, play is not the opposite of medicine.

It is medicine.

Designing for the Body—and the Brain

Therapeutic VR isn't just about beautiful graphics or gamified scoring. The best interventions are grounded in biobehavioral design:

- Short burst challenges to accommodate fatigue.
- Breath-paced levels that sync with autonomic calming.
- Rewards that reinforce adherence to exercises—not just performance.

It's behavioral science meeting clinical need.

And, importantly, it's personal.

A patient with fibromyalgia might get a soothing forest walk with birdsong challenges. A kid with scoliosis gets a surfing game that improves posture while chasing dolphins. Every detail—from music to challenge to narrative—is tailored not to entertain, but to engage the healing brain.

The Unseen Outcome: Dignity

A nurse once told me, "When kids use these VR headsets, it's not just that they stop crying. It's that they stop feeling like patients."

They become heroes, warriors, adventurers. They forget the fluorescent ceiling lights. They forget the IV line. And in that forgetting, they recover something even the best pharmacology can't deliver:

A sense of self beyond suffering.

From the Clinic to the Industry

Pharma has traditionally been distant from VR. But that's changing.

- Roche partnered with VR startup MindMaze for post-stroke motor rehab.
- Novartis explored gamified VR environments for pediatric glaucoma therapy.
- AppliedVR gained FDA breakthrough device designation for chronic low back pain.

What used to be fringe experiments are now structured digital therapeutics—reimbursable, regulated, and real.

This chapter is no longer optional.

Gamified VR is becoming a pillar of next-generation care.

The Deeper Question

What if recovery isn't just about reducing pain, but changing the experience of healing itself?

What if, instead of asking "What's your pain score?"

We ask:

- "What level did you reach today?"
- "Which part of the story did you unlock?"
- "How did you surprise yourself?"

That's the promise of gamification.

Not just to manage pain.

But to re-author the patient's role.

From victim to player.

From sufferer to strategist.

From endured to engaged.

Case Study: Johns Hopkins – Bandit's Shark Showdown (Stroke Rehab)

Rewiring the Brain, One Virtual Fish at a Time

Rehabilitation is often dull.

Not because it lacks importance—but because it lacks story.

Day after day, a stroke survivor is asked to reach, grip, release. Again and again.

Fingers that once buttoned shirts and lifted spoons are now learning to obey… like toddlers with no language.

And that's where Bandit comes in.

Meet Bandit: Not a Dog, but a Game-Changer

Johns Hopkins researchers didn't invent video games. But they reimagined one—for the brain that had lost its map of the body.

"Bandit's Shark Showdown" looks like a cartoon.

You play a pink and yellow fish with an eyepatch, helping a robot dolphin fight off robotic sharks.

But the stakes are anything but imaginary.

The only way to make Bandit swim, dodge, or zap a shark is to move your paralyzed arm—with motion sensors tracking every micro-motion, every angle of effort.

Patients who couldn't lift their arms more than 15 degrees soon found themselves chasing sharks through virtual coral reefs.

They weren't just complying with therapy.

They were competing.

The Neuroscience of a Game

What the Johns Hopkins team understood—better than most—is that the brain craves context.

Ask someone to stretch a limb 30 times and it's a chore.

But wrap it in a narrative—defend Bandit, score points, beat your last level—and it becomes a goal.

Stroke rehab demands neuroplasticity—the ability of the brain to rewire itself, to assign new regions to take over damaged functions. But neuroplasticity doesn't flick on automatically. It needs:

- Repetition.
- Reward.
- Emotional engagement.

That's where Bandit thrives.

It gives the brain a reason to try.

The Story of Mary

Mary was 63 when a clot in her left brain paralyzed the right side of her body.

For months, she stared at her right arm as though it belonged to someone else. It lay there, inert, a stranger in her own body.

Therapy was slow, frustrating. She would cry during sessions, apologizing to the therapists for her failure.

Then, they gave her Bandit.

At first, she didn't understand. "A game?" she asked. "At my age?"

But after the second session, something shifted.

She didn't want to stop.

"Wait, I almost beat the last score," she insisted. "Let me try again."

Her therapists didn't argue.

Two weeks in, she could reach a cereal box on a shelf she couldn't even point at before.

By week four, she lifted a half-filled cup and drank from it—with the same hand that hadn't moved in months.

Mary didn't just recover movement.

She rediscovered herself.

What makes this Work?

Unlike passive rehab, Bandit's Showdown is an active engagement platform. Its design integrates:

- Motion-sensing hardware calibrated for small, incremental improvements.
- Progressive difficulty that adapts to the user's ability.
- Feedback mechanisms that reward effort, not just achievement.

The game doesn't penalize you for failing.

It nudges you gently—"Try again, just a bit higher."

In doing so, it encourages persistence.

This is not gamification for novelty's sake.

It's behavioral therapy in disguise.

Clinical Outcomes that Speak

A Johns Hopkins pilot trial showed that patients using Bandit's game for just 5 hours across 2 weeks had measurable improvements in upper-limb coordination—equivalent to several weeks of standard physical therapy.

But here's what's more telling:

92% of patients reported enjoying therapy.

When was the last time anyone said that about post-stroke recovery?

Beyond the Game: A Shift in Mindset

We often think of medical breakthroughs in terms of molecules and machines.

But sometimes, the real breakthrough is imagination.

What the Johns Hopkins team accomplished wasn't just a software hack. It was a paradigm shift in how we think about healing:

That restoring function isn't about compliance.

It's about giving the patient a reason to play.

And in play, the body remembers what it forgot.

Final Thought: The Game of Life

We like to think life is serious. That illness should be met with solemnity.

But ask any child how they learn to walk, to talk, to become who they are—and they'll tell you:

They played.

"Bandit's Shark Showdown" brought that wisdom back to medicine.

In doing so, it made healing not only effective—but human.

Case Study: SnowWorld VR – Easing Burn Pain with a Snowball Fight

There's something oddly cruel about burn injuries.

They don't just destroy skin—they erase comfort.

Every nerve, left raw and exposed, becomes a live wire.

Even a gust of air can feel like fire.

And then comes the real pain—not from the injury, but from its treatment.

Debridement. Dressing changes. Hydrotherapy.

Necessary procedures. But each one a ritual of agony.

Doctors learned to steel themselves. Nurses braced for screams.

And patients?

They clenched fists, gritted teeth, and waited for the worst to pass.

Morphine helped—but not always.

And certainly not enough.

Then, unexpectedly, came a snowball fight.

What if Pain could be Distracted?

At Harborview Burn Center in Seattle, a team of researchers led by psychologist Hunter Hoffman and physician Dr. David Patterson asked a deceptively simple question:

Could pain be hacked—by the mind?

They knew that pain isn't just a signal.

It's a construction of the brain—amplified by attention, emotion, memory.

So they wondered:

If you could pull the mind somewhere else—someplace cold, fun, immersive—might it turn down the volume on pain?

And so, in the middle of a trauma ward, they introduced SnowWorld.

Welcome to SnowWorld

It wasn't high-tech by today's standards.

Blocky graphics. Cartoonish penguins. A blue sky filled with falling snowflakes.

But to the burn victims who donned the clunky VR headsets, it was another planet.

In SnowWorld, they weren't lying on a hospital bed.

They were flying down an icy canyon, pelting snowmen and polar bears with snowballs, riding over ice bridges, and listening to Paul Simon's Graceland.

The cold colors. The cheerful sounds. The simple goal—hit the targets.

It didn't look like medicine.

But what it did to pain?

That was nothing short of miraculous.

Pain Relief beyond the Pill

Clinical trials showed something stunning.

When patients played SnowWorld during wound care:

- Pain dropped by up to 50%.
- They reported less anxiety, fewer screams, and even fewer requests for opioids.

This wasn't placebo.

Functional MRI scans later showed reduced activity in the pain-related areas of the brain—the somatosensory cortex, insula, anterior cingulate.

The brain, immersed in a vivid, engaging experience, simply couldn't process pain at full volume.

It had better things to do.

A Patient's Story: Noah's Escape

Noah was 12 when an accident with scalding soup left him with third-degree burns across his chest and arms.

For weeks, he dreaded the daily dressing changes.

They meant pain—searing, unbearable pain.

His parents tried everything—distraction, singing, stories. Nothing worked.

Then a nurse brought in a strange-looking headset.

"Wanna try a game?" she asked.

He nodded, skeptical.

Within minutes, Noah was floating above icy ravines, laughing as he launched snowballs at penguins.

His heart rate dropped. His grip on his mother's hand loosened.

When the session ended, he asked:

"Can I play again tomorrow?"

The nurse smiled.

They had found a better way.

The Science of Play and Pain

Why does it work?

Because immersion matters.

SnowWorld isn't passive like TV or distraction like counting ceiling tiles. It's interactive, cognitively demanding, and emotionally cooling.

It hijacks attention, engages spatial memory, and—most importantly—it feels real.

In burn care, the brain is usually taught to fear the procedure room. But when you're inside a snowball fight, the world shifts.

You're not a patient.

You're a player.

What this Means for Medicine

SnowWorld didn't cure burns.

But it healed something deeper—the relationship between patient and pain.

It proved that technology, when built with empathy, could be more than distraction. It could be medicine itself.

Atul Gawande once asked: "What if we stopped thinking of patients as broken bodies to fix—and started seeing them as people navigating the unknown?"

SnowWorld did just that.

It didn't just reduce suffering.

It restored agency.

The Bigger Picture

As healthcare increasingly adopts AI, robotics, and pharmaceuticals, it's easy to overlook the low-tech power of presence.

SnowWorld taught us that where we place the mind, the body often follows.

In that lesson lies the future of pain care.

Not just how we heal—but how we help people endure the process of healing.

And sometimes, all it takes is a snowball.

Rewiring Pain and Possibility: How Immersive Games Engage the Brain

When I first watched a burn patient smile during a wound-cleaning session—laughing as they tossed virtual snowballs at penguins—it struck me not as a miracle, but as a redefinition of medicine.

Because here was a young girl who had once screamed at the sight of sterile gauze, now giggling inside a headset.

Not sedated.

Not medicated.

But immersed.

What changed?

The wound was still there. The nerve endings still raw.

But the brain—the ultimate processor of pain, attention, and experience—had been hijacked by a game.

This wasn't escape.

It was engagement of the most intelligent kind.

The Brain, as Game Designer

To understand what happened, you have to understand the brain not just as a bundle of neurons, but as a living, adapting, rewiring machine.

Our brains, like seasoned editors, constantly filter, prioritize, and compose what we call experience.

Pain, as it turns out, is just one output.

And it's not always objective.

It's modulated—increased or decreased based on what else the brain is doing.

And that's where games come in.

Not just any games.

Immersive ones.

Ones that pull you in and won't let go.

Immersion: The Brain's Full Bandwidth

Think about what happens when you're fully immersed.

Your visual cortex lights up with rich imagery.

Your motor cortex prepares your thumbs to aim.

Your hippocampus maps the world.

Your prefrontal cortex strategizes.

Your reward system—dopamine-fueled—ignites with every small win.

You are not passively observing.

You are doing.

You are being.

And in that moment, the brain simply has no resources left to process pain or fear.

It's like trying to sing a song while reading a physics textbook.

Something's got to give.

With immersive games, what gives is the grip of pain, the loop of anxiety, the helpless script of the patient identity.

Neuroplasticity in Action

Here's where it gets more fascinating.

Repeated immersion doesn't just distract.

It rewires.

Neuroscientists call it experience-dependent plasticity.

The idea that whatever you do repeatedly, your brain begins to encode and prioritize.

In therapy games for stroke rehab, motor neurons begin to fire in response to imagined movement.

In PTSD exposure games, the amygdala learns to quiet itself in the face of simulated threat.

And in pain games, such as SnowWorld, the very networks responsible for amplifying suffering begin to reroute.

Pain becomes not a permanent presence, but a volume knob—and the player learns how to dial it down.

Attention Is the Gatekeeper

One of the most overlooked truths in medicine is this:

Where attention goes, pain flows—or doesn't.

Immersive games are the most advanced tools we have for training attention—not to ignore, but to engage differently.

In virtual environments, patients practice agency. They move. Explore. React. Win.

Each level played, each badge earned, builds not just confidence but new neural highways.

It's not gamification for the sake of fun.

It's serious neurorehabilitation—disguised in snowball fights and spaceship rides.

A New Kind of Doctor's Tool

When we think of medical interventions, we think of pills, scalpels, catheters.

But what if the future also includes headsets, VR joysticks, and reward dashboards?

What if the most powerful tool we had to help a child with cancer cope with chemo wasn't a drug—but a game where they become the hero, collecting courage coins along the way?

That's not science fiction.

That's science, finally applied with human imagination.

Closing the Loop: From Reaction to Redirection

The power of immersive games is not that they numb reality.

It's that they give the mind something new to do with it.

They allow a patient to become a player.

A sufferer to become a strategist.

A frightened child to become a champion.

The brain doesn't just cope—it learns.

And in learning, it heals.

Not by forgetting the pain.

But by replacing the script that surrounds it.

From "I am broken" to "I am playing."

From "I can't endure this" to "I'm leveling up."

And maybe, just maybe, that's where medicine has always wanted to go.

We just needed a controller in hand to show us the way.

PART IV: DESIGNING FOR IMPACT

Chapter 12: The Science of Engagement – Metrics that Matter

Chapter 13: Ethics in the Game

Chapter 14: Where Gamification Fails – Lessons from Misfires

Part IV

Designing for Impact

There is a moment in every surgeon's training when the scalpel stops being just a tool, and begins to feel like an extension of intention. The cut becomes cleaner. The decisions more nuanced. You don't just operate—you start to shape outcomes.

That moment is not about knowledge.

It's about designing with purpose.

And in many ways, gamification in healthcare has now reached a similar threshold.

It's no longer enough to ask: Can games engage patients, doctors, or reps?

The question now is:

How do we design these experiences to deliver real, measurable, lasting impact?

Not once.

Not just with excitement.

But sustainably, scalably, ethically.

Beyond Points and Prizes

In the early days of gamification, the assumption was simple: add points, badges, and leaderboards—and engagement will follow.

And for a while, it worked.

But medicine is not marketing.

Health is not a slot machine.

We are dealing with human fragility, fatigue, and fear. We're operating within systems where stakes are not user metrics—but suffering and survival.

Designing for healthcare impact requires a new kind of rigor—one that blends behavioral science, ethical frameworks, clinical objectives, and emotional intelligence.

It's not about what's fun.

It's about what works—and why.

The Architect's Challenge

Think of the gamified experience as a building.

- The mechanics are the structure.
- The dynamics are how people move through it.
- And the aesthetics are what make them want to stay.

But the real question is:

Does this space serve its purpose?

Does it improve medication adherence over months, not days?

Does it reduce dropout from therapy?

Does it make the rep or MSL want to learn, even when tired?

Does it help the physician retain complex information in a high-pressure environment?

True impact is measured in changed behavior, not app downloads.

Empathy as Design Principle

What the best health-focused games understand—and what this part of the book will explore—is that empathy is the cornerstone of effective design.

Empathy not just for the user's frustration, but for their story.

- A mother juggling chemo schedules and school runs.
- A sales rep managing quotas and depression.
- A doctor who hasn't had a full night's sleep in weeks.

Designing for impact means designing for their lives, not just their screens.

From Systems Thinking to Soul Thinking

Part IV dives deep into this critical juncture—where theory meets therapy, where design choices ripple out into real-world outcomes.

We'll explore:

The design frameworks that work in pharma.

- The role of AI and personalization in maintaining engagement.
- The pitfalls of gamification misuse—and how to avoid them.
- How to build for diverse populations and needs—from rural India to inner-city clinics in Detroit.
- And how to measure what matters: health outcomes, not just leaderboard scores.

We'll examine failures, too. Because in medicine, it's the complications that teach us the most.

Design, Not Decoration

In surgery, the best outcomes often come not from the most aggressive technique, but the most elegantly appropriate one.

In gamification, it's the same.

The most powerful experiences are those thoughtfully calibrated—to nudge, not manipulate; to challenge, not overwhelm; to encourage, not coerce.

And that requires design thinking with a soul.

This part of the book is not just about how to make games that work.

It's about how to make games that matter.

Because if we're going to play in the realm of health, we better be sure we're playing to heal.

Chapter 12

The Science of Engagement – Metrics that Matter

There is a quiet moment that surgeons learn to look for after an operation.

The patient breathes easier.

The monitor readings stabilize.

The hands unclench.

It's not a dramatic moment. No applause. No fanfare. Just a subtle shift. But it tells you the truth:

Something worked.

In healthcare, we're trained to listen for those moments. And in the world of gamification, we must do the same. Amidst the swirl of clicks, streaks, badges, and bounce rates—we must ask a deceptively simple question:

"Did it make a difference?"

Vanity Metrics vs. Vital Signs

In the early days of gamified health platforms, it was easy to get dazzled.

Downloads. Play counts. Leaderboard logins.

Executives cheered. Designers felt triumphant.

But a game that is played… isn't always a game that matters.

A patient might open an app every morning—but still miss doses.

A rep may earn every badge—but forget the core product claim.

Just as in medicine we distinguish between symptom relief and curative action, so in gamification we must distinguish between vanity metrics and vital signs of engagement.

We need to know not just who played, but:

- Who changed?
- Who stayed?
- Who improved—measurably and meaningfully?

The Metrics that Heal

In clinical medicine, we measure impact in mmHg, mg/dL, bpm, % HbA1c. Numbers with teeth. With consequences.

In gamified health interventions, we must identify our own equivalents. Not abstractions, but indicators tethered to outcomes.

Some of these may include:

- Adherence uplift: Was medication taken more regularly? For how long?
- Retention of information: Did reps recall key product facts after 3 weeks?
- Guideline compliance: Did HCP behavior align more closely with standards?
- User engagement depth: Did the player return not just often, but meaningfully?
- Emotional resonance: Did patients report feeling more supported or less alone?
- Behavioral milestones: Were health goals actually achieved—sleep improved, HbA1c reduced, steps walked?

Each of these metrics isn't just a number. It's a heartbeat—a signal of whether the gamified layer moved the needle on real-world health.

The Data behind the Delight

Consider the Mango Health app.

Its playful reminders and reward system led to a 20–30% boost in adherence among users with chronic conditions. But the real win was persistence: adherence was sustained for over 6 months. Not because it was flashy—but because it felt personal.

Or take AstraZeneca's gamified MSL training: 97% of users continued engaging well beyond mandatory modules. The badge was not the point—the sense of mastery was.

In Brazil, Abbott saw a 20% spike in sales force knowledge retention in just 5 days using gamified microlearning. No 200-slide deck needed. Just curiosity, challenge, and smart feedback.

These aren't anecdotes. They're clinical-grade signals of success.

How we Fail?

We've also learned from failures.

One oncology education app saw impressive signups—but HCP drop-off within 48 hours. Why?

The metrics said "engagement."

The experience was "confusing."

There was no feedback loop. No reward for reflection. Only content.

For example, in surgery, doctors learn: if the bleeding doesn't stop, the stitch didn't work—no matter how well it was tied.

In gamification, if behavior doesn't change, the game didn't work—no matter how well it looked.

Closing the Loop: Learning from the Metrics

Metrics, when done right, do more than evaluate. They inform the next design.

- A user disengages after level 2?

You redesign level 2.

- Reps game the quiz without reading?

You introduce scenario-based learning.

- Patients forget to log after week 3?

You personalize triggers, not push notifications.

Measurement is not the end of the design process. It's the engine of empathy-led iteration.

The Human behind the Number

Consider a physician treating a diabetic patient who never missed his appointments, smiled through sessions, and said all the right things. His charts, however, told a different story.

HbA1c: 9.1

Medication pickups: erratic

Step count: near zero

The doctor was not treating a body—he was treating a life in chaos.

The same applies to gamification. A 100% daily login means little if the patient still feels lost.

Real metrics must ask:

- Is the person thriving—not just complying?
- Is this intervention helping them live—not just log in?

What we Owe the Players?

Gamification isn't about making healthcare fun.

It's about making it bearable, motivating, empowering.

And that means holding ourselves to the same standard as medicine itself:

Evidence-based, outcome-driven, human-centered.

In the end, we measure not because we distrust our work, but because we care enough to know the truth.

And when the metrics tell us we've moved someone—even one step closer to health—that's not just a win.

That's a life changed.

Measuring Engagement: DAUs, MAUs, Stickiness, Compliance

There's a rhythm every surgeon learns to respect.

The pulse.

The breath.

The lab values that tell you whether your intervention is working—not just in theory, but inside a living, complex system.

In gamified health systems, we must look for that same rhythm.

Not in heartbeats—but in habit beats.

Because engagement is not about whether the app was downloaded.

It's about whether it became a part of someone's life.

And so, we measure.

But the truth is—just like vitals on a chart—numbers can deceive if we don't know what to ask of them.

The Myth of the Daily Active User (DAU)

Daily Active Users. It sounds reassuring.

Like checking in on a patient and finding them awake and talking.

Except—what if they're awake, but in pain? Talking, but disengaged?

A DAU tells us someone opened the app.

But not what they did.

Not whether it mattered.

Not if they came back tomorrow out of habit or obligation.

We've seen DAUs spike during marketing campaigns—only to fall like a stone after the rewards dried up.

A better question might be:

"What was the quality of that activity?"

Did the user complete a module? Enter meaningful data? Feel something?

DAU is a thermometer.

But we need to know if there's an infection or a healing response.

Monthly Active Users (MAU): The Long View

MAU gives us the broader landscape. The ability to say: this is not a passing fever. It's a trend.

In a diabetes gamification app, MAU stayed constant at 32,000 over six months. But deeper review showed a revolving door—old users dropped off, replaced by new ones drawn by ads.

It looked stable.

But it was, in truth, a churn machine.

In medicine, we track long-term outcomes—amputations prevented, complications reduced.

In gamification, we need the same: Are our MAUs the same people? Are they improving?

Stickiness: Where the Pulse Holds Steady

There's a term I love in behavioral design: stickiness.

It's not about glue.

It's about meaning.

Stickiness is the DAU/MAU ratio. In simple terms:

"Of all the people who use this app monthly, how many come back every day?"

In clinical terms, it's like asking:

"How often does the patient take their medicine?"

"Are they following the protocol not because they must, but because they want to?"

A 0.15 ratio is industry average.

But we've seen apps—like MySugr or Headspace—reach 0.30 or higher. Why?

Not because of badges.

Because of trust.

Because the app wasn't a task—it was a companion.

Compliance: The Metric with Consequences

Now we arrive at perhaps the most consequential metric in health gamification: compliance.

It's a loaded word. In medicine, it has often carried a paternalistic tone.

"Why didn't the patient comply?"

"Why didn't they follow instructions?"

But in gamification, compliance isn't about obedience.

It's about alignment.

Alignment between what the system prompts and what the user actually does.

- Did the patient take their medication at the right time?
- Did the rep complete the training and retain the knowledge?
- Did the doctor apply the guideline in a real patient case?

Compliance is where games cross into behavior change.

And behavior change is the holy grail.

What the Numbers Can't Say

I once talked to a young man after surgery for ulcerative colitis. He used an app to log symptoms, track diet, and monitor meds. His DAU? 100%.

Stickiness? Off the charts.

But he was also anxious, depressed, and exhausted by "doing it all right."

The metrics told one story.

His life told another.

Engagement is more than frequency.

It is agency, autonomy, emotion.

That's why the best-designed systems use qualitative feedback too.

Surveys.

Comments.

Biometrics.

Smiles.

Designing for Meaningful Engagement

Numbers matter. But not all numbers are equal.

- DAU tells us we were seen.
- MAU tells us we were remembered.
- Stickiness tells us we were relied upon.
- Compliance tells us we were trusted.

When all four align, it's like that moment in the OR when the bleeding stops, the vitals stabilize, and the team shares a quiet glance.

You don't need to say it.

You just know:

This worked.

KPIs in Gamification: What we Measure is What we Become

We often think of metrics as cold, clinical things.

But in surgery, as dotors have learned—what you choose to measure changes how you operate.

If you measure how fast you finish, you cut faster.

If you measure complications, you slow down and think.

Metrics are not neutral.

They shape behavior. They nudge culture.

In the world of gamification in pharma, KPIs are no different.

What we measure for a sales rep is not what we measure for a physician, or a patient managing a chronic disease.

Each comes with different motivations, limitations—and possibilities.

For Reps: From Script Pushing to Skill Building

I once spoke to a sales rep at a training session where the usual incentives—certificates, quiz scores, cash bonuses—were swapped out for an app that let them level up their product knowledge like it was a role-playing game.

She told me, "I'm competing with my own best version now."

That's a KPI shift.

What Matters?

- Knowledge Retention Rate

Not just "Did they read the slide?" but "Can they explain the MOA two weeks later?"

- Module Completion Time

How long does it take to internalize complex concepts?

- Peer Benchmarking

Not as punishment, but as friendly friction.

- Practice Simulations

Can the rep handle objections in virtual scenarios?

- Engagement Continuity

Are they returning even without rewards?

What it Tells Us

These KPIs show whether training is a checklist or a mindset shift.

When reps are voluntarily reviewing mechanisms of action at midnight on a Sunday… the game is working.

For HCPs: Precision, Not Points

Doctors don't have time.

They also don't suffer fools—or games that feel like games.

And yet, when one hospital introduced a gamified clinical guideline adherence tool, something fascinating happened.

Compliance with evidence-based treatment jumped by 40%.

Why?

Because the game wasn't a distraction.

It was a mirror—showing HCPs where they stood.

What Matters?

- Clinical Scenario Accuracy

Are they choosing treatments aligned with guidelines?

- Time-to-Decision

Especially in simulations—does speed affect correctness?

- CME Credit Accumulation

Is the platform fulfilling educational needs?

- Peer Comparison (Anonymized)

Are they willing to benchmark themselves?

- Guideline Adherence Delta

Behavior before vs. after gameplay.

What it Tells Us

For HCPs, the KPI is not volume—it's quality of cognition.

They want meaningful, case-based learning that doesn't feel like pandering.

The right KPIs here create clarity, not clutter.

For Patients: From Pill Reminders to Life Empowerment

Here's the hard truth: we can't gamify someone into wanting to be well.

But we can make the path to wellness feel less lonely.

A Type 2 diabetes patient I know once showed me their dashboard on MySugr:

"Your monster is shrinking!" it read.

She laughed. But she also started taking her meds more consistently.

It wasn't the leaderboard.

It was the story of her progress—told back to her.

What Matters?

- Adherence to Medication Schedule

The foundational metric.

- Self-Reported Symptom Logging

Frequency and completeness.

- Steps Taken / Activity Logs (via Wearables)

Movement is medicine.

- Engagement with Educational Content

Are they just clicking? Or completing?

- Mood/Emotion Check-Ins

Especially in mental health or oncology support apps.

- Challenge Completion

Did they finish a 7-day streak? Did they come back after failure?

What it Tells Us

Patient KPIs must honor vulnerability.

Each data point is not a judgment—it's a breadcrumb on a journey back to self-efficacy.

And sometimes, the most powerful metric isn't how often they showed up, but whether they believed they could.

Beyond Numbers: The Shared Thread

In all three groups—Reps, HCPs, Patients—there is one golden KPI that cannot be coded.

It's the unprompted return.

When someone comes back not because they were told to…

But because they wanted to.

That's engagement. That's trust. That's behavior transformed.

That's what every good surgeon, every honest designer, and every ethical marketer is really aiming for.

The Infinit Study: When Research became a Game—and a Habit

In medicine, we often ask:

What makes patients stick with the plan?

We create protocols. We schedule follow-ups.

We prescribe medications, deliver printed handouts, set up hotlines.

But sometimes, what holds everything together is something simpler.

A nudge. A narrative. A point scored on a screen.

That was the premise behind the Infinit Research Study.

It began in the quiet corridors of a Canadian hospital and ended up making waves across the world of clinical adherence science.

The Problem: When Participation Fades

Clinical trials struggle with retention.

Not because patients don't care—but because life gets in the way.

Reminders get ignored. Diaries stay blank.

Even the most altruistic participants—those who sign up for science—can forget to log in, weigh themselves, report symptoms.

The Infinit study asked:

What if participation didn't feel like compliance?

What if it felt like play?

The Experiment: A Gamified App for Patients with Hypertension and High Cardiovascular Risk

The researchers built a mobile app, but this one came with missions and milestones.

Patients could:

- Log their blood pressure
- Track medication intake
- Complete health quizzes

- Earn badges for consistent entries
- Compete gently on anonymous leaderboards
- Set streak goals—"7 Days of Success," "BP Ninja," "Hydration Hero"

The game mechanics were not ornamental—they were intentional behavior design tools.

But this wasn't just about bells and whistles.

The app was integrated into the trial protocol for chronic disease management.

This was not a side experiment.

This was the study.

The Outcomes: When Games become Daily Rituals

The results were more than promising.

They were clinical.

- Medication Adherence improved by 25% in the gamified cohort compared to standard digital reminders.
- Blood Pressure Control saw significant improvements, particularly in the subgroup that completed more than 80% of the missions.
- Time-in-App far exceeded projections—some participants spent 10+ minutes per day engaging voluntarily, compared to 2 minutes for non-gamified versions.

But more importantly:

Patient Self-Efficacy Scores increased.

People reported feeling in charge—not managed.

One patient said, "This is the first time I felt like my blood pressure was mine to beat, not just a number my doctor shook his head at."

That's not just engagement.

That's ownership.

The Narrative behind the Numbers

Gamification didn't just boost compliance.

It built connection—between patient and purpose, between daily choices and long-term outcomes.

In one of the interviews, a 52-year-old man with previously uncontrolled hypertension said:

"Every time I completed a week, I felt like I was leveling up—not just in the app, but in my life."

Another participant said she didn't care about points—

but she did care when her app said:

"You just hit a 14-day streak. Your future heart thanks you."

What it Means

The Infinit Study didn't find a magic trick.

It found something more durable: a framework for behavioral scaffolding.

It reminded us that in medicine, what works often lies just outside the clinic—in the spaces between our visits, in the small feedback loops that keep people returning to themselves.

Gamification, at its best, isn't about making disease fun.

It's about making health a quest worth continuing.

The Telltale Numbers: When 60% More Entries Meant 30% Fewer Goodbyes

It's a quiet but familiar failure in modern medicine.

You start a clinical trial with 500 patients. You end with 312.

No one storms out in protest.

No one slams the app shut in rage.

They just fade.

A missed entry here.

A delayed follow-up there.

Until participation becomes a ghost of its enthusiastic beginning.

That's why researchers in the Infinit Study didn't just count how many participants joined.

They counted how many stayed.

And more curiously—why they stayed.

Logging the Invisible

It turned out the answer wasn't just reminders, or rewards, or reports.

It was something deeper.

Each time a patient completed a log—entered their blood pressure, tapped in their weight, noted how they were feeling—it was more than just data.

It was a vote of intention.

A whisper that said:

"I still care."

And then, the gamified app changed the rules of this invisible game.

Every entry became:

A micro-win ("You're 80% closer to this week's goal!")

A challenge accepted ("Can you go 3 more days without skipping?")

A self-directed act of care

The Numbers Came Alive

Suddenly, data logging didn't feel like homework.

It felt like a ritual.

Patients logged 60% more entries than in the control group.

Sixty. Percent. More.

That's not a marginal gain.

That's a transformation in patient presence.

And here's where it got even more interesting:

The dropout rate?

Down 30%.

A number that stunned even the clinicians, who were used to chalking up attrition to "human nature."

But this time, human nature was nudged differently.

A patient who might've forgotten—or felt overwhelmed—was gently looped back in.

Through a badge. A reminder. A personalized nudge.

Not from a nurse, but from a well-designed system that felt like it was on their side.

Why it Worked?

Not because people became more disciplined.

But because the system became more human.

In exit interviews, participants didn't talk about "compliance."

They talked about confidence.

One patient said:

"It felt like someone noticed when I did the right thing… so I kept doing it."

And another:

"Every time I almost quit, the app said: 'Let's just finish today. 'And I thought, okay—today I can do."

From Numbers to Narratives

That's the secret gamification offers to healthcare:

Not manipulation.

Motivation.

Not gimmicks.

Guidance.

In the end, 60% more data entries told us less about dashboards, and more about hearts and habits.

And 30% fewer dropouts?

That's not a statistic.

That's hundreds of patients who stayed in the story.

Who chose to keep playing.

Who, for one more day, didn't give up.

Chapter 13

Ethics in the Game

We tend to think of games as innocent.

Harmless fun. A reward after the hard work is done.

But what if the game is the work?

What if the very act of taking your medicine, logging your symptoms, or answering an oncology quiz was turned into a game—complete with points, streaks, leaderboards, badges?

That's the frontier we've arrived at in pharmaceutical marketing.

And as with any new frontier, there's power.

And there's peril.

The Design that Nudges—and Nudges Too Far

I met a digital strategist who once proudly said,

"We can keep a patient engaged longer than Netflix can."

He wasn't joking.

Using variable rewards, progress bars, and even peer pressure mechanics, the gamified app his team built doubled patient interaction time.

But I found myself asking: At what cost?

If a pharma-sponsored app keeps a hypertensive patient logging in twice a day—but won't let them skip a screen without watching an ad for a new combination therapy—is that education? Or exploitation?

The Slippery Slope of Manipulation

Gamification works because it understands psychology.

- And psychology, as it turns out, is vulnerable.
- Scarcity dynamics ("Only 3 chances left to earn this badge!")

- Fear of missing out ("Your peers have completed this—have you?")
- Loss aversion ("You're about to lose your 7-day streak!")

These aren't merely persuasive.

They're persuasive technology—a term coined by Stanford's BJ Fogg, who also warned that such systems, when misused, become weapons rather than tools.

What begins as motivation can tilt toward coercion—especially when the player is a patient, vulnerable, or in pain.

Who Owns the Behavior?

There's another question—one less about tactics and more about trust.

When a pharma company uses gamification to drive patient adherence or rep behavior, whose interest is being served?

- Is the game helping the patient get better?
- Or is it optimizing market share?

Often, the answer is both.

But the ethics live in the balance.

And that balance must be transparent.

When a behavior is shaped, the source of the nudge should be visible.

And the intent behind it should be clear.

Because otherwise, we're not treating patients like participants in care.

We're treating them like lab rats with dopamine levers.

Design with Dignity

At Johns Hopkins, during trials of a gamified rehab tool, developers noticed something small but profound:

Patients felt patronized when the app sounded too cheerful, too childish.

"Don't talk to me like I'm five," one stroke survivor told the team.

So they redesigned the voice.

The tone became more respectful, the graphics more mature.

Engagement improved.

But more importantly—so did dignity.

Transparency. Consent. Autonomy.

These are not bonus features in a gamified system.

They are foundations.

Patients must know what data is collected, who sees it, and how it's used.

They must be free to opt out without being punished by the game mechanics.

And the system must allow for autonomy—not just compliance.

Otherwise, we're building systems that don't heal.

They hook.

The Ethics of Winning

In games, someone always wins.

In healthcare, the stakes are different.

If a pharma rep "wins" by mastering product info, if a doctor "wins" by improving treatment adherence, if a patient "wins" by managing their disease better—then the game works.

But when the game is designed solely to capture more attention, more prescriptions, more clicks—without care—then we lose something larger.

We lose the very essence of medicine:

Not just treatment, but trust.

So, What's the Score?

Gamification in pharma is not inherently ethical or unethical.

It is a medium.

Like a scalpel, it can heal—or harm—depending on how it's used.

So, we must ask:

- Does it empower the user?
- Does it support clinical goals?
- Does it preserve patient dignity?

If the answer is yes, the game is worth playing.

If not, it's time to change the rules.

Motivation vs. Manipulation

Some years ago, I sat across from a teenage girl with Type 1 diabetes.

She hated her insulin routine. Hated the reminders. Hated the pokes.

But she loved one thing.

A dragon.

A digital one.

Every time she recorded her glucose, fed herself right, or injected her dose, her dragon grew stronger. It earned wings. Then fire. Eventually, it soared.

The app was part of a clinical trial.

The goal was clear: create motivation where none existed.

And it worked.

But then I asked her: Would you still log your data if the dragon didn't grow?

She thought for a moment.

"No," she said. "What's the point?"

That's when it hit me.

What we call motivation is often something else entirely.

The Invisible Line

In medicine, we strive to inspire people to take agency in their care.

To follow up. To change habits. To listen and adapt.

But in the digital world, persuasion has grown fangs.

Apps are now designed by behavioral psychologists.

Interfaces trigger dopamine hits.

Designs leverage loss aversion, social proof, variable rewards.

It is not always clear anymore:

Are we encouraging behavior?

Or are we engineering it?

The line between motivation and manipulation has become exquisitely thin.

When the Game Plays You

Take the leaderboard.

It works.

We've seen medical reps double their participation in training modules when they can climb ranks.

But what if the leaderboard resets weekly and constantly shows you below your peers?

What if the only way to catch up is to keep logging in late at night?

Now it's no longer about motivation.

It's pressure posing as play.

Or consider streaks—the gold standard of habit design.

They build consistency. But break one, and the app shames you with red flashes, disappearing progress, or even loss of access.

At that point, you're not playing a game.

You're playing not to lose.

And that's manipulation.

The Four Questions

In surgical training, doctors were taught to ask four questions before every decision:

1. Does this benefit the patient?
2. Does it respect their dignity?
3. Does it support autonomy?
4. Would I recommend it to someone I love?

We must ask the same of gamified systems.

- If a patient adheres to medication because an app rewards them with points, is that okay?
- What if the same system sells anonymized behavior data to advertisers?
- What if it nudges a switch to a more expensive brand?

Where, exactly, does motivation end and manipulation begin?

The answer, I suspect, is not in outcomes alone.

It lies in intent.

And in transparency.

Behavioral Design with a Soul

The best systems respect the player.

They don't shame.

They don't trap.

They don't confuse urgency with importance.

Motivation aligns incentives.

Manipulation distorts them.

Motivation says: "You can."

Manipulation whispers: "You must."

The Telltale Signs

When pharma marketers build gamified campaigns—whether for HCP education, patient adherence, or wellness behavior—they must learn to spot the red flags:

- Are we using fear to drive clicks?
- Are we hiding friction behind flashy UI?
- Are we collecting data the user didn't consent to?

These are not merely design flaws.

They're ethical cracks.

Motivation thrives in light.

Manipulation grows in the shadows.

Back to the Dragon

That girl and her dragon?

She eventually transitioned off the app.

But something interesting happened.

She had internalized the habit, even if the dragon vanished.

It didn't matter that it started as a game.

It ended with self-efficacy.

That is the key.

When gamification is done well, it doesn't trap users in a loop.

It frees them from it.

Where we Stand?

In an era of persuasive technologies, we must learn to build not just sticky systems—but ethical ones.

Because in healthcare, the game we're playing isn't about clicks, badges, or dashboards.

It's about trust.

And transformation.

And we should never forget:

Manipulation controls.

Motivation empowers.

And that difference is everything.

When Games Go Too Far: The Perils of Dark Patterns and Over-Gamification

Not long ago, I spoke with a clinical pharmacist who had been piloting a new gamified app aimed at medication adherence in patients with heart failure.

The idea was elegant: patients earned points for every day they logged their weight, took their pills, avoided sodium. These points converted into little digital rewards—badges, fireworks, avatars in white coats applauding.

But something strange began to happen.

One patient—a retired schoolteacher—became obsessive.

He weighed himself three times a day.

He restricted food far beyond clinical recommendations.

He began to game the app—inputting phantom behaviors just to keep his streak alive.

When the app updated its algorithm, wiping his 93-day streak due to "data inconsistency," he stopped using it altogether. And worse—he stopped taking his medication.

He told the pharmacist:

"If I'm just going to lose everything with one slip, what's the point?"

The game that was meant to help had become a trigger.

It wasn't just ineffective. It was harmful.

The Lure of the Loop

Gamification, at its best, is powerful.

It can motivate the unmotivated.

Nudge patients toward better behaviors.

Make clinical education feel like discovery rather than duty.

But behind its colorful surfaces, there's something more primal at play—addiction architecture.

Variable rewards.

Scarcity timers.

Social comparison.

Endless scrolling mechanics.

What works in mobile gaming—to keep thumbs twitching and eyes glued—doesn't always belong in healthcare.

And when we blindly import these designs, we invite dark patterns in.

What are Dark Patterns?

Coined by UX designer Harry Brignull in 2010, dark patterns are designs that trick users into actions not in their best interest.

In pharma gamification, they wear lab coats:

- A streak counter that resets without warning.
- A leaderboard that shames more than it inspires.
- Consent forms buried three clicks deep in animated rewards.
- Notifications that mimic alerts from clinicians but are really marketing nudges.

The user is drawn in not by purpose, but by deception.

It's not motivation.

It's manipulation.

And worse—it's cloaked in the name of health.

The Tyranny of the Badge

Consider the badge.

It sounds harmless. Encouraging, even.

But I once encountered a nurse practitioner who told me about a training module that gamified continuing medical education. Practitioners earned a digital badge for every completed course.

The twist?

Their completion rate and badge count were displayed on an internal leaderboard. Managers began using those numbers for performance reviews.

One HCP confided:

"I wasn't learning. I was skimming just to get the badge."

The system rewarded completion, not comprehension.

The game was being played—but the purpose was lost.

When Engagement becomes Exploitation

Every time a pharma marketer uses game mechanics, they must ask:

Who benefits from this loop?

If a diabetes app rewards blood glucose logging, but hides upsells for premium insulin reminders behind the next level—whose interest is it serving?

If a digital platform gamifies adherence but collects behavioral data for marketing segmentation—where's the ethical boundary?

Engagement, in and of itself, is not the goal.

Health is.

Trust is.

Patient empowerment is.

And when engagement becomes exploitation, we haven't just failed the user.

We've violated the sanctity of healthcare.

The Myth of "More is Better"

Over-gamification is often driven by a seductive idea:

If a little game works, a lot must work better.

But the truth is more nuanced.

- Too many mechanics create cognitive overload.
- Too many rewards dilute meaning.
- Too much competition fosters anxiety, not collaboration.

A gamified oncology simulation tried to include leaderboards, timers, badges, peer chats, boss levels, and story arcs—all in one interface.

One physician's feedback?

"It felt like trying to solve cancer while inside a pinball machine."

Gamification must simplify, not scatter.

It should serve the learning, not steal attention.

Toward Ethical Gamification

So what do we do?

We design for dignity.

We audit our assumptions.

We test for harm, not just engagement.

And we remember:

- A game mechanic is not just a feature. It's a force.
- Once unleashed, it shapes behavior—sometimes subtly, sometimes profoundly.
- And like any medicine, it must be dosed responsibly.

A Closing Thought

A game is not just play.

It's architecture for behavior.

And in the temple of healthcare, we are not just builders.

We are custodians of trust.

So when we gamify, we must ask:

- Are we lifting patients and professionals toward better choices?
- Or are we nudging them toward outcomes that suit us more than them?

Because in the end, it's not about how clever the game is.

It's about whether it helps someone heal.

The Fine Print of Trust: Data Privacy, Consent, and Fairness in the Age of Health Gamification

In the early days of surgical residency, doctors learn that the most important part of a procedure wasn't the scalpel. It was the informed consent.

Before touching a patient's body, they had to sit down—face to face—and explain. Not just what they were going to do, but why. What could go wrong. What their other options were. And, most importantly, that they had the right to say no.

That's what gave the profession its moral spine.

And now, in the gleaming world of digital health and gamified pharma tools, I wonder:

Are we honoring that same principle? Or are we slicing deeper than we realize—without permission?

The Data that Smiles Back

Imagine a teenager with epilepsy, using a gamified app to track medication adherence. It's clever—animated rewards for every dose, mini-games that reinforce safety tips, friendly avatars reminding them to log side effects.

But behind the scenes, that app is collecting data.

- Timestamps.
- Dosage adherence.
- Mood scores.
- Even device location.

None of that is inherently unethical.

But what if that data is sold to an analytics company…

Which sells it to a marketing agency…

Which then uses it to profile the teen's household for targeted ads?

All without the patient—or their parent—truly understanding.

The game gave them a badge.

But took their privacy.

And unlike a scalpel, this cut is invisible.

Consent isn't a Checkbox

We live in an era of "click to agree."

And nowhere is that more dangerous than in healthcare.

Gamified apps often present long, legalistic privacy policies buried under layers of colorful interface design. The dopamine hits of points and progress can drown out the gravity of what's being signed away.

Consent becomes a formality.

Not a conversation.

But health data isn't like music preferences or shopping history.

It's sacred. It's sensitive.

It can shape how you're treated by insurers, employers, even governments.

When a parent consents to a gamified asthma tracker for their child, do they know the data may be used to evaluate medication efficacy—and shared with payers?

When a patient logs their anxiety levels in a wellness app that rewards journaling streaks, do they realize that aggregated insights might train a model used to target vulnerable users?

If they don't know, can we call it consent at all?

The Uneven Playing Field

Gamification often relies on patterns—what people do, when, and how often.

But what if those patterns reflect privilege?

A digital platform might reward patients who log symptoms daily.

But what about the ones who can't afford a smartphone? Or those living in areas with unstable internet?

It might score physicians on how many CME modules they finish each week.

But what about the rural doctor with night shifts and no time to "play"?

Suddenly, what began as a motivational tool becomes a sorting mechanism.

One that rewards the already advantaged, and punishes the marginalized—quietly, systematically.

A patient's behavior isn't just a signal.

It becomes a score.

A judgment.

Fairness, in gamification, is not just about giving everyone the same game.

It's about understanding the context in which they play.

From Data Points to People

We like to believe that more data means better decisions.

But in medicine, data divorced from empathy is dangerous.

A rep's response rate.

A physician's completion metric.

A patient's login streak.

These are numbers.

Useful, yes.

But incomplete.

They don't tell you the rep was caring for a sick parent.

That the physician was in the field with Doctors Without Borders.

That the patient's depression made it hard to get out of bed—let alone click a screen.

Gamification risks reducing life into leaderboards.

But people are not just players.

They are human beings with stories.

And if we forget that, we lose the very essence of healthcare.

The Real Game

Ultimately, this isn't a question of technology.

It's a question of values.

We must design systems where:

- Consent is ongoing, not one-time.

- Privacy is the default, not an opt-out.
- Fairness is built in, not retrofitted.

We must be willing to slow down the game—to ask what kind of behavior we are shaping, and for whose benefit.

Because trust, once broken, cannot be gamified back.

A Closing Reflection

There's a saying in surgery:

"You can fix a mistake with a scalpel. You cannot fix betrayal."

Gamification in pharma can be revolutionary.

But it walks a tightrope.

Between motivation and manipulation.

Between support and surveillance.

Between innovation and intrusion.

We must choose wisely.

Because the game we're designing is not just for profit or performance.

It's about people's lives.

And in that game, the stakes couldn't be higher.

The Hidden Rulebook: Playing by Regulations in the Game of Health

When asked what do you think is the hardest part of becoming a surgeon, the leading surgeon replied, "When I was in medical school, I thought the hardest part of becoming a surgeon would be the knowledge—the anatomy, the physiology, the dexterity of the hands. But, it wasn't.

The hardest part was learning the rules.

Not just of surgery, but of the system that surrounded it.

Rules of what you could say, document, share, disclose, hide.

Rules written in codes—ethical, legal, bureaucratic."

And now, as gamification becomes the new language of patient engagement, those rules are being tested again.

Apps that reward behavior.

Platforms that nudge decisions.

Games that collect, analyze, adapt.

They look like fun.

But beneath the surface, there's a tightrope of regulation.

And those who walk it must learn a new kind of balance.

The FDA: Between Innovation and Oversight

The U.S. Food and Drug Administration is not a villain.

It's a reluctant referee in a game that moves faster than it ever expected.

Traditionally, the FDA regulated drugs, devices, diagnostics.

But what happens when a mobile app offers a cognitive behavioral game to reduce anxiety—and actually works?

Is it a toy?

A treatment?

A medical device?

The line is blurry.

That's why the FDA created its Digital Health Software Precertification Program—an attempt to understand, assess, and approve software that behaves like medicine but evolves like technology.

Take Akili's EndeavorRx, the first FDA-approved prescription video game for ADHD in children.

It wasn't reviewed like a toy. It underwent clinical trials. It produced measurable outcomes.

But the FDA faces a dilemma:

Gamified tools often update in real-time.

Algorithms adjust. Interfaces change. Features evolve weekly.

How do you regulate a moving target?

The FDA is trying.

But it's like drafting traffic laws while riding shotgun in a self-driving car.

HIPAA: Guarding the Sanctity of the Health Record

In America, there's a law that stalks every hospital hallway and healthcare startup:

HIPAA—the Health Insurance Portability and Accountability Act.

It tells us what we can do with Protected Health Information—names, test results, insurance IDs, diagnoses, device data.

It's a guardian of confidentiality.

But here's the catch:

HIPAA applies only to covered entities—hospitals, insurers, and the vendors they contract.

That diabetes app you downloaded?

If it's not directly linked to your hospital or doctor, it might not be bound by HIPAA at all.

Gamified health tools live in this strange space.

They straddle the line between healthcare provider and consumer tech.

Between medical adherence tool and wellness platform.

They may collect heart rate, sleep patterns, medication logs—but unless tethered to a healthcare provider, HIPAA might look the other way.

And that creates a troubling loophole.

Because patients—especially vulnerable ones—don't read terms of service.

They trust the design.

They believe in the badge and the buzz.

But what happens to their data—who sees it, sells it, or mines it—is often unclear.

In gamification, HIPAA doesn't always whistle the foul.

GDPR: Europe's Game-Changer

If the FDA is a referee and HIPAA is a fence, GDPR—the General Data Protection Regulation of the European Union—is a full-blown rulebook with penalties.

In 2018, GDPR changed the world.

It made data ownership a citizen's right.

It required explicit consent, data minimization, purpose limitation, and the right to be forgotten.

For gamified pharma tools in Europe, this is serious business.

Imagine a gamified platform that tracks pill intake, offers rewards for streaks, and sends reminders via WhatsApp.

Under GDPR:

- You must state what data you collect, why, and for how long.
- You must obtain freely given, specific, informed consent—not buried in small print.
- You must allow users to opt out, access, and erase their data.
- You must disclose if algorithms make automated decisions.

If you fail, the consequences aren't a slap on the wrist.

They can be 4% of your global revenue.

GDPR doesn't care how innovative your app is.

It cares whether you treated the person behind the data as a person, not just a data point.

And in that, it reminds us of something medicine sometimes forgets.

The Ethical Thread Across them All

Whether it's FDA approval, HIPAA compliance, or GDPR enforcement, these regulations share a common thread:

They are not just about what we can build.

They are about what we should build.

Regulations, at their best, are the guardrails of innovation.

Not to stifle creativity, but to channel it responsibly.

Gamification in healthcare is seductive.

It can motivate, engage, and transform.

But it can also manipulate, distract, and exploit.

The rules are there not to punish risk—but to prevent harm.

And when we build within those boundaries, we do more than protect ourselves legally.

We protect the trust that underpins healthcare.

A Final Thought

In surgery, when a new tool arrives—a new stapler, a robotic arm, a laser—the surgeons don't just ask if it works.

They ask:

- Is it safe?
- Is it proven?
- Are we using it for the right reasons?

Gamification needs that same scrutiny.

Because in the game of health, the players are real people.

And the outcomes are not just points—but lives.

Chapter 14

Where Gamification Fails – Lessons from Misfires

In medicine, doctors are taught that failure is a teacher.

You dissect what went wrong.

You trace the missed cues.

You examine the flatlines not to place blame—but to learn.

Gamification in healthcare—when it fails—leaves no postmortem on the screen. But if you listen closely, you can still hear the heartbeats of good intentions that went silent.

These are not cautionary tales meant to scare us off.

They are meant to tune our ears to what truly matters.

The Game No One Played

At a conference in Barcelona, a digital health company unveiled a gleaming app for medication adherence. It had the works—points, progress bars, leaderboards, a friendly avatar who reminded users to "take your statin!"

The company had partnered with a major pharmaceutical player. The budget was generous. The interface was gorgeous. But three months in, 80% of users had stopped using the app.

Not because it crashed.

Not because it was confusing.

But because it didn't matter.

It hadn't asked why patients forget pills. It hadn't addressed fatigue, fear, financial strain. It had gamified the wrong pain point.

The game mechanics were solid.

The human mechanics were not.

When Competition Undermines Care

In another case, a hospital network introduced a gamified CME platform for physicians. They could earn badges, climb a leaderboard, and receive recognition at grand rounds.

But something odd began to happen.

Doctors started skipping modules that weren't scored.

They focused on "winning" points instead of absorbing nuance.

Peer rivalry edged out collaboration. The "why" was replaced by the "how fast."

What had been designed as a tool for mastery devolved into a race for metrics.

Gamification, it turns out, can produce the opposite of what you intend—when the goal becomes the game.

The Overjustification Trap

There's an old concept in psychology: the overjustification effect.

It's what happens when external rewards crowd out internal ones. A child who loves to draw starts getting gold stars for every sketch—and suddenly, drawing feels like work.

In health gamification, this happens quietly.

A wellness app gave users points for walking 10,000 steps. It worked—until the points stopped. So did the walking.

Behavior change collapsed when the rewards stopped arriving. There was no lasting transformation—just conditional compliance.

Because badges can't replace belief.

And points don't build purpose.

The Avatar that Mocked You

One mental health app used an animated avatar that cheered users when they completed emotional check-ins. But it also frowned when they skipped days.

One patient reported feeling judged by the cartoon face.

Another said the avatar's disappointment reminded her of her father.

The design was clever.

But the impact was cruel.

What began as a behavioral nudge became a source of shame—a gamified trigger that deepened emotional distress.

This is where gamification tiptoes into dangerous terrain.

When empathy is replaced by emotionless interaction, we build walls instead of bridges.

The Story behind the Numbers

A pharmaceutical rep once told me about a training module her company gamified.

It was fast-paced, full of interactive quizzes, and designed to mimic real-life scenarios. Reps scored well. The completion rate was high. The dashboard was green.

But out in the field, reps faltered.

Why?

Because the game had trained recall, not resilience.

It hadn't prepared them for rejection, for the tough questions, for the human complexity of HCP conversations.

Learning is not the same as mastery.

And simulation is not the same as preparation.

The game had taught the answers.

It hadn't taught the work.

The False Promise of Universality

A final example: a global pharma campaign rolled out a gamified app across 17 countries. It worked brilliantly in Western Europe. But in rural India, adoption was dismal.

Why?

The app assumed smartphones.

It assumed high-speed internet.

It assumed that cultural norms embraced competitive play.

In reality, some users shared devices. Some felt alienated by leaderboards. Some found the visual design juvenile or Western.

Gamification, when treated as universal, fails at the level of lived experience.

Designing games without context is like writing prescriptions without taking a history.

What we Learn from the Misfires

When gamification fails in healthcare, it often fails because:

- It prizes engagement metrics over meaningful connection.
- It builds incentives but forgets empathy.
- It pursues scale but ignores story.
- It uses mechanics without understanding motives.

The lesson is not to gamify less.

The lesson is to gamify with care.

To start with the human.

To understand the burden, not just the behavior.

To build play, not pressure.

Because in healthcare, the point is not the points.

It's the people.

A Closing Reflection

In surgery, doctors don't abandon a tool because it failed once.

They review.They adapt. They ask better questions.

We get closer to what matters.

Gamification is a tool.

When it works, it inspires.

When it fails, it teaches.

And if we're willing to listen to its misfires, it can become not just a game we play—but a practice we refine.

Tokenization without Motivation: When the Game Loses its Soul

Not long ago, I spoke with a patient—let's call her Maria—who had been prescribed a mobile health app to manage her hypertension. Every time she logged her blood pressure, the app gave her a little gold token. When she completed five days in a row, the tokens stacked. There were fireworks on the screen. A digital confetti explosion. It was all very… cheerful.

But Maria wasn't smiling.

She told me:

"I'm not sure what those coins are for. They just show up. But nothing changes."

She had the tokens.

What she didn't have was the will to care about them.

The Illusion of Engagement

In our rush to gamify health, we often conflate activity with engagement.

We think that if a screen flashes or a badge dings, behavior has changed.

But the reality is subtler—and more sobering.

Tokens, points, badges—they are symbols.

They're supposed to represent progress.

But if they're not anchored in meaning, they become noise.

Noise that clutters the interface.

Noise that clouds intention.

Noise that masks the fact that nothing, deep down, has actually shifted.

The Empty Trophy Syndrome

This happens in surgical training, too.

Residents now earn points for completing simulation modules. Their names go up on a board. They win lunch with attendings. On paper, they're more "engaged" than ever.

But when the OR doors swing open and the scalpel is in their hand, the real test begins.

Did they just chase points?

Or did they absorb purpose?

You can earn a hundred digital tokens and still fail to care.

Because trophies without triumph are just trinkets.

Designing for Checklists, Not Change

Many digital health tools are designed like checklists with sparkle.

Take your meds? ✔

Log your steps? ✔

Watch a video? ✔

Here's a coin. Here's a badge. Here's an avatar dancing.

But ask the user what it's all for, and the answers taper off.

Gamification has become, in too many cases, a layer of glitter on an unchanged habit. It lacks narrative. It lacks emotional arc. It lacks why.

Motivation is a Story, Not a Score

What drives real health behavior isn't accumulation—it's meaning.

It's the father who wants to walk his daughter down the aisle.

The young woman who wants her skin to clear before her wedding.

The retired teacher who wants to feel sharp enough to finish the novel he's started three times.

These are stories.

They have stakes.

They can't be replaced with tokens.

If gamification doesn't tap into that story—if it substitutes trinkets for transformation—it becomes a hollow exercise.

A machine that prints stickers no one sticks to.

The Work of Real Motivation

Designing for motivation is harder. It requires:

- Listening before coding
- Purpose before platform
- Empathy before engine

It asks:

"Why should this matter to the person using it—on the worst day, not just the best?"

A leading doctor told me, "In my practice, I've seen patients who ignore flashing red reminders... but perk up at a note from their doctor that says, 'You've done so well this month. Keep going—I'm proud of you."

That's human motivation.

And it cannot be tokenized.

The Better Game

If gamification is to be part of the future of health—and I believe it should be—it has to evolve.

Not by stacking more tokens.

But by asking:

"What does this person care about—and how can we help them get there?"

In medicine, doctors learn the hard way that numbers don't always mean health.

Vitals can look stable while the soul collapses.

In gamification, the same holds true.

You can have all the tokens in the world—and still be losing the game.

Unless we build in meaning.

Unless we build in motivation.

Bad Game Design: When the Game Itself is the Problem

We've all done it.

Downloaded an app that promised to make life easier, healthier, more fun.

And then—five minutes in—we closed it.

Uninstalled.

Forgot it ever existed.

The problem wasn't our attention span.

It was the game.

When Play Feels Like Work

I remember visiting a health tech startup in Boston, where a young team had designed a gamified physical therapy app for post-operative patients. It had all the bells and whistles—points for movements, animations to guide exercises, a virtual mascot that cheered you on.

But by week two, dropout rates were soaring.

One patient said:

"I kept doing the same stretch… and it kept giving me the same badge. Nothing changed. I didn't even know if I was doing it right."

Another added:

"It felt like being graded by a robot… with no teacher in the room."

What had been intended as encouragement became surveillance.

What was supposed to be engaging turned repetitive.

And worse—unrewarding.

Gamification, in this case, became chore-ification.

The Tyranny of Leaderboards

One oncology rep told me about a learning module where sales reps across regions were ranked on a leaderboard after completing training tasks.

At first, it sparked excitement.

But soon, the top spots were dominated by a handful of over-achievers.

The rest saw no way to catch up.

"It just made me feel worse," she admitted.

"I stopped opening the app."

What began as friendly competition devolved into status anxiety.

And instead of fostering participation, the game design inadvertently enforced disengagement.

Too Much, Too Soon

There's a subtle art to designing games that ramp up—that build mastery and challenge over time.

But some apps throw everything at the user at once—buttons blinking, timers ticking, levels unlocking in a cascade of confusion.

One MSL training program had a mini-game embedded inside each chapter.

Within ten minutes, you had to collect molecules, dodge virus particles, drag data points into line graphs, and answer trivia—all in rapid succession.

The intent was noble: to reinforce learning.

But the outcome?

"I felt like I was playing a game inside a game inside a spreadsheet," one user wrote in their feedback.

"I just wanted to understand the drug's mechanism of action."

In medicine, doctors often discuss the cognitive load—how too much information, delivered too quickly, can lead to shutdown.

Bad game design forgets that principle.

When Design Ignores the Human

Great games—even simple ones—feel alive. They speak to you. They adapt. They respect your time.

Bad game design doesn't.

It assumes that all users are the same—with the same attention span, goals, needs.

It forgets that patients in pain don't want fireworks.

That HCPs juggling back-to-back appointments don't want puzzles.

That sales reps on the road need clarity, not complexity.

And most of all—it forgets why people came to the app in the first place:

Not to be impressed.

But to be helped.

Games that Frustrate are Games that Fail

The danger in pharma gamification isn't just wasted effort.

It's the erosion of trust.

When users feel confused, they disengage.

When they feel patronized, they rebel.

And when they feel nothing at all, you've lost them for good.

Because if a game is boring, users blame themselves.

But if a game is frustrating—they blame you.

The Way Forward

Gamification isn't a panacea.

It's a design choice. And like all choices in healthcare, it must be guided by:

- Empathy for the person using it
- Clarity about what the experience is trying to accomplish
- Humility to admit when the design isn't working

Games are not about technology.

They're about humans in motion—their motivations, rhythms, and realities.

Design for those.

Design with care.

And maybe, just maybe, the game will be worth playing.

When we Forget why the Game Works

In 2018, A health-tech company in San Francisco did a design sprint.

Their goal: to create a gamified app for improving adherence among adolescents with asthma.

There were UI designers, machine learning engineers, product managers—even an Oculus developer.

Everyone was speaking in acronyms:

APIs. DAUs. UX flows. XR simulations.

The energy was palpable.

But there was one person missing from the room.

A behavioral psychologist.

And before long, it showed.

The Shiny Object Problem

They built an elegant interface.

Push notifications appeared like magical reminders.

There were rewards, avatars, even virtual pets that "thrived" when you took your medication.

But users dropped out.

Fast.

Some found the app annoying.

Others didn't understand what the rewards meant.

One teen said flatly:

"I don't care about fake pets. I just want my lungs to work."

It was a classic mistake.

Designing for the platform, not the person.

Tech Can't Outsmart Psychology

Gamification is a beautiful confluence of science and art—of interface and insight.

But in the rush to build "the next big thing," pharma marketers often lean heavily into the tech—algorithms, dashboards, token systems—assuming technology is motivation.

It's not.

Behavioral change isn't engineered. It's nurtured.

It unfolds through friction, emotion, habit, and reward—all of which are deeply human, irrational, and contextual.

BJ Fogg called it "the trigger–ability–motivation loop."

But a predictive algorithm doesn't feel frustration.

It doesn't understand shame.

It doesn't celebrate the small wins that make change sustainable.

In other words, it doesn't know what it means to be human.

Data ≠ Desire

One large pharma firm launched a beautifully engineered app for statin adherence.

It had gamified challenges, synced wearables, medication scanners—the whole tech stack.

But they overlooked one thing:

Why people stop taking statins in the first place.

Fear of side effects.

Lack of symptoms.

Mistrust in pharmaceutical companies.

No tech can fix that if it isn't acknowledged.

Behavioral science tells us this:

Adherence is emotional. Not logical.

And yet the app spoke only in numbers, scores, reminders.

It lacked empathy.

It lacked narrative.

It lacked soul.

The Misguided Faith in "More Tech"

We in healthcare have a recurring tendency—what you might call "technological substitution bias."

We think if something isn't working, it's because it's not tech enough.

So we add layers.

More interactivity.

More sensors.

More AI.

But sometimes the answer isn't more tech.

It's less friction, more meaning.

Sometimes what users need is a reason—not a reward.

When behavioral Science Leads, Tech Amplifies

Consider the success of the MySugr app for diabetes.

It's gamified, yes. But its real genius lies in its tone—playful, nonjudgmental, gently reinforcing.

Why?

Because it was co-created with patients.

Because it was built on theories of motivation, not just software.

Because the developers asked not only what users do, but why they don't.

Gamification isn't a Game of Code

In surgery, doctors learn quickly that tools don't save patients—judgment does.

A scalpel in the wrong hands can do damage.

So can a badge system that rewards clicks, but not change.

Tech without behavioral grounding is like surgery without diagnosis.

In gamification, it's tempting to lead with the latest platform, the latest buzzword.

But if we forget cognitive load, intrinsic vs. extrinsic motivation, social identity, loss aversion, and self-efficacy, then we're building monuments to cleverness—not care.

The Quiet Power of Knowing what Drives Us

Gamification done right begins not with code, but with questions:

- What do patients fear?
- What do reps hope for?
- What do physicians ignore—and why?

You don't find these answers in a database.

You find them in conversation. In observation. In stories.

That's where the real design begins.

And when the tech comes later—guided by that wisdom—it doesn't replace humanity. It elevates it.

PART V: FUTURE HORIZONS

Chapter 15: Playing it Right — A Strategic Playbook for Pharma Brand Managers

Chapter 16: The Next Level

Part V

Future Horizons

What Comes After the Game?

In medicine, doctors often overestimate what can be achieved in a year, and underestimate what can change in a decade.

A decade ago, I watched a teenage boy named Sean, recovering from a traumatic brain injury, use a clunky Wii controller to play Mario Kart in a rehab center.

The game was rigged, not in his favor—but to challenge his coordination, train his cognition, and track his progress.

His therapist sat beside him, not holding a clipboard but a second controller.

Sean was smiling.

He was recovering.

And he didn't know he was in therapy.

That was the promise of gamification before it had a name.

What Now?

Since then, we've gamified pill-taking, hand-washing, CME credits, and even oncology sales simulations.

We've turned learning into missions, adherence into streaks, and wellness into social quests.

But now we stand at the edge of something deeper.

- What if AI doesn't just personalize the game—but learns from the player's emotion in real time?
- What if wearables become portals—not just trackers—into adaptive, supportive health ecosystems?

- What if play isn't just a strategy—but a language of care?

The future of gamification in pharma is not just more apps.

It's not more points or badges.

It's more humanity, mediated through smarter technology.

Three Emerging Currents

In this final section, we explore three currents shaping the next decade:

1. **AI + Neurogaming:** Not just predictive. But responsive. Emotional. Human-aware.

   Games that listen, adapt, and grow alongside the user.

2. **Digital Twins & Behavioral Modeling:** Virtual avatars of patients or providers, simulating reactions to nudges, therapies, and even storytelling.

   What if we could test engagement itself before launching?

3. **Gamification as Therapy:** Not a wrapper around health, but health itself.

   VR for PTSD. Games for cognition. Movement for mood.

   Play becomes medicine.

A Word of Caution

The frontier dazzles. But it also deceives.

Not everything that can be gamified should be.

We must not lose sight of ethics, privacy, and dignity in our pursuit of delight.

A bad game can do harm.

An ungrounded one can waste millions.

A well-crafted one?

It can give a child with cancer a smile.

Or an elderly woman with dementia a moment of agency.

These are not features.

They are futures.

Where we're Going?

This section is not a forecast. It's a conversation with the possible.

- You'll meet startups building empathy engines.
- You'll see pharma pilots exploring digital micro-dosing of feedback.
- You'll learn how narrative, neuroscience, and nudge theory are converging in virtual clinics.

The question is no longer "Can games help?"

The question is:

What kind of world are we building—when healing itself becomes playable?

And more quietly:

Will we still remember to listen, even as the game speaks louder?

Chapter 15

Playing it Right – A Strategic Playbook for Pharma Brand Managers

In 2019, a mid-sized European pharma company launched a medication adherence app with gamified reminders—colorful badges, a streak calendar, even a virtual pet that cheered patients for taking their meds on time. It seemed like the perfect storm of digital health and engagement science.

Three months later, it quietly vanished.

When a post-mortem was conducted, the problem wasn't the technology. It was the absence of strategy. No clearly defined patient behavior goal. No alignment with brand messaging. No measurable KPIs. What was meant to spark motivation turned into noise.

Gamification, like surgery or drug discovery, demands rigor. Not just enthusiasm.

This chapter outlines a step-by-step strategy blueprint for pharma brand managers—turning play into purpose, pixels into progress.

1. **Diagnose Before You Prescribe: Identify the Engagement Problem**

   All strategy begins with a diagnosis.

   Is the goal to improve HCP awareness of updated treatment protocols? To reduce patient non-adherence in chronic conditions? To elevate rep training retention for a new product?

   Start with a brutally honest question: "What behavior is currently not happening that we want to encourage—and why?"

   Case in Point: Novo Nordisk launched "Cornerstones4Care" to tackle low patient engagement in Type 2 diabetes. Their insight? Education fatigue. The fix? Bite-sized, reward-driven microlearning journeys.

2. **Understand Your Player: Build Personas with Behavioral Data**

   Who are you gamifying for?

   Patients with low digital literacy and high symptom burden? MSLs overwhelmed with onboarding modules? Pediatricians juggling high caseloads?

   Leverage:

   - Patient journey maps
   - Field force feedback
   - CRM data
   - Behavioral science principles (like BJ Fogg's Motivation-Ability-Prompt model)

   Example: AstraZeneca's "Go to Jupiter" used fun planetary metaphors and gamified quests tailored for new MSLs—who, as research showed, craved mastery and peer recognition.

3. **Set SMART Objectives Aligned with Brand Strategy**

   Gamification must ladder up to business impact, not vanity metrics.

   ✓ Specific: Increase medication adherence among 18–35 age group with asthma

   ✓ Measurable: Improve refill rates by 20% over 6 months

   ✓ Achievable: Pilot with 5,000 users before scaling

   ✓ Relevant: Supports brand's patient-centric positioning

   ✓ Time-Bound: Tracked quarterly via pharmacy data

   Infinit App Study: Gamification led to a 60% increase in data logging and a 30% decrease in dropout rates—because metrics were defined upfront and rigorously tracked.

4. **Design with Intention: Mechanics + Emotions**

   - Use Octalysis Framework (Yu-kai Chou) as a design lens:
   - Core Drive 2: Development & accomplishment → Level badges
   - Core Drive 5: Social influence → Peer competitions
   - Core Drive 3: Empowerment → Custom avatars, decision trees

   But beware: Game mechanics without emotion are like pills without a purpose.

Mango Health used real-time medication tracking + reward systems. But what made it sticky? Emotional design—a pet avatar that grew healthier with the user.

5. **Choose the Right Channel & Tech**

   Web? Mobile app? WhatsApp bot? Smartwatch?

   Choose based on user behavior, not tech trends.

   ✓ HCPs → E-detailing tablets, email nudges

   ✓ Reps → Mobile-first, offline-compatible

   ✓ Patients → App stores, wearables, SMS for low-tech markets

   Integrate with:

   - CRM (Veeva)
   - LXP (for reps)
   - Patient support programs (PSPs)
   - AI personalization engines

   Headspace + Fitbit leveraged wearable sync for gamified sleep hygiene challenges—lowering anxiety scores in pilot studies.

6. **Pilot Relentlessly: Test Before Scale**

   Run A/B tests with variations in:

   - Mechanics (points vs. challenges)
   - Onboarding flows
   - Feedback language (encouraging vs. directive)
   - Timing (morning vs. evening nudges)

   Use Engagement KPIs:

   - DAUs, MAUs
   - Session duration
   - Feature adoption
   - Drop-off points

   Abbott Brazil reduced knowledge gaps from 27.5% to 7.5% in 5 days with the Atrivity platform—thanks to tight pilot loops and rapid iteration.

7. **Regulatory & Ethical Guardrails**

   ✓ Ensure GDPR, HIPAA, and FDA compliance

- ✓ Avoid dark patterns—no hidden rules, coercive nudging, or exploitation of vulnerable states
- ✓ Get informed consent for behavioral tracking

Johns Hopkins 'Bandit VR Rehab passed institutional ethics boards by anchoring gamified stroke rehab in measurable patient outcomes and consent frameworks.

8. Measure What Matters: Outcomes, Not Just Output

Create layered metrics:

- Engagement (usage, time-in-app)
- Behavior (adherence, HCP completion)
- Clinical proxies (refill rate, AE reporting)
- ROI (cost savings, revenue lift, brand recall)

Use control groups where possible.

US HCP Gamified Platform: Delivered 40% guideline adherence increase—not just clicks or logins, but clinical relevance.

9. Iterate and Scale with Stories

Every engagement loop yields insight. Use qualitative feedback loops from:

- Patients ("What made you return?")
- Reps ("When did it feel tedious?")
- HCPs ("Was it intuitive?")

Build internal dashboards. Share wins. Publish white papers.

Because what gets celebrated, scales.

10. Embed It in the Brand Culture

Gamification isn't an app. It's a mindset.

Train cross-functional teams—Med Affairs, Training, Marketing, Digital—to understand game psychology.

Frame it not as fluff, but as behavioral science in action.

AstraZeneca's MSL program saw 97% participation—even after hours—because play was reframed as professional mastery.

Closing Reflection: Serious Work Needs Playful Minds

The best gamified experiences are not entertainment. They are catalysts for change.

When done right, they build habits, reinforce knowledge, and deepen human connection—precisely what pharma marketing often lacks.

Brand managers who learn to use game mechanics wisely will not just launch better campaigns. They'll move people—patients, HCPs, colleagues—toward better outcomes.

Because in the end, the best game is the one that plays back with purpose.

Defining the Strategic Objective: Start with Why

There's a story that circulates among pharma brand managers—one of those quiet cautionary tales no one wants to own. A multinational company once built a sleek, expensive adherence app for a blockbuster oncology drug. It had points. It had badges. It even had animations of cells regenerating when you logged your daily pill.

Three months in, engagement dropped off a cliff.

Not because the tech was flawed. Not because patients weren't digitally savvy.

But because no one could answer a simple question: "Why was this made in the first place?"

Gamification, like a treatment plan, must begin with diagnosis. And the first diagnostic test is clarity of purpose.

Why are you Gamifying at All?

This isn't about adding bells and whistles. It's about changing behavior in service of better outcomes—clinical, commercial, or both.

Ask:

- What is the core behavior we are trying to encourage?
- Who is exhibiting the undesired behavior—and why?
- What is the cost (human, financial, operational) of that behavior not changing?
- What is the desired end state?

If you can't articulate these clearly, gamification becomes ornamental. And in healthcare, ornamentation without impact is waste.

Case in Point: MySugr

When MySugr entered the diabetes management space, they didn't say: "Let's make diabetes fun." They asked:

Why do patients stop logging their glucose?

The answer was simple: Logging felt like scolding. A negative feedback loop. The "why" was not about features, but emotion—shame, fatigue, disconnect.

So they built a system that made data entry rewarding, non-judgmental, even playful. The "why" was to transform a chore into a companion. Everything flowed from that.

Don't Confuse Objectives with Tactics

"Improve adherence" is not a strategic objective. It's an outcome. The strategic objective is the behavior shift required to reach that outcome, in context

Instead of:

"We want to improve adherence."

Try: "We want 18–35-year-olds with mild asthma to consistently take controller medication, by reinforcing the short-term benefits of adherence in a context that feels empowering rather than parental."

That specificity is what allows game design to serve strategy—not the other way around.

Pharma's Strategic Whys (and the Hidden Traps)

Strategic Why	Common Trap
Improve HCP engagement with new data	Mistaking novelty for relevance
Increase Rep knowledge retention	Confusing access to content with asssimilation
Enhance patient adherence	Assuming all patients are motivated by points
Boost AE reporting	Designing systems that feel punitive

The Emotional Underpinning of why

Gamification is not just a logic model. It's an emotion engine.

The most successful pharma gamification projects tap into intrinsic motivators:

- Mastery (HCPs leveling up in expertise)
- Autonomy (Patients choosing their path)
- Connection (Reps collaborating in social quests)
- Purpose (Feeling part of a patient outcome ecosystem)

Define your why in both strategic and emotional terms. Marry metrics with meaning.

Closing Thought: Start with the Heart

When Simon Sinek said, "Start with Why," he wasn't selling a motivational poster. He was pointing to an essential truth of human behavior:

People don't buy what you do. They buy why you do it.

And in healthcare, where every behavior carries consequences, that "why" must be both felt and measurable.

So before you sketch your first badge or avatar, ask the one question that changes everything:

"Why would this matter to the person we're trying to reach?"

If you answer that with clarity, everything else—design, technology, measurement—has a spine to build on.

Mapping the Player Types and Motivation Models

There's a moment in every strategy meeting where someone asks, "What do our users want?"

And someone else—often the analytics lead—starts pulling up dashboards of clicks, opens, bounce rates.

But here's the truth: People are not spreadsheets. They're players in a story you're asking them to join.

If gamification is your tool, then understanding who's playing—and why—is your first surgical incision.

Why Knowing Your Players Matters

In medicine, we wouldn't give the same therapy to every patient just because they have the same disease.

We segment by phenotype, genotype, lifestyle.

In gamification, your audience segments aren't just "patients" or "reps" or "HCPs."

They are players—each with their own motivational architecture.

Understanding that architecture is how you turn participation into persistence.

The Four Player Types (Bartle Taxonomy – Simplified for Pharma)

1. Achievers – thrive on mastery, completion, and goal-setting.
   - In pharma: The rep who wants to be top of the leaderboard or earn advanced certifications.
2. Explorers – enjoy learning, discovering, testing systems.
   - In pharma: An HCP interested in digging deep into MOA mechanisms or rare side effects.
3. Socializers – seek connection, collaboration, recognition.
   - In pharma: Patients in support groups, reps on team quests, MSLs sharing knowledge.
4. Killers (reframed as Competitors) – love challenge, dominance, proving superiority.

- In pharma: HCPs in diagnostic quizzes, reps in regional competitions, peer-to-peer clinical case debates.

Note: Most players are not just one type—but knowing which dominates helps you design accordingly.

Real-World Example: AstraZeneca's "Go to Jupiter" Rep Training

They segmented reps into:

- Achievers – driven by badge tiers and fast progress
- Explorers – drawn to optional deep dives and "hidden" facts
- Socializers – who thrived on team missions and shared chats

The result?

- 97% engagement rate—even after work hours.

Because each rep felt like the game was designed for them.

Motivation Models: Going beyond Points

If player types are the "who," motivation models explain the "why they keep playing."

1. Self-Determination Theory (Ryan & Deci)

   Humans need:

   - Autonomy – control over choices
   - Competence – sense of improvement
   - Relatedness – connection to others

   In Pharma:

   Patients logging mood or pain levels should feel in control, not judged.

   Reps completing a training quiz need to feel smarter, not just scored.

   HCPs in forums want to feel part of a clinical tribe, not isolated.

2. Fogg Behavior Model

   Behavior = Motivation × Ability × Trigger

   If your game isn't working, one of those three is misfiring:

   - Low motivation? It's not meaningful.
   - Low ability? It's too hard or clunky.
   - No trigger? It's invisible or forgettable.

Example: A COPD app that gamified spirometry tracking failed. Why? Triggers were missing. No reminders, no context, no urgency. The patients didn't forget the disease. They forgot the game.

Building Your Player Map

Let's say you're planning a gamified patient journey for a chronic skin condition.

Segment	Dominant Player Type	Motivation Anchors	Game Tactics
Teen patients	Socializer + Achiever	Peer interaction, progress streaks	Streak counters, social shareables
Elderly patients	Explorer + Autonomy	Learning, control over treatment	Unlockalbe education paths
Caregivers	Achiever + Socializer	Progress for loved ones, social support	Team goals, shared dashboards
Dermatologists	Explorer + Competitor	Clinical mastery, case-based validation	Peer leaderboards, unlockable CME

Final Insight: Design for people, not just at them

The biggest mistake in pharma gamification is designing for a generic user—the "average" HCP, the "typical" patient.

But there's no such thing.

There's only the player in front of you—with their own fears, drives, and reasons to keep going.

Understand who they are.

Speak to what moves them.

Design an experience that feels like it knows them.

That's not just strategy.

That's empathy in action.

Designing Mechanics Aligned with Behavior Science

In medicine, we've learned that even the most elegant treatment fails without patient behavior.

You can prescribe the gold standard therapy—but if the patient never fills it, or forgets it, or fears it—biology bows to psychology.

Gamification faces the same truth.

The prettiest points and flashiest badges won't work if they misfire against human behavior.

To work, the mechanics must do more than engage. They must align with how people change.

Start With the Brain, Not the Interface

Behavioral science teaches us this: humans are not always rational, but they are predictably irrational.

We procrastinate.

We overvalue rewards now over rewards later.

We fear loss more than we desire gain.

We don't do what's best—we do what's easiest, or most reinforcing, or most immediate.

So, a good gamified mechanic doesn't just incentivize. It corrects cognitive biases.

Mechanic 1: Progress Bars & Completion Bias

Ever noticed how people finish books faster when they can see a % completion?

That's completion bias—a psychological nudge that says, "You've come this far. Might as well finish."

In Pharma:

The Pfizer Oncology app used a progress bar for patient onboarding.

Once patients reached 60%, 85% went on to finish.

Just that tiny bar changed drop-off behavior.

Why? Because we are wired to finish what we see ourselves finishing.

Mechanic 2: Variable Rewards & Dopamine Loops

Slot machines are addicting not because they always win—but because you never know when you might.

That's the variable ratio schedule, the most powerful reward mechanic in behavior psychology.

In Pharma Education:

The "Go to Jupiter" MSL game from AstraZeneca gave unpredictable quiz bonuses—sometimes 1 point, sometimes 10, sometimes an Easter egg video.

MSLs kept returning—not for content, but for the thrill of maybe.

You can't do this recklessly. In healthcare, we design for reinforcement, not addiction.

But you can still harness uncertainty to drive curiosity.

Mechanic 3: Leveling & Mastery Pathways

Humans seek mastery.

We want to feel we are getting better—not just busier.

In Rep Training:

Abbott Brazil's Atrivity platform let reps unlock "expert" levels after basic product modules.

No one told them to.

They just wanted to prove they could.

Why? Because achievement unlocked isn't just a phrase—it's a feeling.

And that feeling drives repetition and retention better than any KPI ever has.

Mechanic 4: Feedback Loops (Positive & Negative)

Feedback is how humans learn.

Too little, and we get bored.

Too harsh, and we shut down.

Too vague, and we never improve.

In Gamified Adherence Tools:

The MySugr app gives instant visual feedback on each blood glucose entry.

Instead of judgment, it offers reflection:

"Looks like a spike. What happened here?"

Patients stayed longer because the game spoke with them, not at them.

Mechanic 5: Daily Missions & Microcommitments

Big behavior change? Intimidating.

But a 3-minute quiz? A badge for walking 500 steps?

That's microcommitment—and it works.

In Behavior Adherence Tools:

Mango Health had a "streak" mechanic—log your medication 3 days in a row, win a bonus.

That single mechanic lifted adherence in hypertensive patients by 23% in one pilot study.

Because humans will do a little every day for the reward of feeling on track.

Design Rule: Every Mechanic Must Map to a behavioral Goal

Game Mechanic	Behavioral Principle	Desired Outcome
Progress bars	Completion bias	Task persistence
Variable rewards	Dopamine loops	Repeat engagement
Levels & achievements	Mastery + self-efficacy	Knowledge retention
Feedback loops	Reflective learning	Better decision-making
Streaks / missions	Commitment bias + consistency	Daily engagement, habit formation

If your mechanic doesn't map to a known behavior principle—you're designing by hope.

And hope is not a strategy.

Final Insight: Behavior First, Technology Second

Too often, brand managers are shown a tech demo and asked,

"Can we build this into our campaign?"

But the right question is:

"What do we want them to do differently—and how does this mechanic nudge them there?"

The tech is just the delivery system.

Behavior is the payload.

Design from that, and you won't just build games.

You'll build habits that heal.

Prototyping, Testing, and Regulatory Alignment

In surgery, doctors never go from textbook to operating table in one step.

They simulate.

They practice on cadavers.

They build muscle memory before lives depend on it.

Gamification in pharma is no different.

An idea on a whiteboard—however inspired—needs to survive contact with three realities:

1. The user
2. The system
3. The law

That's where prototyping, testing, and regulatory alignment come in.

It's not just a phase.

It's the difference between novelty that fizzles and intervention that scales.

Prototyping: Build the Experience, Not Just the App

Too many gamification projects start with tech.

"We need an app," they say.

But the real question is:

What does the user feel while using it?

Prototyping isn't about code. It's about emotion in motion.

Use simple tools: clickable wireframes, paper sketches, Miro boards, even Figma mockups.

Put it in front of the user as soon as it's coherent enough to provoke a response.

A pharma company in Germany once used LEGO bricks to simulate a patient adherence journey.

They mapped mood states, touchpoints, and friction zones—before a single line of code was written.

Why? Because gamification is a story with rules.

If your prototype doesn't convey the journey, the game won't either.

Testing: It's not what You Think Works, It's what they Do

In medicine, we test new therapies in phases:

Phase I: Safety.

Phase II: Efficacy.

Phase III: Generalizability.

Gamified tools need a similar discipline.

Phase 1: Usability testing

Does the user know what to do?

Do they want to do it again?

Phase 2: Behavioral outcomes

Is knowledge retention higher?

Are pill logs more consistent?

Phase 3: Real-world integration

Does the tool fit into the workflow—for patients, HCPs, or reps?

Case Example:

In AstraZeneca's "Go to Jupiter" onboarding game, they tested early versions with small MSL cohorts.

Result:

- Confusion over badge meaning? Fixed.
- Reps skipping instructions? Added a forced tutorial.
- Drop-off after Day 3? Introduced a mystery bonus challenge on Day 4.

Testing isn't a hurdle.

It's a mirror.

And often, that mirror is brutally honest.

Regulatory Alignment: Guardrails, Not Roadblocks

The fear in pharma is real:

"What if the game violates FDA guidance?"

"Will GDPR shut us down for tracking behavior?"

That fear, while valid, is manageable—if you plan early.

Here's what works:

1. Bring legal and compliance in at the design table.

   Not at the end. Not after the build.

   At the start.

   Let them see the why—and they'll help you shape the how.

2. Know the rules for each audience:

Audience	Regulatory Focus
Patients	Informed consent, data minimization (GDPR/HIPAA), fairness
HCPs	Promotional boundaries (FDA, MCI), fair balance, CME rules
Reps	Internal compliance, learning data privacy

3. Document intent, process, and safeguards.

   Why you built it, how you're measuring efficacy, and how user data is protected.

4. Test for unintended consequences.

   Could the leaderboard shame underperformers?

   Could streak mechanics penalize chronic illness flare-ups?

   Ethics is a form of safety.

   And in pharma, safety is never optional.

The Gold Standard: Regulatory Co-Design

Some of the most successful gamified tools in pharma didn't just comply with regulation—they were co-designed with regulators in mind.

Example:

The SnowWorld VR therapy, used for burn victims, was built with clinical validation from the start.

It wasn't a cool game with a medical claim slapped on.

It was a medical tool designed to be proven.

That approach turns regulators from gatekeepers into collaborators.

Final Insight: Treat the Prototype Like a Patient

In the OR, surgeons scrub, check, rehearse—because small flaws have large consequences.

In gamification, that same ethic applies.

Prototype with humility.

Test with curiosity.

Align with integrity.

Because in the end, this isn't just a game.

It's someone's medication.

It's someone's training.

It's someone's trust.

And trust, once lost, is the hardest behavior to rebuild.

Execution Blueprint: From Concept to Launch

Atul Gawande once said that even the best plans in surgery are worth little unless they are carried out with steady hands, a watchful eye, and an openness to adjust mid-stream. Gamification in pharma—though often conceived in digital war rooms and branded strategy decks—demands no less discipline in its execution.

There is no single "right way" to execute a gamified experience. But there is a rigorous way.

Here's how brand managers who succeed do it—not with flash, but with focus.

1. **Lock the Core Loop: The Heartbeat of Your Game**

   Every effective game—whether for diabetes adherence or MSL learning—has a core loop:

   - The action (what the user does)
   - The feedback (what they receive)
   - The reward (why they return)

   Example:

   In MySugr, the loop was:

   Log data → Receive monster cheer + insights → Feel accomplished → Repeat.

   Before launching anything, you must build and refine this loop.

   Test it with your team.

   Test it with 5 real users.

   If they don't instinctively smile, pause, or lean in—it's not ready.

2. **Align the Team: Marketing, Medical, Legal, Tech**

   Gamification is not a "marketing campaign." It's a cross-functional effort.

   Too many brand managers push ahead solo, only to be derailed later.

   Checklist for alignment meetings:

   - Medical Affairs: Is the content clinically accurate and balanced?
   - Legal/Compliance: Is it non-promotional, non-coercive?

- IT/Tech Partner: Can it scale securely?
- Market Access/Pricing: Could it influence behavior in a way that has implications for coverage?
- Sales Ops/MSL Training Leads: Is it integrated into their daily flow?

Execution is a relay race, not a sprint.

Get all runners in the same lane.

3. **Develop in Iterations, Not Fireworks**

   Think of game development like iterative treatment—phased, observed, adjusted.

   Use agile sprints:

- Sprint 1: Build the onboarding flow
- Sprint 2: Core mechanics
- Sprint 3: Rewards logic
- Sprint 4: Analytics hooks

Each sprint should end with testing + learning.

Don't wait for a "big reveal."

In pharma, surprises rarely end well.

4. **Integrate into Existing Ecosystems**

   A standalone app, no matter how beautiful, is often a ghost town.

   Successful gamification lives where the user already lives:

- For patients: Tie into reminder apps, wearables, or telehealth platforms.
- For HCPs: Embed in CME portals or e-detailers.
- For reps/MSLs: Integrate into Salesforce, Viva, or LMS.

The most elegant solution dies if the user forgets to log in.

5. **Launch with a Story, Not a Feature List**

   People remember stories. Not mechanics.

   Don't launch with:

   "Earn badges while learning."

   Launch with:

   "Every rep who completes the Jupiter mission helps bring a life-saving drug closer to launch readiness."

Frame the game as part of a larger purpose.

In healthcare, meaning is the best fuel.

6. **Monitor Real-Time Metrics – Then Act**

Set up dashboards not just to see data—but to respond to it.

Watch for:

- Drop-offs during onboarding? → Simplify steps.
- Leaderboard inactivity? → Refresh the reward structure.
- Too many users plateauing early? → Add surprise bonuses or new levels.

Execution doesn't end at launch.

That's where it begins to learn.

7. **Plan the Exit – or the Scale**

Not every gamification initiative should be eternal.

Some are seasonal.

Some tie into a product lifecycle.

Three pathways:

- Retire (sunset with a thank-you reward or community closure)
- Repeat (seasonal refresh, new challenges)
- Scale (local to regional, regional to global)

AstraZeneca's MSL onboarding game started in one region.

Once 97% engagement hit, they scaled it globally—with translations, local compliance, and fresh avatars.

8. **Document, Debrief, and Learn**

Just like post-op analysis, debrief every gamification effort.

Ask:

- What worked—and why?
- What fell flat—and why?
- How did behavior actually change?

Document it.

Not just for records—but for the next brand manager who follows you.

That's how pharma marketing gets better. Not with trends, but with transparency and transmission.

Final Insight: Execution is the Moment of Truth

Strategy is your diagnosis.

Gamification design is your treatment plan.

Execution? That's surgery.

It's where precision meets uncertainty.

Where plans face reality.

Where outcomes are made—or missed.

Treat it with the care of a surgeon.

Not just for ROI.

But because in pharma, every well-executed engagement may lead to something deeper:

A better-trained rep.

A more adherent patient.

A more informed physician.

And when that happens, everyone wins the game that really matters.

Measuring what Matters – KPIs, ROI, and Continuous Optimization

"We count what we can measure. But we must also measure what truly counts."

— A lesson from both medicine and marketing

You can dress a wound, close an incision, even remove a tumor—but if you don't track recovery, infection rates, readmissions, or patient-reported outcomes, you've done half the job.

In pharma gamification, it's the same. You can launch the flashiest app, give away the best-designed badges, run a month-long HCP trivia campaign—but unless you measure what moved the needle, you're just decorating.

Measurement is not a post-mortem.

It's a living, breathing instrument panel.

Here's how great brand managers measure gamification—like clinicians measure healing.

1. **Define Success Early—In Behavioral Terms**

   Don't measure just downloads or clicks.

   Start with:

   - What behavior are we trying to change?
   - How will we know it changed?

   Examples:

Examples	Behavior Metric
Increase adherence	% of patients logging doses daily
Improve rep knowledge	Quiz scores before vs. after module
Boost HCP-engagement	Time spent in content + repeat logiins
Encourage MSL activity	Average daily app opens during field use

2. **Track the Right Metrics – Not Just the Easy Ones**

   Don't settle for vanity metrics:

   - Installs
   - Opens
   - Badge counts

Track impactful engagement:

DAUs / MAUs (Daily/Monthly Active Users)

- Session duration and frequency
- Completion rates of missions, modules, or checklists
- Behavior change signals (e.g., refill rates, log-ins over 30+ days)
- Stickiness Index = DAU ÷ MAU (above 0.2 = healthy retention)

Case in Point:

In a gamified COPD adherence program, patients who reached Level 3 showed 41% higher refill rates than those who dropped out at Level 1.

It wasn't the leaderboard that mattered—it was sustained behavior.

3. **ROI: From Engagement to Outcomes**

Gamification is not immune to the CFO's scrutiny.

You must show ROI in business and clinical terms.

Example Metrics:

Cost per engaged user vs. traditional campaigns

- Time to rep readiness (training hours saved)
- HCP re-engagement rate after gamified touchpoint
- Patient LTV (lifetime value) increase from better adherence
- % Increase in script lift in pilot vs. control regions

AstraZeneca's "Go to Jupiter" campaign saw not just 97% engagement—but a measurable reduction in training time by 28%.

Gamification isn't fluff. It's friction-reduction at scale.

4. **A/B Test and Optimize Continuously**

Like adjusting a medication dose, great gamified systems are tuned over time.

Run controlled tests:

- Leaderboards vs. private progress
- Narrative-driven vs. reward-driven
- Avatar customization vs. static UI

Track what nudges behavior—and what wears thin.

Just because users liked Level 1 doesn't mean they'll return for Level 10.

Game fatigue is real. So is motivational decay.

5. **Use Qualitative Feedback to Fill the Gaps**

Quantitative data tells you what happened.

But only users can tell you why.

Ask questions:

- What made you come back?
- What frustrated or confused you?
- Did this help your real-life decisions?

Patient in MySugr study:

"It felt like the app was cheering me on, not just watching me fail."

That's not in any chart—but it's everything.

6. **Benchmark, Share, and Create a Feedback Culture**

Just as morbidity and mortality conferences help surgeons improve, pharma teams must share gamification learnings openly.

- Build a post-launch dashboard.
- Publish internal case studies.
- Invite reps, MSLs, patients to roundtables.

Make gamification not just a tactic—but a culture of engagement excellence.

7. **Don't Just Report, Reflect.**

Sometimes, a campaign performs modestly—and that's okay.

Ask:

- Did it change anyone's behavior meaningfully?
- Was it deployed to the right audience?
- Was the strategy sound but the delivery weak?

Gamification is still new in pharma.

Every effort teaches us something.

Even a 3% improvement in adherence can save lives.

So measure well. But also listen deeply.

Because at the end of the game, it's not just about scores.

It's about impact.

It's about habits that heal.

It's about humans who stay engaged—because we met them where they were, and nudged them forward with care.

Agile Rollouts and Metric Dashboards – Learning while Doing

"In medicine, we don't wait for perfect data to act. We treat, observe, and adjust. Iteration saves lives. It also builds better systems."

—A mindset equally vital in healthcare and marketing

The Fallacy of Final

Pharma is often a victim of its own perfectionism. We want the training module to be flawless. The adherence app to be bug-free. The HCP platform to have all the bells and whistles from day one.

But gamification, by nature, is not waterfall. It's not meant to be planned for 12 months and launched in one heroic sprint.

It thrives when built like software and evolved like treatment protocols:

→ Prototype. Pilot. Measure. Tweak. Relaunch.

That's what the agile model allows—experiments at human scale.

The Power of Pilots

Let's take a real case:

A European biopharma company wanted to gamify HCP engagement for a rare autoimmune drug. Instead of deploying a full-fledged app across the continent, they launched a limited pilot in Italy.

The MVP (Minimum Viable Product) was simple:

- 3 guideline quizzes per week
- Peer comparison leaderboard
- Micro-rewards: CME points and badge tiers

Within 30 days, repeat log-ins were 2.4x that of their prior email campaigns.

But more importantly:

Users said they stayed not for the badges, but for the "gamified reinforcement of clinical reasoning."

They re-launched in 3 other countries, adapting difficulty, language tone, and even badge names per region—because agile gave them insight velocity.

Build → Measure → Learn → Iterate

The lean-agile loop applied to pharma gamification:

1. Build: Launch the lightest version that can test your hypothesis.
2. Measure: Track key behavioral metrics (adherence, engagement depth).
3. Learn: What's sticky? What's skipped? What's sparking comments or drop-offs?
4. Iterate: Change. Re-measure. Repeat.

Even FDA digital health guidance encourages "real-world evidence evolution."

Gamification deserves the same scientific humility.

The Dashboard That Saves the Campaign

Behind every successful gamified initiative is a dashboard that tells a story.

Not a spreadsheet of opens and clicks.

A living monitor of user psychology in motion.

What to track dynamically:

- Onboarding friction: Where do users drop off in the first 5 minutes?
- Session depth: Are they browsing, or completing?
- Challenge attempts vs. success: Too easy? Too hard?
- Feedback loops: Are users responding to nudges? Ignoring them?
- Time of day activity: Are patients engaging before bed? Are reps logging in between calls?

Real Insight:

A migraine management app saw 45% higher challenge completions on Sundays—users engaged during downtime, not weekdays. They moved key nudges to Saturdays. Engagement rose by 29%.

That kind of insight doesn't come from reports.

It comes from responsive design fed by real data.

Make Dashboards Collaborative, Not Clerical

A dashboard isn't just for the brand manager.

- ✓ It's a shared cockpit.
- ✓ Product team sees user paths.
- ✓ Medical team flags red-line content risks.
- ✓ UX team sees where emotion dips.
- ✓ Data science predicts dropout windows.
- ✓ Field reps offer anecdotal clues:

"Dr. Patel said he liked the leaderboard… but found the badges 'juvenile.'"

You wouldn't fly a plane solo without instruments.

You shouldn't fly a campaign without shared telemetry.

Agile is a Philosophy, Not a Process

Gamification isn't a bolt-on tactic.

It's a behavioral operating system.

And agile isn't just about how fast you deploy.

It's about how honestly you learn.

Because in the end, pharma is about trust.

And gamification, done right, isn't about playing games.

It's about playing fair—and improving lives one iteration at a time.

"Leveling Up Adhera™: A Gamified Cardiovascular Drug Launch"

A fictional case based on real principles and outcomes

The Problem:

When Cardovia Inc. prepared to launch Adhera™, its new once-daily cardiovascular pill targeting stage 1 hypertension in adults under 50, it knew the landscape had changed.

Doctors were overwhelmed with promotional clutter. Patients — especially younger adults — often ignored lifestyle warnings and stopped medications as soon as they "felt fine." The sales force was tired. Adherence across similar drugs hovered at 55% within three months. The stakes weren't just commercial; they were clinical.

And so, Cardovia asked a simple, heretical question:

"What if our launch felt like a game worth playing?"

Step 1: Defining the Strategic Objective – Start With Why

Dr. Malini Rao, Cardovia's brand lead, reframed the team's objective: "Not just brand awareness. Not just prescriptions. But sustained habit formation — for patients, for doctors, and for our field force."

That meant the goal wasn't impressions. It was impact. Measured not just in sales but in completed onboarding, pill-taking streaks, educational unlocks, and behavior nudges.

Step 2: Mapping Player Types and Motivation Models

Using BJ Fogg's Behavior Model and Yu-Kai Chou's Octalysis Framework, they segmented stakeholders into player types:

- HCPs (Physicians, Cardiologists): Status-driven achievers.
- Patients (25–50 yrs): Habitual explorers, novelty-seekers.
- Sales Reps: Competitive collaborators with peer visibility needs.

Each had different motivations. But they shared one thing: the desire to feel progress and purpose without extra friction.

Step 3: Designing Behavior-Aligned Game Mechanics

The gamified launch experience was split across three verticals:

1. HCP Engagement Portal: "The Adhera League"
   - Points for attending webinars, completing knowledge quizzes, submitting case reports.
   - Badges unlocked for first prescriptions written, referrals made, and e-consent obtained.
   - Leaderboards displayed by region (anonymized).
2. Patient Companion App: "HeartQuest"
   - Users created avatars and daily health quests (pill taken, BP logged, 10-min walk).
   - Each success filled up their "Heart Shield."
   - Weekly challenges offered digital collectibles and partner discounts (e.g., with Fitbit).
   - Motivational messages crafted using Self-Determination Theory: autonomy, competence, relatedness.
3. Sales Rep Learning Game: "Mission Adhera"
   - Mobile-first modules with scenario simulations (e.g., handling objections from skeptical cardiologists).
   - Peer competitions: regions competed based on in-field quiz completions and HCP feedback.
   - Avatars leveled up with completed missions.

Step 4: Prototyping, Testing, and Regulatory Alignment

Everything was prototyped with co-design workshops involving reps, patients, and physicians.

Privacy risks were addressed using GDPR-consistent opt-ins, with HIPAA compliance for all logged health data. The FDA's evolving guidelines on digital engagement tools were consulted.

All content was modularized to allow easy decoupling if any feature ran afoul of compliance teams.

Step 5: Agile Rollout and Live Dashboard Tracking

The rollout happened in three waves:

- Wave 1: Beta region with 30 reps and 500 patients.
- Wave 2: Full regional deployment post-feedback.
- Wave 3: National scale-up.

Live dashboards tracked:

- HCP education module completion (↑ 89%)
- Patient onboarding via app (↑ 73%)
- Adherence at 90 days (↑ 72% vs 55% baseline)
- Rep engagement post-hours (↑ 82%)

Human Narrative:

Priya, 34, Lawyer, Hypertensive.

Priya hated meds. "I'm too young for this," she said. But she loved games. When her doctor invited her to "HeartQuest," she downloaded it reluctantly.

Three days in, she got a digital badge for her "BP log streak." Then came a challenge: Beat your week 1 record. She unlocked a virtual companion: a small animated heart that pulsed when she completed her daily routine. She smiled.

Two months later, she hadn't missed a pill. Not one.

And when she saw her BP normalize, she whispered, "I'm winning."

The Measurable Impact

Metric	Before Adhera™ Launch	After Gamified Launch
90-day Patient Adherence	55%	72%
HCP Guideline Quiz Completions	28%	91%
Sales Rep Product Knowledge Scores	Avg. 67%	92%
App DAUs (Week 6)	-	9,800
NPS (Physician Portal)	14	38

Lessons Learned

- Gamification didn't replace education — it scaffolded it.
- The best mechanics weren't flashy — they were frictionless.
- Empowering patients made them better partners, not just end-users.

Conclusion

Adhera™ succeeded not just because it worked biochemically — but because it played psychologically. It didn't bribe people into compliance. It invited them into mastery, progress, and story.

Sometimes, what saves lives isn't just medicine.

Sometimes, it's a game — thoughtfully played.

Chapter 16

The Next Level

Gamification and the Future of Pharma

In 2015, I met a young man in Hyderabad who had recently been diagnosed with early-stage Parkinson's disease. He was 39. A software engineer. A new father.

The tremor began in his left hand.

He knew enough to Google his symptoms before the neurologist did.

But what changed his life wasn't the medication.

It was a mobile game.

Not a cure. Not a miracle. A tool.

A game that tracked his tremors through micro-movements on the touchscreen. That offered him cognitive puzzles tied to motor feedback. That nudged him to move, meditate, and message his doctor when thresholds were breached.

"It made me feel like I was doing something," he told me.

"It gave me a way to fight."

A New Kind of Pharma

What if feeling like you're doing something is part of the treatment?

For most of the 20th century, the pharmaceutical industry saw itself as a supplier of molecules—bioactive compounds that altered the physiology of the body.

But the 21st century has brought a shift.

- From molecules to models.
- From interventions to interactions.
- From prescriptions to experiences.

Gamification, in this light, is not just a communication tool or a marketing ploy.

It's a behavioral interface between science and human nature.

It's where efficacy meets engagement.

The End of the One-Size-Fits-All Pill

In the traditional pharma model, we develop a drug, package it, label it, and push it to market.

We hope the patient swallows it. We hope the HCP recommends it. We hope the rep explains it.

And we measure success in volume, not value.

But gamification changes the equation.

- A gamified asthma app not only tracks inhaler use—it learns why it's skipped.
- A VR module for chemotherapy patients reduces anticipatory nausea through distraction and agency.
- A sales rep simulation reveals knowledge gaps before they cost us a prescriber.

It's not just adherence. It's alliance.

Beyond Adherence: Towards Empowerment

Gamification invites the user to be more than a recipient.

- The patient becomes the protagonist.
- The doctor becomes the strategist.
- The rep becomes the learner.
- The brand becomes the game master.

It's a radical redefinition of roles.

One where pharma stops speaking at people, and begins building with them.

Where the question isn't just "Did they take the drug?"

But: "Did they feel part of the solution?"

What the Future Demands

As AI personalizes the challenge, as wearables stream data in real-time, as digital twins allow us to simulate entire patient journeys—we enter a new paradigm:

Therapy is not just what the drug does to the body.

It's what the experience does to the person.

The implications are profound:

- Clinical trials become quests.
- Medical education becomes sandboxed simulations.
- Market access becomes behavioral design.
- Regulatory frameworks must now ask not just is it safe and effective?

But also: is it fair, ethical, meaningful, and inclusive?

The Danger of Missing the Point

There will be gimmicks.

Bad games.

Points-for-the-sake-of-points.

The future of gamification is not about gamifying everything.

It's about gamifying what matters—skillfully.

It's about motivating action while honoring complexity.

Designing delight without dumbing down.

Crafting choice without coercion.

A Final Reflection

When I think about the future of pharma, I don't picture a molecule.

I picture a dashboard.

An avatar.

A decision made with a nudge, not a push.

A patient not merely taking control—but feeling in control.

And somewhere in that system, a small reward.

A star.

A progress bar.

A message: “You’ve completed your streak.”

We laugh at such things. But we shouldn’t.

Because they whisper what medicine too often forgets to say:

“I see you.

You’re trying.

You’re not alone.”

And sometimes, that’s what healing sounds like.

Hyper-Personalized Gamified Care Pathways

A new frontier in medicine, where healing learns who you are.

In medicine, doctors often build systems for the average.

The average diabetic. The average hypertensive. The average patient with breast cancer, or COPD, or depression.

They map out care pathways—clinical guidelines, checklists, regimens—and we walk patients down them like a path through the woods.

But here's the problem.

No patient is average.

The Day My Father Skipped his Meds

My father was a meticulous man.

An accountant by profession.

The kind of person who counted his pills twice after filling the weekly pillbox.

But one winter, after a bout of bronchitis, he missed his blood thinner for three days straight.

When I asked why, he said:

"I just didn't feel like a patient anymore."

There was no trigger. No reminder. No reinforcement that connected the 'why' of his treatment to the 'who' of his identity.

And that's the central failure of one-size-fits-all medicine.

It knows the disease.

It forgets the person.

Enter: Gamified, Hyper-Personalized Pathways

Now imagine a system that remembers.

That learns, in real time, not just what medications you're on—but how you respond to them, when you're most likely to skip, what motivates you, and what story you're telling yourself about your illness.

This is not science fiction.

It is the merging of behavioral design, AI, and gamification—crafted into what we now call hyper-personalized care pathways.

These systems do not offer static checklists.

They offer dynamic narratives.

- For the competitive user: a streak system that rewards consistency.
- For the socially driven: a community board with peer encouragement.
- For the cognitively fatigued: fewer choices, clearer visuals, shorter sessions.
- For the anxious: soothing affirmations, guided steps, and "safe zones" within the experience.

Every interaction is adjusted, like a good coach tailoring training to the player.

Games that Listen

The beauty of well-designed gamification is not in the points or badges.

It's in its attunement.

When a gamified app senses you're stressed—by tapping into wearable heart rate variability or typing speed—it may dial down the challenge.

If you're engaged, it nudges you a little further.

If you're discouraged, it celebrates small wins.

It does what medicine has struggled to do at scale: be present, responsive, and personalized.

The Shift from Prescription to Participation

These pathways shift the paradigm.

Instead of medicine being something done to you, it becomes something you shape.

- A patient with type 2 diabetes doesn't just track glucose—they play a story where blood sugar is a dragon to tame, and each meal a weapon or weakness.

- A cancer survivor undergoing rehab doesn't just fill a boring pain log—they complete quests, earn avatars, see progress arcs.
- A caregiver gets feedback not just on "compliance," but on emotional tone, burnout risk, and resilience-building micro-goals.

This is not frivolous.

It's behavioral neuroscience, artfully delivered.

Why this Matters?

The average medication adherence rate in chronic disease hovers around 50%.

But in gamified, personalized systems like Mango Health, Omada, or MySugr, we're seeing:

- Adherence rates rise to 70–80%.
- Dropout rates cut by a third.
- Patient satisfaction scores resembling those of entertainment platforms—not hospital wards.

People stay engaged because they feel seen.

Because the care path bends toward them, not the other way around.

The Ethical Compass

Of course, with personalization comes risk.

- Are we nudging… or manipulating?
- Is the game empowering… or addictive?
- Are we treating the person… or just optimizing the data?

These are not trivial questions. But they are solvable—with transparency, consent, and dignity as the design principle.

One Final Image

Picture a young girl with juvenile arthritis.

Every day she logs her symptoms through an app shaped like a magical forest.

When she stretches, she helps a tree grow.

When she breathes deeply, the wind picks up.

When she endures a tough day, a bird lands beside her to say, "You are brave."

This isn't just a game.

This is medicine—not only as pharmacology, but as poetry.

And perhaps that's the future we're called to create:

A healthcare system that not only knows what works—but remembers who it's for.

AI Co-Pilots and Adaptive Challenges

A medicine that watches, learns, and adjusts in real time.

The Piano Teacher Who Never Gave Up

When I was ten, I had a piano teacher named Mr. D'Silva.

He was patient—almost unnervingly so.

He noticed when I got bored and slipped in a jazz riff.

He noticed when I got frustrated and slowed the tempo.

He gave me harder pieces when I was curious. Easier ones when I was overwhelmed.

It was only much later that I realized what made him so effective.

He wasn't teaching piano.

He was teaching me.

And that's what AI, done right, can do in healthcare.

Not treat "the diabetic." Not "the rep who needs training."

But treat the person—where they are, with what they need, at the exact moment they need it.

The Rise of AI as Co-Pilot

In the operating room, we've long relied on checklists.

In the clinic, on protocols.

But in a world where no two patients, reps, or learners are quite alike, we are now turning to AI co-pilots—systems that augment human decision-making, not replace it.

These systems:

- Observe behavior in real time.
- Predict the likelihood of disengagement or error.
- Adjust challenge levels to match cognitive load or emotional state.
- Deliver feedback that's timely, precise, and empathetic.

They don't just watch you—they walk with you.

The Right Challenge at the Right Time

In behavioral science, there's a concept called the Zone of Proximal Development.

Too easy, and we tune out.

Too hard, and we shut down.

The sweet spot—the "stretch zone"—is where growth happens.

AI co-pilots excel here.

They learn:

- When a patient logs meals diligently, it's time to introduce sleep tracking.
- When a rep masters one therapeutic area, the next quiz includes edge cases.
- When a depressed user shows signs of cognitive fatigue, the app eases up on daily goals and adds a supportive message instead.

It's medicine with a feedback loop.

It's learning with a pulse.

An MSL's Game, Rewritten by AI

Take the case of an MSL onboarding program gamified on the Atrivity platform.

Instead of a fixed training path, the AI learned which kinds of questions each learner struggled with—and reshaped the next day's challenge accordingly.

It even adjusted difficulty based on time of day and device usage pattern.

The result?

Engagement soared.

Knowledge retention deepened.

And reps began… playing after hours.

Why? Because the game knew them.

It made them feel competent, not judged.

Challenged, not cornered.

The Promise for Patients

In adherence programs, AI co-pilots do more than remind you to take your pill.

They contextualize your behavior.

- If you're skipping doses on weekends, they check for social triggers.
- If your wearable flags increased heart rate variability, the system might delay a cognitive challenge and nudge toward mindfulness instead.
- If you succeed five days in a row, it celebrates—then raises the bar just enough.

This is not compliance.

This is conversation.

And Yet—We Must be Careful

With such power comes responsibility.

An AI co-pilot can nudge or nag, depending on design.

It can motivate or manipulate.

The key lies in its ethics—and its humility.

- Is it learning to help—or to sell?
- Is it adapting for engagement—or for data extraction?
- Is it empowering the user—or engineering behavior for someone else's gain?

These questions must not be afterthoughts.

They must be baked into every line of code.

Back to the Music

In medicine, doctors are used to the idea that challenge builds resilience.

But in gamified healthcare, challenge must also build trust.

And trust comes from feeling known.

The best piano teachers don't just teach notes.

They teach at your tempo.

They know when to push and when to pause.

AI co-pilots have the potential to be just that kind of teacher.

To become adaptive guides, whispering:

"I've seen where you've been.

I know what you're capable of.

Let's take the next step together."

Blockchain and Reward Tokenization in Healthcare

What if health had its own currency—and trust was built into the system?

A Visit to the Village Store

Years ago, I visited a rural village in Andhra Pradesh where a local clinic had a curious incentive system.

Patients who showed up for their check-ups on time, took their medications regularly, or attended health workshops earned tiny colored coupons—small tokens of acknowledgment.

These tokens could be redeemed for food grains, soap, or sometimes even a bus ticket to the nearest city.

It was crude, simple, almost childlike.

And yet—it worked.

People cared. They showed up. They stuck to treatment plans. They talked about "earning health."

I remember thinking: What if we could do this at scale?

Today, that possibility doesn't sound so quaint.

It sounds like blockchain and tokenization.

Why Trust is Broken

Healthcare systems run on promises—of privacy, fairness, accountability. But in reality:

- Patients rarely control their own data.
- Adherence is monitored top-down, with little incentive for participation.
- And health engagement programs often feel more extractive than empowering.

Enter blockchain—a system designed not to assume trust, but to earn it.

At its core, blockchain is a ledger of truth: decentralized, tamper-proof, transparent. It lets you record, track, and validate actions without a central authority.

In pharma, that opens new doors:

- Every dose taken could be logged and verified.
- Every clinical milestone could be rewarded.
- And every reward could be securely owned, transferred, or spent—by the patient, not the platform.

The Currency of Engagement

Now add reward tokenization.

Imagine a gamified app where:

- A hypertensive patient gets 2 tokens for daily BP logging.
- A diabetic caregiver earns 5 tokens for consistent meal planning.
- A cancer patient gets bonus tokens for completing a mindfulness session.

These tokens aren't just vanity points.

They're digital assets—blockchain-certified, unique, and usable.

- Redeemable for discounts on health products.
- Tradable for services like teleconsultations.
- Donatable to charities or community health funds.

Health becomes a mutual investment, not a prescription.

Case in Point: Healthereum & Solve.Care

Take Healthereum, a blockchain-based platform that rewards patients with HEALTH tokens for showing up to appointments or completing health tasks. Those tokens are traceable, transparent, and patient-controlled.

Or Solve.Care, which allows healthcare services to be paid using tokens, while integrating smart contracts that ensure services are only paid for if they're delivered properly.

This isn't hypothetical. These are working systems—with live users.

The question is not if tokenization will reach healthcare, but how ethically and meaningfully it will do so.

From Gamification to Autonomy

The beauty of blockchain is not just in what it tracks, but in who owns the game.

A traditional gamification system might reward you—but the data is theirs. The rules, theirs. The agenda, theirs.

But a tokenized, blockchain-based system flips the power.

It's you who logs your health.

You who owns the token.

You who decides where it goes.

Suddenly, the game is no longer something played on you—but by you.

But Let's not be Naïve

There are caveats.

- Is a token truly valuable—or just digital candy?
- Will the poor be gamified into compliance while the rich opt out?
- Can blockchain scale without burning the planet or the pocket?
- And who governs this new economy of health?

The answers matter. Because health is sacred. And so is dignity.

Tokens should never be used to manipulate behavior.

They should affirm effort, reward participation, and empower autonomy.

Back to that Village

I still remember the glint in the eyes of an elderly woman who had saved up enough clinic tokens to get a small bag of rice.

It wasn't the rice that mattered.

It was that someone had noticed.

That her effort had been seen.

That she had earned something—not just health, but respect.

That's what blockchain and tokenization can do, if done right.

They can restore trust.

They can turn patients into partners.

They can make health not just a goal—but a game worth playing.

Predictive Analytics and Real-Time Gamification

When the system learns you better than you know yourself—and nudges you just before you falter.

The Missed Turn on an Empty Highway

A few years ago, I was driving through the backroads of New Hampshire, long after sunset, following directions on a GPS app. It was pitch dark. No streetlamps. No houses. Just me, the road, and the voice in my dashboard.

At one point, I missed a turn. Just a brief moment of inattention. The app recalculated instantly, as if it knew this would happen. A calm voice redirected me: "Turn left in 400 feet."

It wasn't surprised. It was prepared.

And I remember thinking—what if healthcare worked like that?

What if predictive analytics in a gamified system could detect when a patient, or a rep, or a caregiver was about to veer off course—not after the fact, but just before?

And what if, instead of punishment or silence, there was a voice—not scolding, but encouraging—nudging them gently back on track?

That's not just a dream anymore.

That's what predictive analytics and real-time feedback loops are doing in gamified pharma experiences.

The Old Model: Static Paths for Dynamic People

Traditional training programs and adherence protocols were built like one-way highways.

- Fixed routes.
- Fixed milestones.
- Everyone treated the same.

But human behavior isn't static. It's contextual, emotional, fluid.

Patients don't fail because they lack information.

They fail because life gets in the way.

And that's where predictive systems enter—systems trained on patterns, timing, behavior histories, even micro-interactions.

They don't wait for a crash.

They predict the slippage—and adjust the game before it's lost.

The Nudge Before the Fall

Imagine a patient with chronic heart failure using a gamified self-care app.

- For 21 days, she logs weight, sodium intake, and daily walks.
- On day 22, she hesitates. Doesn't log breakfast.
- The system flags this as a dropout risk pattern—based on thousands of similar trajectories.

Within minutes:

- She receives a motivational badge: "21-Day Champion!"
- A pop-up challenge appears: "One more log today and you unlock a new health badge."
- Her phone buzzes with a brief, encouraging message: "You've come this far. You've got this."

It's not random. It's algorithmic empathy.

The Rep who was About to Tune Out

Now picture a medical sales rep learning a new oncology product.

The system detects that he's:

- Taking longer to answer certain question types,
- Avoiding simulation rounds after 6 PM,
- And skipping the pharmacodynamics module.

Rather than penalize him, the platform adapts:

- Reorders the learning sequence.
- Introduces spaced repetition for weak areas.
- Sends a well-timed push notification with a mini-challenge and peer leaderboard snapshot.

The rep doesn't feel watched. He feels seen.

And more importantly, he stays in the game.

The Brain Loves Feedback

In the OR, surgeons crave feedback—blood loss, vitals, oxygenation, surgical depth.

In behavior change, it's no different.

We thrive on:

- Instant feedback ("You completed your challenge!")
- Visual progress (bars filling, avatars advancing)
- Adaptive encouragement ("You're in the top 30% of learners this week.")

The key is timing.

Too late, and it's meaningless.

Too early, and it's annoying.

Done right, real-time feedback becomes a whisper, not a whistle.

A whisper that says: "Keep going."

Patterns Become Prevention

Predictive gamification doesn't just observe—it anticipates.

It sees:

- That a patient tends to skip meds on Mondays.
- That a rep disengages after three incorrect quiz attempts.
- That a caregiver shows signs of digital fatigue when stress peaks in wearable data.

And then, it acts.

It offers a shorter challenge. A badge for consistency. A breathing exercise. A message from a digital coach. A reset button.

Every nudge becomes a chance to stay in motion, not spiral.

But Beware the Overreach

Here's where we must tread carefully.

Predictive analytics is not about predicting failure.

It's about enabling resilience.

When real-time feedback becomes surveillance, trust erodes.

When gamification becomes coercion, dignity is lost.

We must ask:

- Who controls the algorithm?
- Who benefits from prediction?
- Is this empowerment, or subtle engineering?

The line is fine. And sacred.

Back to the Road

I think about that missed turn often.

How the app didn't blame me.

Didn't freeze.

Just recalculated—and kept me going.

In healthcare, that's all people need sometimes.

Not a perfect plan.

Just a path that adjusts when we stumble.

And a system that says: "You're not lost. You're learning. Let's try again."

That's predictive gamification.

Not the game of punishment.

But the game of progress.

Epilogue

The Joy of Play in a Serious World

What if healing didn't have to feel so heavy?

The Puzzle in the Waiting Room

A few years ago, I walked into a pediatric oncology ward and noticed something odd.

Not the machines. Not the IV poles.

But a jigsaw puzzle.

Scattered across a table, half-done. Cartoon animals. Bright colors.

Beside it, a 9-year-old boy, bald and smiling, focused not on the chemotherapy that dripped into his arm—but on finding the corner piece to complete a giraffe's ear.

A nurse told me the puzzle wasn't part of the protocol.

It wasn't therapeutic. It wasn't evidence-based.

It was just there.

And yet, that puzzle had become ritual.

Each child added a piece. Each family left something behind.

It was a game. But it was also a way through.

I've never forgotten that boy—or that moment.

Because amidst the buzzwords and dashboards, the AI and IoT, the compliance rates and KPIs, we often forget something simple:

The human instinct to play—to try, to fail, to try again—is not trivial.

It's how we survive. It's how we heal.

Medicine is not just Molecules

Not very long ago, a surgeon told me "In my surgical training, we were taught to value precision.

Protocol. Planning. Procedure.

And yet, the longer I've practiced, the more I've come to see that health isn't built solely on rules. It's built on engagement. On meaning. On emotion."

And nothing taps into these better than play.

Not just games with points, badges, or avatars.

But games that give people back a sense of agency.

A sense that they're not being acted upon, but are active players in their own story.

The Seriousness of Joy

- Play is not frivolous.
- It teaches risk in safety.
- Builds habits through repetition.
- Trains the mind to focus through joy—not force.

Even in intensive care units, we use distraction games to ease pediatric pain.

Even in medical education, we simulate crises so that we may one day avert them.

We play to learn.

We play to adapt.

We play to remember what matters.

So why should pharma marketing, patient engagement, or physician training be any different?

The Point is not the Points

Gamification has brought points, leaderboards, and levels into the halls of pharma.

But the real win is not scoring higher.

It's staying longer.

It's caring more.

It's returning tomorrow.

A diabetic who logs meals for 90 days because a cartoon dragon smiles when she does it—that's not childish. That's triumph.

A sales rep who plays a scenario game late into the night—not for approval, but for mastery—that's not frivolous. That's commitment.

A cancer patient who journeys through an app where their avatar overcomes firestorms and fear—that's not escapism. That's empowerment.

In a world of crushing seriousness, play reminds us we are still alive.

The Game is not the Goal

Atul Gawande once said, "Better is possible. It does not take genius. It takes diligence. It takes moral clarity. It takes ingenuity. And above all, it takes a willingness to try."

Gamification, done well, is exactly that: a willingness to try again. And again. And again.

To build systems that adapt.

To design journeys that inspire.

To remember that behind every dosage, every dashboard, every decision——there is a human being, hoping to make it through.

Let them Play

In that pediatric ward, I watched a child in pain laugh.

Not because the pain was gone.

But because he had something to build. Something to control. Something to enjoy.

That puzzle wasn't medicine.

But it was healing.

And maybe that's the lesson.

In healthcare, we don't just need more rules.

We need more puzzles.

More quests.

More dragons.

More joy.

Not to make light of suffering—but to bring light into suffering.

So let the games begin.

Not for fun alone.

But for hope.

Gamification is not a Gimmick

It's a return to what truly moves us—purpose, progress, and play.

The Surgeon and the Checklist

Years ago, when Atul Gawande began writing about the use of checklists in surgery, people laughed.

A checklist? Really? For trained professionals?

It sounded like a gimmick—an insult to expertise.

But over time, the data told another story.

Surgical complication rates dropped. Communication improved. Teams became... teams.

Not because the checklist was clever, but because it tapped into something essential:

- A shared purpose—we all want the patient to live.
- A sense of progress—tick by tick, we move forward.
- And strangely, a kind of play—the way routines, when done with mastery, become like choreography.

It wasn't a gimmick.

It was a rediscovery.

And I've come to believe that's what gamification truly is—not the addition of fluff, but the restoration of focus.

What we Think Gamification is

We've all seen the worst of it:

- Toothbrushes that cheer you on like you won a Nobel Prize.
- Health apps that give out "water intake badges" like candy.
- Point systems that feel more like distractions than support.

It's easy to dismiss it all as shallow. Manipulative. Juvenile.

But the best gamification—especially in health and pharma—isn't about turning life into a video game.

It's about turning life back into a journey. One where you matter.

Where you know why you're doing what you're doing.

Where you see that you're making progress.

And where you're allowed to enjoy the ride, even when it's hard.

The Three Things that Still Motivate Us

If you strip away jargon, platforms, badges, and behavioral science frameworks, you're left with three primal motivators:

1. **Purpose**

   We want our actions to matter.

   Whether it's a patient logging blood sugar or a rep mastering a new oncology molecule—there is a deep need to feel that what we're doing contributes to something beyond ourselves.

   Gamification—done well—reconnects the task to the mission.

   A digital coach that reminds you why your steps help your heart.

   A leaderboard that isn't about ego, but about impact.

2. **Progress**

   We crave momentum.

   Our minds are wired to respond to forward motion.

   This is why a partially filled progress bar is more motivating than a blank one.

   Gamification lets people see their own growth:

   - "You completed 6 out of 10 modules."
   - "You've taken your meds 14 days in a row."
   - "You're 3 points away from your personal best."

   The magic isn't in the numbers.

   It's in the feeling that we're getting somewhere.

3. **Play**

   We are, at heart, playful creatures.

   Even in war zones, children play.

   Even in ICUs, patients joke.

   Play is not the opposite of seriousness—it's the companion of resilience.

Gamification isn't about turning illness into entertainment.

It's about making health feel human again. Light where there was only weight.

The Real Gimmick? Pretending We're Rational Robots

For decades, we designed healthcare interventions assuming people would act logically.

"Take this pill. It helps."

"Attend this training. You need it."

"Read this leaflet. It's important."

But humans don't run on logic alone.

We run on emotion, connection, stories, goals, surprises.

Gamification is not an add-on to these truths.

It is an expression of them.

Ten Real-World Case Studies of Gamification in Pharma

1. **Mango Health " –Reminders with Rewards"**

   In a healthcare landscape where nearly 50% of patients with chronic illnesses fail to take their medications as prescribed, Mango Health emerged with an innovative solution: gamify the act of taking pills. The app uses mobile reminders combined with reward systems to encourage consistent medication adherence.

   Here's how it works: users receive reminders to take medications, log vital signs, or engage with educational content. Each successful action earns them points. These points can be redeemed for real-world incentives—like gift cards and charitable donations. More importantly, the feedback loop instills a habit. The more they engage, the more they win—not just rewards, but better health outcomes.

   Clinical data reported a 27% increase in medication adherence among chronic condition cohorts, such as hypertension, diabetes, and high cholesterol. This improvement, though seemingly small, can translate to fewer hospitalizations and improved quality of life.

   What's particularly unique about Mango is how it transforms routine compliance into something more emotionally resonant. Adherence isn't portrayed as a moral failing or obligation—it becomes a game. A bit of dopamine enters the discipline. By shifting its mindset from compliance to accomplishment, Mango taps into the core insights of behavioral psychology—reward loops, goal-setting, and reinforcement.

   Ultimately, Mango Health doesn't just remind users to take pills—it helps them take control.

2. **mySugr – Taming the Diabetes Monster**

   "Diabetes is tedious, frustrating, and invisible. So what if we made it visible—and gave it a face?"

   —Frank Westermann, Co-founder of mySugr

   The act of logging blood sugar is mundane. Even exhausting. And for millions with diabetes, it's a constant reminder of failure—of how the body betrayed them and how managing it has become a second job. The folks behind mySugr understood this—not just clinically, but humanly.

So they turned management into a game. Not just any game—but one where you tame a monster.

The app introduced a small, animated creature—quirky, expressive, part coach, part conscience. Each time a user logged a blood glucose reading, recorded a meal, or tracked insulin doses, the monster responded. It calmed down, smiled, celebrated. Miss an entry? It sulked. It became a kind of pet—but one that demanded discipline in exchange for joy.

But the brilliance wasn't in the cuteness. It was in the behavioral psychology. What mySugr did was invoke what psychologist BJ Fogg might call "tiny habits" wrapped in emotional rewards. Every action reinforced a loop—cue, behavior, feedback—that over time became routine. They made glucose tracking feel like progress, not punishment.

The numbers backed it up. Users who interacted daily with the app logged over 75% of their recommended entries. A study by the University of Graz found that consistent use of the app significantly improved HbA1c levels—one of the gold standards of diabetes control. It wasn't just engagement for engagement's sake. It was clinical impact, translated through playful interaction.

More importantly, mySugr rewired the emotional narrative. People stopped seeing their diabetes as a silent adversary and started seeing themselves as active players in a game of mastery. A monster was no longer a metaphor for disease—it was one for empowerment.

As one patient put it: "Before mySugr, diabetes ruled my day. Now I rule it—with a smile, and a monster on my side."

3. Abbott + Atrivity " –Game On, Brazil"

In pharma sales, training often feels like a compliance checklist—long slide decks, dense PDFs, monologues posing as webinars. And in a country as vibrant and diverse as Brazil, where reps crisscross urban sprawl and rural frontiers, keeping them aligned, trained, and motivated is no small feat.

Abbott's Brazil division faced this exact challenge. Their reps needed rapid upskilling for a complex product portfolio in an increasingly competitive marketplace. The stakes weren't just academic—they were commercial. But there was a deeper issue: knowledge decay. What was taught on Monday faded by Thursday.

So they tried something radical.

They partnered with Atrivity, a mobile gamification platform designed to convert training into bite-sized challenges. Instead of pushing static materials, Atrivity pulled reps into an interactive game: quizzes, missions, competitions—all designed to reinforce brand knowledge, objection handling, and product features.

The game lasted just five days. But in those five days, something unexpected happened. Knowledge gaps—measured by pre- and post-assessments—dropped from 27.5% to 7.5%. That's not a marginal gain—it's a pedagogical breakthrough. Over 90% of reps participated actively, and many logged in during off-hours—on buses, during lunch, even at night.

Why did it work?

Because Atrivity didn't just present content—it engineered a behavior loop. It used competition, social proof, and instant feedback to convert passive learning into active retrieval. Reps weren't just memorizing—they were mastering. More importantly, the game created psychological buy-in. Learning felt less like school and more like sport.

For Abbott, it wasn't about digital flash. It was about results. Reps who scored higher in the game consistently outperformed peers in subsequent field performance, showing better recall during HCP visits and greater confidence in positioning complex therapies.

In a landscape where attention is fleeting, Abbott found a way to make learning contagious—and fun. They didn't just gamify training. They transformed it into a competitive advantage.

4. **AstraZeneca: "Go to Jupiter" – MSL Onboarding Takes Off**

When AstraZeneca set out to revamp its medical science liaison (MSL) onboarding, they weren't just trying to train—they were trying to prepare a new class of scientific professionals for the complex, high-stakes conversations that define medical affairs.

MSLs are not typical field reps. They engage with key opinion leaders, explain mechanistic pathways, discuss clinical data, and handle nuanced queries that often go beyond the product into therapeutic ecosystems. Standard training modules—lengthy eLearning, static PDFs, and multi-day workshops—left little room for real-time cognitive agility.

So the team posed a radical question: What if we treated onboarding not as a course, but as a journey?

The answer became "Go to Jupiter"—a gamified onboarding simulation set in a space exploration narrative. Each module was framed as a "mission," and the MSLs were cast as interstellar navigators, tasked with exploring unknown clinical landscapes, decoding scientific signals, and navigating decision trees with alien-like ambiguity (not unlike real-world HCP interactions).

Behind the playful metaphor sat robust pedagogical engineering:

- Case-based branching scenarios that mimicked HCP conversations.
- Time-pressured quizzes that demanded application, not recall.
- Peer competition in the form of leaderboards and badges.
- Knowledge libraries disguised as "data stations" for just-in-time learning.

But the impact wasn't fiction. It was measurable:

- Engagement rates hit 97%, a figure previously unheard of in traditional onboarding.
- MSLs logged back into modules even after certification, treating the experience more like a toolkit than a test.
- Field performance, especially in early HCP interactions, showed faster confidence ramp-up and higher scientific fluency, per manager evaluations.

One senior MSL said, "I didn't feel like I was being trained. I felt like I was already doing the job—with less fear."

In transforming onboarding from a checklist to a space odyssey, AstraZeneca didn't just improve retention—they redefined readiness. "Go to Jupiter" proved that gamification, when done with care and narrative craft, can elevate not just engagement but professional identity.

5. Pfizer's Oncology Simulation Platform – 3D Roleplay, Real-World Readiness

Where immersive experience replaces slide decks, and memory follows motion.

Oncology is among the most scientifically complex and emotionally nuanced therapeutic areas. For pharmaceutical reps and medical teams, mastering its language requires more than memorizing mechanisms—it demands an empathetic, systems-level understanding of patients, pathways, and the shifting treatment landscape.

Pfizer recognized this challenge when launching a next-gen oncology portfolio. Traditional training—PowerPoint slides, expert-led lectures, annotated PDFs—simply wasn't enough. The information stuck, but not deeply. Reps could recite facts, but struggled with synthesis under pressure.

So Pfizer flipped the script.

They designed an immersive, VR-enabled training platform that placed learners inside a fully realized 3D simulation—a virtual hospital, complete with patient profiles, interactive treatment decision trees, stakeholder roleplay, and dynamic oncology dashboards.

The name wasn't as important as the experience:

- Reps were not passively watching; they were walking through disease progression—tumor staging, diagnostic challenges, treatment responses.
- They engaged in simulated dialogues with virtual oncologists, nurses, and even caregivers, each scenario branching based on their responses.
- Clinical trial data came alive not in a table, but as a narrated progression of patient cohorts, response rates, and side effect profiles, visualized in motion.

The platform wasn't a "game" in the traditional sense—but it was undeniably gamified:

✓ Progress tracking with visual dashboards.

✓ Scenario-based feedback after each session.

✓ Replay and level-up modes to refine weak spots.

✓ Peer benchmarking and leaderboard-driven motivation.

And the outcomes were dramatic:

- Ramp-up time for new hires dropped by 40%—from 10 weeks to just 6.
- Reps demonstrated 20% higher retention of key clinical concepts at the 3-month mark.
- Managers reported increased confidence and fluency in early HCP engagements.

One rep put it this way:

"Instead of telling me what a tumor does, they let me walk through a tumor board. That changed everything."

This case study didn't just validate immersive tech. It illustrated a core principle of effective gamification: when users learn through doing, the brain doesn't just remember—it rehearses for real life.

In Pfizer's world, the playbook became a place. And in that place, reps practiced for the most serious performance of all—talking to doctors about saving lives.

6. **Novartis " –Galaxies of Hope" – Emotional Gamification for Rare Cancer Awareness**

When facts don't resonate, stories take flight. When pain isolates, games connect.

Neuroendocrine tumors (NETs) are rare, complex, and poorly understood—even within oncology. For patients newly diagnosed with NETs, the experience is often alienating: misdiagnoses are common, symptoms are vague, and the emotional toll of navigating a rare disease can be profound. Traditional patient education—pamphlets, videos, whitepapers—struggled to connect in a meaningful way.

Novartis chose a different path: story-driven emotional gamification.

Rather than presenting NET information clinically, the company developed "Galaxies of Hope"—a mobile-first, interactive journey built like a graphic novel meets a visual game. But there were no points. No badges. No timers. This was gamification without gameness—where narrative immersion replaced mechanics, and connection replaced competition.

The Narrative Arc:

Players took on the role of a traveler navigating mysterious galaxies—each one symbolizing a phase in the NET journey:

- The Nebula of Symptoms: ambiguous, confusing signals.
- The Black Hole of Diagnosis: waiting, uncertainty, fear.
- The Constellation of Care: options, choices, and difficult trade-offs.
- The Orbit of Support: community, caregivers, clinicians.

With each interaction, players unlocked stories voiced by real patients, caregivers, and doctors. It wasn't fictionalized—it was empathetically reframed. Users could choose pathways, make decisions, and hear reflections. The goal wasn't education through explanation—it was education through emotion.

Real-World Impact:

- Engagement rates were 2x higher than traditional educational content.
- Patients reported feeling "understood," "less alone," and "emotionally connected"—rare outcomes in patient materials.
- HCPs found the tool useful in initiating conversations about NETs, particularly for newly diagnosed patients and caregivers.
- It became a catalyst for community, with patient advocacy groups integrating it into their support toolkits.

One caregiver described it as:

"The first time I saw my brother cry wasn't after diagnosis—it was after seeing someone else walk through it in that galaxy."

The Gamification Insight:

Gamification is often reduced to incentives—but "Galaxies of Hope" reminds us it can also be a mirror. When done with care, game-based storytelling becomes a form of emotional scaffolding, helping patients process grief, uncertainty, and even hope.

In the end, it wasn't a game for play—it was a game for belonging.

7. **Janssen " –RA Game App" – Turning Injections into Milestones**

In the battle against chronic illness, victory often lies not in the cure, but in consistency.

Rheumatoid arthritis (RA) is more than just joint pain. It is a relentless, progressive disease that demands strict adherence to biologic injections or disease-modifying treatments—many of which come with their own complexity, fear, and psychological resistance. For patients, especially the newly diagnosed, each injection feels like an event, often clouded with anxiety or avoidance.

Janssen, a leader in immunology, recognized a gap in this adherence journey: despite clinical efficacy, drop-off rates remained troubling. So, they leaned into behavior science and developed a mobile gamification platform, known informally as the "RA Game App."

But this wasn't Candy Crush in a lab coat. It was a clinically informed, behaviorally intelligent tool, designed to motivate without overwhelming, and to celebrate milestones without trivializing the condition.

Game Mechanics, Thoughtfully Designed:

- **Mission-Based Framework**: Each injection was reframed as a "mission accomplished" rather than a medical procedure.
- **Level Progression**: Patients advanced through levels that mirrored their real-world clinical milestones—first month, third month, symptom control, and mobility gains.
- **Doctor Customization**: Physicians could tailor the app's motivational cues to each patient's treatment plan—some saw affirmations, others got educational nudges.
- **Social & Emotional Layering**: The app offered private "diary unlocks" where patients could log pain levels, journal feelings, or reflect on their journey—gamified, but not gamed.

Impact That Mattered:

- Medication adherence rose by 19% within three months of app adoption.
- Patients reported greater emotional ownership of their health outcomes.
- Clinician-patient dialogue improved, with providers using app data to have more empathetic and specific conversations.
- Notably, patients who had previously missed 2+ doses in a quarter reduced their non-adherence rate by 42%.

One patient described it best:

"The injection stopped being something I feared. It became something I conquered. Each time I leveled up, I knew I was doing my part."

The Strategic Lesson:

This wasn't about extrinsic motivation—it was about reframing behavior through meaning. Where traditional reminder apps failed with their sterile notifications, Janssen's game created a micro-world where progress was personal, and each clinical step felt like narrative progression.

Gamification, done right, isn't a distraction from medicine. It's a bridge to participation.

8. **Takeda " –IBD&Me" Simulation – Empowering Patients Through Choice**

In a chronic illness, it's not just the disease that's complex—it's the daily decisions.

Patients with Inflammatory Bowel Disease (IBD), such as Crohn's disease or ulcerative colitis, live in a state of continuous negotiation—with their symptoms, treatments, routines, and expectations. The burden is not only biological; it's deeply psychological. Every flare, every medication switch, every scan triggers a question: Am I doing the right thing?

Takeda, a company deeply engaged in gastroenterology, saw a persistent pattern in its patient research: patients often arrived at the physician's office uninformed, overwhelmed, or underconfident. Shared decision-making, while clinically recommended, was rarely realized in practice. This insight led to the creation of "IBD&Me"—an interactive, quiz-based simulation platform that gamified decision preparation for patients.

But this wasn't a trivia app. It was a serious game grounded in empathy, designed with gastroenterologists, patient advocacy groups, behavioral psychologists, and UX designers.

Game Structure: Simulating the Real, Respectfully

- **Scenario-Based Play**: Patients navigated through realistic decision trees—"You're experiencing new symptoms. Do you call your doctor, increase your meds, or wait it out?"—with each choice branching into new outcomes.
- **Quiz-Style Modules**: Each simulation reinforced key education about biologics, flare triggers, surgery options, and long-term management.
- **Risk-Reward Feedback**: Unlike scare tactics, the feedback loops highlighted the pros, cons, and long-term implications of each decision.
- **Custom Tracks**: Users could select paths based on their current stage in the treatment journey—such as newly diagnosed, post-surgery, or considering escalation.

Tangible Outcomes:

In a pilot study of 800 patients:

- 82% felt more confident about discussing treatment options with their physician after using the app for just two weeks.
- 76% reported higher satisfaction with their clinical consultation.
- Shared decision-making scores, as measured by the SDM-Q-9 tool, improved by 31%.
- Gastroenterologists noted more engaged and question-asking patients, particularly among younger adults who had previously avoided clinical follow-up.

A Patient's Reflection:

"Before IBD&Me, I just nodded along in consults. Now, I show up with questions, preferences, and a plan."

The Strategic Lesson:

Takeda didn't gamify IBD. It gamified decision fluency. In doing so, it transformed a passive patient population into active participants in their own care. The app didn't dictate what to choose—it taught how to choose. And that shift—from compliance to collaboration—is where true patient empowerment begins.

9. **Roche " –Pathways Challenge" – Gamified HCP Education That Sticks**

Learning in oncology is never static—and Roche didn't want it to be silent either.

Oncology is one of the fastest-evolving fields in medicine. New biomarkers, treatment pathways, resistance mechanisms, and therapeutic combinations emerge with increasing speed. For busy healthcare professionals (HCPs), keeping up is a challenge—not due to lack of interest, but because time, mental fatigue, and dry formats hinder engagement.

Roche, a global leader in oncology, recognized this cognitive overload early. Their internal analytics revealed that completion rates for online modules in continuing medical education (CME) hovered around 27%—even when incentives were offered. It wasn't the content that was lacking. It was the experience.

So Roche reimagined CME as a game—not in the superficial sense, but as a deeply motivating, adaptive, and community-driven experience. Enter the "Pathways Challenge."

What Made it a Challenge Worth Playing?

Modular Game Design: Each treatment pathway (e.g., HER2+ breast cancer, non-small cell lung cancer) became its own self-contained level, complete with branching case studies, quizzes, and evidence trails.

Time-Limited Leaderboards: HCPs competed asynchronously—completing modules during breaks or after hours—unlocking badges and climbing specialty-specific leaderboards.

CME Credits as Power-Ups: Completion translates into tangible rewards—certificates, CME points, and access to exclusive content or expert roundtables.

Peer Learning Loops: HCPs could see how others responded to clinical scenarios (anonymized), sparking discussion and challenging assumptions.

Impact in Numbers:

- 42% increase in module completion across regions within three months.
- Oncology specialists spent 34% more time engaging with the material compared to previous static formats.
- Post-module surveys showed a 61% rise in content recall, especially in guideline updates and diagnostic algorithm use.

A particularly telling insight? Many oncologists reported revisiting modules just before patient consultations—a sign that the format had moved from passive education to point-of-care utility.

The Strategic Insight:

Roche didn't treat HCPs as content consumers—they treated them as players in an ever-changing diagnostic game. The real innovation wasn't just in the gamification mechanics—it was in mapping them to real-world cognitive challenges of oncology care.

By transforming passive learning into problem-solving under pressure, Roche proved that the future of medical education isn't about dumping knowledge. It's about activating it.

10. GSK " –Meningitis Educator" Simulation – Field Force Enablement Through Serious Play

Before you walk into a clinic, try walking into the story first.

GSK's vaccine portfolio has long included protection against meningitis—a disease that is often fast-moving, emotionally charged, and difficult to explain in standard sales visits. Field reps often found themselves facing questions that went beyond the science: parental fears, vaccine hesitancy, misinformed HCP perceptions, and time-crunched appointments.

Traditional training—slide decks, medical brochures, and memorized objection handling—didn't always prepare reps for this human complexity.

So GSK took a radical step.

They developed the "Meningitis Educator," a serious game that placed reps in the hot seat of a virtual consult room. Using branching narratives, real-world clinical objections, and timed dialogue simulations, the experience mimicked conversations reps would have with pediatricians, family doctors, and even caregivers.

Game Mechanics That Trained Empathy and Strategy

- **Role-Play Dialogues**: Reps navigated conversations with realistic virtual HCPs who asked tough questions, expressed hesitations, or challenged efficacy claims.
- **Branching Scenarios**: Each choice led to different outcomes. A pushy response could shut down engagement; empathetic framing, on the other hand, opened up new questions.
- **Feedback Loops**: After each interaction, the game provided a debrief to the player, highlighting strengths and missed opportunities, supported by actual market data and behavioral science.
- **Progressive Difficulty**: As reps advanced, the scenarios became more nuanced—featuring combo vaccines, catch-up schedules, and age-specific queries.

Measurable Results, Tangible Change

- Over 1,200 reps across 3 continents completed the simulation within the first 60 days of launch.
- Field readiness scores improved by 38% in post-game assessments.

- Role-play performance during in-person training saw a 50% increase in objection-handling effectiveness.
- Most importantly, real-world feedback from HCPs showed reps were more confident, precise, and persuasive—and more attuned to emotional cues.

Strategic Insight

GSK didn't just teach facts; they simulated empathy. In doing so, they moved beyond knowledge transfer to skill immersion. Field reps stopped being message deliverers and became better navigators of human concern.

By creating a world where mistakes were safe and learning was iterative, GSK used gamification to build competence and confidence in equal measure.

Ten Real-World Case Studies: A Summary

Case Study	Focus Area	Gamification Strategy	Impact
1. Mango Health	Patient Adherence	Points, reminders, rewards	27% increase in adherence
2. mySugr	Diabetes Self-Management	Monster-taming visual narrative	75%+ logging compliance by daily users
3. Abbott + Atrivity (Brazil)	Sales Rep Training	Quiz battles, mobile challenges	Knowledge gap dropped from 27.5% to 7.5%
4. AstraZeneca - "Go Jupiter"	MSL Onboarding	Space-themed simulation, decision trees	97% engagement, repeat usage post-training
5. Pfizer Oncology VR Simulation	Rep Product Training	3D immerssive learning environment	40% faster ramp-up time
6. Novartis - "Galaxies of Hope"	Cancer Patient Support	Empathy-based storytelling game	Increased emotional engagement
7. Janssen - RA Game App	Rheumatology Adherence	Mission-based medicaiton goals	Boosted long-term adherence
8. Takeda - IBD&Me	Shared Decision-Making	Interactive quizzes, consult prep tools	Empowered patients, better consult outcomes

Contd...

Case Study	Focus Area	Gamification Strategy	Impact
9. Roche - Pathways Challenge	HCP Oncology Education	CME-integrated modules, leaderboards	42% increase in module completion
10. GSK - Meningitis Educator Game	Field Rep Enablement	Roleplay simulations with HCP dialogues	Improved sales call confidence / performance

APPENDICES

Appendix A: Glossary of Gamification Terms

Appendix B: Scientific References and Citations

Appendix C: Gamification Templates and Checklists

Appendix A

Glossary of Gamification Terms

This glossary compiles key terms frequently used throughout the book, blending concepts from game design, behavioral science, digital health, and pharma marketing. Each entry includes a concise definition and a note on its relevance in the pharmaceutical context.

Achievement

A recognition for completing a task or milestone, often represented by badges, trophies, or points.

Pharmaceutical Context: Can reinforce medication adherence or rep training goals.

Adaptive Challenge

A dynamic task that adjusts to a user's skill level or performance in real time.

Pharmaceutical Context: Used in rep onboarding, CME modules, or patient apps for progressive learning.

Behavioral Economics

An interdisciplinary field combining psychology and economics to understand decision-making.

Pharmaceutical Context: Powers many gamification principles, such as nudges, reward sensitivity, and loss aversion.

Behavior Loop

The cyclical structure of trigger → action → reward → investment that keeps users engaged.

Pharmaceutical Context: Encourages repeated health behaviors, such as daily medication logging or app engagement.

Badge

A virtual symbol of accomplishment, progress, or status.

Pharma Context: Used in adherence programs, training dashboards, or loyalty campaigns for HCPs.

Compliance Rate

The percentage of users adhering to desired behaviors, often tracked via logs or interactions.

Pharmaceutical Context: A critical metric for measuring app engagement or digital therapeutic effectiveness.

Dark Pattern

A deceptive design practice that manipulates user behavior through coercion or confusion.

Pharmaceutical Context: Must be avoided—regulators (e.g., GDPR) may penalize manipulative gamification.

Dynamic Difficulty Adjustment (DDA)

Real-time tuning of game complexity based on user performance.

Pharmaceutical Context: Helps tailor learning modules or patient pathways to individual cognitive or clinical profiles.

Game Mechanics

The tools and rules that create gameplay—points, levels, leaderboards, feedback loops, etc.

Pharmaceutical Context: The scaffolding behind most gamified patient/HCP programs.

Goal Gradient Effect

The psychological principle that motivation increases as people approach a goal.

Pharmaceutical Context: Used in titration programs or step therapy adherence campaigns.

Intrinsic vs. Extrinsic Motivation

Intrinsic: Driven by personal growth or purpose.

Extrinsic: Driven by external rewards (e.g., points, money).

Pharmaceutical Context: Effective gamification balances both to avoid dependence on shallow incentives.

Leaderboard

A public ranking of users based on performance metrics.

Pharmaceutical Context: Enhances friendly competition among representatives or healthcare professionals in training environments.

Leveling Up

Progressing to a higher stage of skill or challenge.

Pharmaceutical Context: Maps well to milestone-based engagement (e.g., learning modules, patient education).

Loss Aversion

A behavioral principle where users fear losing something more than they value gaining it.

Pharmaceutical Context: Drives "streak loss" features in adherence or exercise tracking.

Motivation Model (e.g., Octalysis, Self-Determination Theory)

Frameworks used to design for human engagement.

Pharmaceutical Context: Used to map HCP or patient types and create tailored game loops.

Onboarding

The initial phase of guiding users into a gamified system or platform.

Pharmaceutical Context: Crucial for rep training apps or patient therapeutic games.

Player Types

Classifications of users based on how they engage—e.g., achievers, explorers, socializers, competitors.

Pharmaceutical Context: Helps pharma marketers segment users for personalized experiences.

Reward Schedule

The timing and structure of delivering rewards can be fixed or variable.

Pharmaceutical Context: Variable rewards (e.g., random draws) often drive more engagement than predictable ones.

Regulatory Alignment

Ensuring all gamified elements comply with legal and ethical standards (HIPAA, GDPR, FDA, etc.).

Pharmaceutical Context: Especially critical when collecting patient data or incentivizing behavior.

Retention

The ability to keep users engaged over time.

Pharmaceutical Context: Often a primary KPI for patient apps, MSL training platforms, or HCP portals.

Scaffolding

Step-by-step progression that helps users master skills gradually.

Pharmaceutical Context: Often used in tiered learning or therapeutic journey gamification.

Streak

A consecutive streak of completing an action—e.g., taking medication for 7 days.

Pharma Context: Encourages habit formation and builds accountability.

Tokenization

Assigning symbolic or blockchain-based rewards for actions.

Pharmaceutical Context: Emerging area—used in digital health wallets or reward redemption.

User Journey Map

A design tool that visualizes user touchpoints, goals, and emotional states across a gamified experience.

Pharmaceutical Context: Crucial for mapping patient or HCP engagement in branded ecosystems.

Virtual Simulation

Immersive environments where users engage in role-playing, training, or behavioral challenges.

Pharmaceutical Context: Used in VR training (e.g., oncology pathways, vaccine counseling).

XP (Experience Points)

Points earned by users for participating or progressing in a system.

Pharmaceutical Context: Often used as a non-monetary progress indicator in e-learning or wellness apps.

Closing Note

Understanding these terms is essential not only to speak the language of gamification but to design and evaluate with confidence and responsibility. Whether you're mapping patient pathways, training reps, or launching adherence apps, a solid grasp of these core concepts ensures your strategy is both effective and ethical.

Appendix B

Scientific References and Citations

This appendix presents a curated list of the scientific, technical, and industry references that informed the research, frameworks, and case studies in this book. They span disciplines including behavioral science, game design, pharmaceutical marketing, digital health, and data ethics.

Wherever possible, references are peer-reviewed, evidence-based, and relevant to real-world applications in the life sciences.

Gamification Theory and Behavioral Science

1. Deci, E. L., & Ryan, R. M. (2000). The "What" and "Why" of Goal Pursuits: Human Needs and the Self-Determination of Behavior. Psychological Inquiry, 11(4), 227–268.
2. Werbach, K., & Hunter, D. (2012). For the Win: How Game Thinking Can Revolutionize Your Business. Wharton Digital Press.
3. Deterding, S., Dixon, D., Khaled, R., & Nacke, L. (2011). From Game Design Elements to Gamefulness: Defining "Gamification". Proceedings of the 15th International Academic MindTrek Conference, 9–15.
4. Hamari, J., Koivisto, J., & Sarsa, H. (2014). Does Gamification Work? – A Literature Review of Empirical Studies on Gamification. Proceedings of the 47th Hawaii International Conference on System Sciences, 3025–3034.
5. Fogg, B. J. (2009). A Behavior Model for Persuasive Design. Proceedings of the 4th International Conference on Persuasive Technology, ACM.
6. Cialdini, R. B. (2007). Influence: The Psychology of Persuasion. Harper Business.

Gamification in Healthcare and Pharma

7. Chiauzzi, E., Rodarte, C., & DasMahapatra, P. (2015). Patient-centered activity monitoring in the self-management of chronic health conditions. BMC Medicine, 13(77).
8. Kvedar J., Coye, M. J., & Everett, W. (2014). Connected health: a review of technologies and strategies to improve patient care with telemedicine and telehealth. Health Affairs, 33(2), 194–199.
9. Morrison, D., et al. (2012). Digital health behavior change interventions that use gamification: systematic review. JMIR Serious Games, 3(1).
10. Lister, C., et al. (2014). Just a fad? Gamification in health and fitness apps. JMIR Serious Games, 2(2).
11. Khalil, H., & Fakih, W. (2017). Gamification in medication adherence. Journal of Pharmacy Practice and Research, 47(4), 338–342.

Digital Therapeutics, Mobile Health, and VR Use Cases

12. Digital Therapeutics Alliance. (2020). Defining DTx – Digital Therapeutics Defined. https://dtxalliance.org
13. Eichenberg, C., et al. (2017). Virtual Reality in Health Care: A Review of Recent Literature. Journal of Medical Internet Research, 19(10).
14. Shah, R. A., & Nogueras, D. (2020). Immersive VR for Pain Management in Burn Victims: A Meta-Review. Pain Management Nursing, 21(2), 147–154.
15. Johns Hopkins Medicine. (2021). Stroke Rehabilitation and VR Integration – Bandit's Shark Showdown Case Study.

Gamification Case Studies in Pharma (Referencing Real-World Examples)

16. Mango Health. (2016–2020). Medication adherence app data, user engagement metrics. [MangoHealth.com]
17. mySugr. (2018). Case studies and behavioral adherence metrics. Roche Group.
18. Abbott + Atrivity. (2017). Sales Training Gamification in LATAM Markets. Atrivity Corporate Blog.

19. AstraZeneca. (2019). Gamification in MSL onboarding – Internal Corporate Training Report.
20. Pfizer Oncology. (2021). VR-Enabled Oncology Simulation Platform – Learning and Development Impact Report.
21. Novartis. (2018). Galaxies of Hope – Empathy-driven storytelling app for NET patients. [PatientResource.com]
22. Takeda. (2020). IBD&Me Shared Decision Tool – User Experience Evaluation. UEG Journal.
23. Janssen Immunology. (2021). RA App – Adherence and App Engagement Metrics.
24. Roche Pathways Challenge. (2022). CME Module Completion Rate Data. Roche Medical Affairs Division.
25. GSK. (2019). Meningitis Vaccine Roleplay Training App – Case Study. GSK Learning & Development Division.

Ethical and Regulatory Frameworks

26. U.S. Food & Drug Administration (FDA). (2023). Digital Health Software Precertification Program. [www.fda.gov]
27. Health Insurance Portability and Accountability Act (HIPAA). U.S. Department of Health & Human Services.
28. General Data Protection Regulation (GDPR). European Commission. https://gdpr.eu
29. Gamification and Behavioral Design Code of Ethics. Behavioral Science & Policy Association.

Metrics, Engagement, and Measurement

30. Google Firebase Analytics. (2022). Health app user engagement metrics: DAU, MAU, retention. [firebase.google.com]
31. Singh, K., et al. (2016). Measuring engagement with mobile health apps: DAU, MAU, churn, and stickiness metrics. mHealth Journal.
32. Gartner. (2023). Gamification in Enterprise: Adoption Metrics and Best Practices.

Citations in Context

All in-text references in Chapters 1–16 and Case Study sections refer to the above numbered entries. Where real-world case studies were cited, the data have been either:

- Drawn from public company reports,
- Referenced via peer-reviewed literature, or
- Validated through corporate whitepapers, interviews, or trade publications.

Appendix C

Gamification Templates and Checklists

From Complexity to Clarity—A Field Manual for Brand Teams

The theory is inspiring. The case studies are convincing. But at the coalface of pharma brand management, inspiration often needs scaffolding. Appendix C bridges the knowing-doing gap. It offers a field-tested toolkit—templates, checklists, and planning canvases—that pharma marketers, training leads, MSL managers, and CX strategists can use to design, develop, and deliver gamified programs with precision and purpose.

This appendix is not a theoretical dump—it's a starter kit for action.

1. **Gamification Strategy Canvas**

   A one-page visual planning tool to align:

   - Strategic objectives
   - Player personas (HCPs, patients, reps)
   - Motivation triggers
   - Game mechanics
   - Key success metrics

   Use when: Initiating a new gamified campaign or pitching to internal stakeholders.

2. **Player Persona Worksheet**

   Capture detailed personas for:

   - Healthcare Providers (Specialty, digital fluency, learning preferences)
   - Patients (Condition, tech comfort, support needs, adherence triggers)
   - Sales Reps/MSLs (Experience, content needs, training gaps)

   Use when: Defining player types and aligning mechanics with behavioral goals.

3. **Behavior Design Checklist**

   Grounded in Fogg's model and Octalysis principles:

- Does the challenge match ability?
- Are motivation boosters baked in?
- Are nudges and feedback loops seamless?
- Is progression visual and rewarding?

Use when: Finalizing game flow or evaluating early prototypes.

4. **Regulatory Alignment Template**

Ensure compliance with:

- HIPAA (for patient data)
- GDPR (for EU markets)
- FDA Guidelines (for digital tools and adherence programs)

Includes prompts for privacy notices, opt-ins, and adverse event monitoring.

Use when: Collaborating with legal and regulatory before launch.

5. **Engagement KPI Tracker**

Includes fields for:

- DAUs / MAUs
- Completion rates
- Challenge participation
- Post-game survey insights
- Behavior changes (e.g., refill rates, training completions)

Use when: Running a live dashboard to monitor campaign health.

6. **Agile Sprint Tracker for Gamified Projects**

Kanban-style worksheet to manage:

- Storyboarding → Prototype → Test → Iterate → Launch
- Cross-functional task ownership
- Sprint retrospectives

Use when: Managing the game development team or coordinating vendors.

7. **Post-Mortem Review Checklist**

After every campaign:

- What engaged? What fell flat?
- Was learning retained?
- Did behavior change happen?

- Were unintended consequences noted?

Includes prompts for team reflection and stakeholder debriefs.

Use when: Wrapping up a pilot or preparing for scale.

8. **Real-World Case Study Planning Template**

   Replicate success stories by capturing:

   - Objective
   - Target audience
   - Mechanics used
   - Outcomes measured
   - Lessons learned

   Use when: Documenting internal successes or preparing conference abstracts.

Final Note

Like a surgical checklist in the OR, these tools don't replace strategy—but they make sure nothing mission-critical is forgotten. They invite rigor, clarity, and a shared vocabulary for teams navigating the exciting, uncertain terrain of gamification in pharma.

In pharmaceutical marketing, precision must meet play. Appendix C is how you get there.

About the Author

Subba Rao Chaganti is a pioneering voice at the intersection of pharmaceutical marketing, behavioral science, and emerging technologies. With over three decades of industry experience and a prolific portfolio of 30+ groundbreaking books on pharmaceutical strategy, Chaganti is widely regarded as a thought leader who redefines how pharma educates, engages, and empowers.

He began his journey as a marketing educator and practitioner, driven by a singular mission: to bridge the gap between science and storytelling in pharma. Today, his work spans disciplines—from sales force effectiveness and key account management to digital therapeutics, wearable tech, internal branding, and AI-powered brand strategy.

In Level Up: Gamification in Pharma Marketing, Chaganti brings his signature clarity, real-world pragmatism, and narrative depth to a topic often misunderstood as frivolous. Drawing on cutting-edge behavioral models, compelling case studies, and pharma-specific implementation frameworks, he demonstrates why gamification is not a gimmick—but a strategic tool that taps into the deepest drivers of engagement: purpose, progress, and play.

Beyond the books, Chaganti is a mentor to brand managers, a respected voice on LinkedIn and Substack, and an unwavering advocate for ethical, patient-centered innovation in life sciences marketing. His ability to translate complexity into actionable strategy makes his work not just readable—but indispensable.

He lives in Farmington, Connecticut, USA, and can be reached at: subbarao.chaganti@gmail.com.

Here is a list of his publications:

1. Pharmaceutical Marketing in India: Concepts, Cases, Strategy
2. Game Plans for Post-GATT Era: Action Agenda of the Indian Pharmaceutical Industry
3. Compete or Forfeit: Strategies for Sustainable Competitive Advantage in the Pharma Product Patents Era

4. Pharmaceutical Marketing in India for Today and Tomorrow - 25th Anniversary Edition
5. Bullseyes and Blunders: Lessons from 100 Cases in Pharma Marketing
6. Digital Pharma Marketing Playbook: Winning With the New Rules of Engagement
7. Cracking the Generics Code: Your Single-Source Success Manual for Winning in Multi-Source Product Markets
8. Reimagine Pharma Marketing: Make It Future-Proof!
9. Brand Positioning in Pharma
10. Transactional to Transformational Marketing in Pharma: The Science of Why and The Art of How
11. A to Z of Pharmaceutical Marketing: World's First and Only Encyclopedia in Two Volumes
12. The Synergy of Minds: Human+AI Orchestrating the Pharma Marketing Revolution
13. Design Thinking for Pharma
14. The Pharma Product Manager: Navigating the Digital Frontier
15. Sentiment Analysis for Pharma Marketers
16. Whispering to AI: Prompt Engineering for Pharma Brand Managers
17. Storytelling in Pharma Marketing
18. Beyond the Molecule: The Art and Science of Metaphors That Matter
19. The Voices Within: Your Body Speaks, When your organs tell their own stories
20. Pharma Archetypes: The Science of Meaningful Healthcare Marketing
21. Navigating the AI Revolution: Human Futures
22. Breaking Through: A Business Novel (based on the theory of constraints)
23. The Wearable Edge: Redefining Pharma Marketing in a Connected and Data-Driven World
24. Code to Cure: Digital Therapeutics and the Future of Pharma

www.ingramcontent.com/pod-product-compliance
Ingram Content Group UK Ltd.
Pitfield, Milton Keynes, MK11 3LW, UK
UKHW021238300926
15471UKWH00013B/338

9 789347 311079